九年义务教育三年制初级中学教科书

英　语

第　三　册

JUNIOR ENGLISH FOR CHINA

STUDENTS' BOOK 3

(中国) 人民教育出版社
　　　　　　　　　　　　合编
(英国) 朗文出版集团有限公司

人民教育出版社

1996 · 北京

（京）新登字113号

九年义务教育三年制初级中学教科书

英　语

第三册

(中国)人 民 教 育 出 版 社
(英国)郎文出版集团有限公司　合编

*

人 民 教 育 出 版 社 出 版
吉林省新闻出版局出版印制处重印
吉 林 省 新 华 书 店 发 行
长 春 新 华 印 刷 厂 印 装

*

开本 787×1092　1/16　印张 18.25　插页 2　字数 390 000
1996 年 10 月第 1 版　　1999 年 3 月吉林第 3 次印刷
印数：1—207 500

ISBN 7-107-02306-3
G·4142(课)　　定价：9.74 元

顾　　问　L · G · 亚历山大　(L. G. Alexander)
邓炎昌　张志公　丁往道

主　　编　N · J · H 格兰特　(N. J. H. Grant)
刘道义

学生用书

责任编辑　董蔚君　魏国栋　（参加编写工作）
J · 特怀曼　(J. Twyman)

绘　　图　高　燕　王惟震　吴　勇

设　　计　P · 布莱斯—史密斯　(P. Price-Smith)
魏国栋

封面设计　P · 布莱斯—史密斯　(P. Price-Smith)
张　蓓

封面图绘制　王惟震

美术编辑　陈出新

练习册

责任编辑　张献臣　张永年（参加编写和设计工作）
J · 特怀曼　(J. Twyman)

绘　　图　姜吉维　刘德臣

设计指导　P · 布莱斯—史密斯　(P. Price-Smith)

说　　明

根据我国政府与联合国开发计划署达成的协议，由联合国开发计划署提供资助，联合国教科文组织任执行机构，人民教育出版社与英国朗文出版集团有限公司合作编写九年制义务教育初中英语教材。本书由人民教育出版社教科书编辑人员、设计人员与英方作者、编辑和设计人员合作编制而成，由人民教育出版社出版。

本册课本供初中三年级使用，第一学期教学第1–14单元，第二学期教学第15–24单元。

本书附录中的课文注释由岳汝梅编。词汇表由刘锦芳编。

在本册课本的编写过程中，王碧霖、龚亚夫等同志参加了审阅工作，提出了宝贵的意见，特此谨表谢意。

本册课本已经国家教委中小学教材审定委员会审查。

CONTENTS

Unit 1 Teachers' Day

Lesson 1

1 Read and say

JIM: Hi, Li Lei! How are you?
LI LEI: Oh, hello, Jim. Glad to see you again. How are you?
JIM: I'm very well. Did you have a good summer holiday?
LI LEI: Yes, thanks. How's Kate?
JIM: She's OK, thanks.
LI LEI: And your parents?
JIM: They're both fine, too. What about your family?
LI LEI: Fine, thanks. Oh, that's the bell. Everyone is going into class. We'd better go too.

2 Read and act

MISS ZHAO: Good morning, class! Who is on duty today?
MA LILI: Good morning. I am. Everyone is here. No one is away. Today is Thursday, September 10th, Teachers' Day. Happy Teachers' Day, Miss Zhao! Here are some flowers for you, with our best wishes.
MISS ZHAO: What beautiful flowers! Oh, a diary, too. Thank you!

3 Read and learn Make a Teachers' Day card in your art lesson.

To our dear teacher,

Happy Teachers' Day!
Thank you for teaching us so well.
We hope you'll have a very happy year in our class.
Good luck! Best wishes!

From your students

Lesson 2

Read Miss Zhao asked Jim to give the class a talk.

TEACHER: Tomorrow I want you to give us a talk, Jim. Please give us a short talk. Nothing difficult!

JIM: A talk? What subject should I talk about?

TEACHER: Choose any subject. Something about England, for example.

JIM: About England? What a good idea! Maybe I could talk about English names.

TEACHER: Yes, do please. That's a good idea.

What subject did Jim choose? He chose to talk about English names. Read his talk below and find out: "What did Jim's parents call him when he was born?" Then answer the questions on page 2 of your workbook.

ENGLISH NAMES

Most English people have three names: a first name, a middle name and the family name. Their family name comes last. For example, my full name is Jim Allan Green. Green is my family name. My parents gave me both of my other names.

People don't use their middle names very much. So "John Henry Brown" is usually called "John Brown". People never use Mr, Mrs or Miss before their first names. So you can say John Brown, or Mr Brown; but you should never say Mr John. They use Mr, Mrs or Miss with the family name but never with the first name.

I think this is different from Chinese names. In China, the first name is the family name, and the last name is the given name. For example, a man called Zhou Jian puts his family name Zhou first.

Sometimes people ask me about my name. "When you were born why did your parents call you Jim?" they ask. "Why did they choose that name?" The answer is they didn't call me Jim. They called me James. James was the name of my grandfather. In England, people usually call me Jim for short. That's because it is shorter and easier than James.

Lesson 3

1 Read and act

A: Excuse me. What is your full name, please?
B: My name is Robert Thomas Brown.
A: Thank you, Mr Robert.
B: No, I'm Mr Brown.
A: Oh, sorry.
B: That's all right. Why don't you call me Robert or Bob? But please don't call me Mr Bob.
A: Thanks, Bob. I won't.

2 Practise

Look at these English names.

Boys' names:			**Girls' names:**		
Thomas	—	Tom	Linda	—	Lin
David	—	Dave	Catherine	—	Kate

A: Is *Linda* a boy's name?
Is *James* a boy's name or a girl's name?
Jill is a girl's name, isn't it?

B: Yes, it is. / No, it isn't.
It's a ... name. / I think it's a ... name.
I'm not sure. / I'm afraid I've no idea.
That's difficult. Let's go and ask our teacher.

3 Read and act

Practise similar dialogues.

A: Excuse me. What's your full name, please?
B: James Allan Green.
A: Shall I call you James or Jim?
B: It doesn't matter. It's not important. But my friends call me Jim for short.
A: OK, Jim.

A: Excuse me. Are you a new student?
B: Yes, I am.
A: Glad to meet you.
What's your name, please?
B: Sun Huifang.
A: May I call you Huifang?
B: Of course, if you wish.

Lesson 4

1 **Listen and answer** Turn to page 4 of your workbook.

2 **Read and act**

Monday

A: What are you going to give our art teacher for Teachers' Day?
B: I'm not sure. Maybe I'll give her some flowers. How about you?
A: I'm going to give her a book.
B: That's a good idea.

Friday

A: Did you give our English teacher a card for Teachers' Day?
B: Yes, I did.
A: What did you write on it?
B: I wrote: "Best wishes for Teachers' Day!"

CHECKPOINT 1

● Grammar

The Present Indefinite Tense 一般现在时态

I usually *rest* on Sundays. Where *does* she *work*?

The Present Continuous Tense 现在进行时态

We *are learning* English. We *are reading* some English words.

The Future Indefinite Tense 一般将来时态

1 用 be going to 表示

We *are going to* work hard this year.

2 用 will 或 shall 表示

He *will come* to see us later. What time *shall* we *meet*?

The Past Indefinite Tense 一般过去时态

He *picked* a lot of fruit yesterday. I *went* to the farm last week.
Where *did* your father *work*? Where *did* he *go* last Sunday?

● Useful expressions

Happy Teachers' Day!	Good luck!	Do please.
Glad to see / meet you again.	Best wishes for ...!	give a talk
Jim is short for James.	Of course.	How about ...?

Unit 2 The sports meeting

Lesson 5

1 Read and learn

Last week No. 14 Middle School held a sports meeting on the playground.

The 100-metre race
Meimei ran fast.
Lucy ran faster than Meimei.
But Wu Dong ran fastest of all.
Who was first? Who was second?
Who was third? So who won the race?

The high jump
Lin Tao did quite well, but Bill did better than Lin Tao. Zhang Jun did best of all. Who was second? Who was third? Who jumped highest? Who won?

The long jump
Huifang jumped quite far, but Ann jumped farther. Liu Mei jumped farthest of all. Did Huifang jump farther than Ann? Who jumped farthest of all?

2 Read and act

A: Which sport are you in today?
B: I'm not doing anything because I fell and hurt my *neck* last week.
A: Bad luck!

foot	back
leg	arm

Lesson 6

 **Read** What is a relay race? Is it a team race?

Look at the pictures of a relay race below. Then read the story quickly and find out: "Which two classes were in front?"

The starting line

Passing on the stick

Dropping the stick

THE RELAY RACE

Mr Hu stood at the starting line. All the runners got ready to run.

"Ready? Go!" Mr Hu shouted, and the boys started to run. Of course, everyone began to shout very loudly.

"Come on!" they shouted.

On the first lap, Class 3 were in front. Li Lei ran much faster than the other boys. At the end of the first lap, Li Lei quickly passed the stick on to Jim. Jim ran very fast, but Yu Yan from Class 1 ran faster. He began to catch up with Jim.

At the end of the second lap, Yu Yan and Jim were neck and neck. They both passed on their sticks at the same time. Class 3 and Class 1 were in front!

"Come on!" shouted everyone, very loudly. On the third lap, the Class 3 and Class 1 runners both ran very fast. They were still neck and neck! But the other runners were not far behind. Then the Class 2 runner dropped his stick on the ground when he was passing it on to the fourth runner. A moment later, the Class 4 runner fell and hurt his leg, but he quickly got up and went on running.

The last lap! Wu Peng from Class 1 and Lin Tao from Class 3 were still neck and neck. But Jiang Honglin from Class 2 was running very fast. He began to catch up with the others.

"Come on!" shouted everyone. "Run! Run!"

Answer the questions on page 6 of your workbook.
Read the end of the story in the next lesson for homework.

Lesson 7

1 **Read** Read the end of the story. Who won?

The finishing line

Now Wu Peng from Class 1 was in front! Not far behind him was Lin Tao. Jiang Honglin was catching up fast, too, but not fast enough. "Come on, Wu!" shouted the Class 1 students. "Oh! Bad luck!"

Wu dropped his stick! He stopped to get it and of course fell behind. Lin Tao ran past him. He was first past the finishing line. Class 3 were the winners!

"Hooray!" shouted Class 3. "Well done, everyone! Congratulations, Lin Tao!"

2 Read and learn

Lucy didn't do very well. She did rather badly.

Meimei did worse than Lucy.

Lily did worst of all. Bad luck!

3 Practise dialogues like these. Take turns to ask the question:

A: Did you win?
B: Yes, I did.
A: Really? Congratulations!
B: Oh, it was nothing, really.

A: Did you win?
B: No, I didn't. I was last.
A: Bad luck!
B: Well, you can't win every time!

4 Read and act

A: Who won the girls' 400 metres?
B: I'm not sure. It was difficult to see. Wei Hua and Sun Meiying were both neck and neck.
A: Oh, listen to the loudspeaker. I think Mr Hu is going to tell us the result right now.

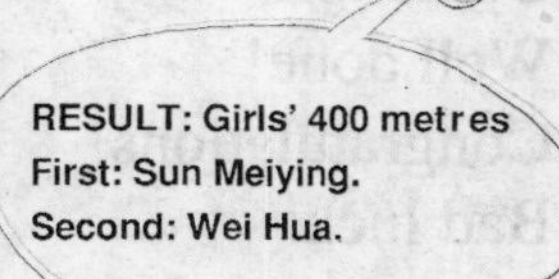

RESULT: Girls' 400 metres
First: Sun Meiying.
Second: Wei Hua.

Lesson 8

1 **Listen** Turn to page 8 of your workbook.

2 **Read and act**

HEADTEACHER: Well done, everyone, and congratulations to the winners. Here are the results. Girls' relay: The winners — Class 4! (*Hooray!*)

FANG MING: Thank you very much!

HEADTEACHER: Boys' relay: The winners — Class 3! (*Hooray!*) Well done!

LIN TAO: Thank you.

HEADTEACHER: Girls' 100-metre race: first — Wu Dong!

WU DONG: Thank you.

HEADTEACHER: Second — Lucy King.

LUCY: Thanks a lot.

CHECKPOINT 2

● **Grammar** **Comparison of adverbs** 副词的比较等级

	Adverb 原级	**Comparative** 比较级	**Superlative** 最高级
Regular forms 规则形式	fast	faster	fastest
	long	longer	longest
	late	later	latest
Irregular forms: 不规则形式	far	farther	farthest
	well	better	best
	badly	worse	worst

Han Meimei did very well in the 100-metre race.
Li Lei jumped farther than Jim (did).
Lin Tao jumped farthest of all.

● **Useful expressions**

Come on!	pass ... on	at the same time
Well done!	catch up with	a moment later
Congratulations!	be neck and neck	right now
Bad luck.	go on doing something	

Unit 3 A good teacher

Lesson 9

1 Listen, read and say

Do you like learning a foreign language? Miss Zhao likes to help her students in the English class. She likes them to ask questions like this:

STUDENT A: Excuse me, what does this word mean?
TEACHER: Which one?
STUDENT A: Er ..., *chick*.
TEACHER: Show me the word, please! Oh, "*quick*"! You say it like this: [kwik]. Say it again, please. *Quick*.
STUDENT A: *Quick*.
TEACHER: That's right! In English, *qu* makes a [kw] sound. Good. What does "*quick*" mean? Who knows? Hands up, please!
STUDENT B: Er ..., "*quick*" means *fast*.
TEACHER: That's right. It's another way of saying *fast*. Good.

2 Read and practise

1

A: What does this word ['iz'lænd] mean?
B: Oh, don't say it like that. Say it like this: ['ailənd].
A: Will you please say it again more slowly?
B: ['ailənd]. Don't say the letter *s*. In Chinese it means *dao*.
A: Oh yes, of course. Thanks.

2

A: What does "*newspaper*" mean, please?
B: "*Newspaper*"? Er ..., in Chinese it means *baozhi*.
A: What do you mean by ..., please?
B: Er ..., look, there's a picture of one.
A: I see. Thanks.

Lesson 10

Read Read this passage and find out:

1 Why was Miss Zhao not pleased?
2 What did Class 3 do last Sunday?

Put your hand up when you find the answers. Then read the passage again and answer the questions on page 10 of your workbook:

IN CLASS WITH MISS ZHAO

Miss Zhao is one of the most popular teachers in the school. Yesterday morning she came into class as usual. There was a big smile on her face.

"Well done, everyone!" she smiled. "Class 3 did very well in the school sports meeting last week. I was very glad when the boys won the relay race. Congratulations! The girls did very well, too.

"By the way, I came into this classroom last Friday morning, and it was not as clean as usual. I'm afraid some people forgot to sweep the floor. There was no excuse — we have new brooms. Will you please sweep the floor and tidy the classroom every day?"

"Yes, Miss Zhao," answered the students.

"Now, who is on duty today?"

"I am, Miss Zhao," said Wei Hua. "Today is Wednesday, September 19th. Everyone is at school today except Lin Tao. The weather today is rather wet. The radio says that it may stop raining later.

"Last Sunday we had a picnic. We visited the Great Wall. We went there by bus. We all took some food and drink with us.

"We had a very nice time. Luckily the weather was not so wet as it is today. We had a long walk along the wall. Later, we ate our picnic under some trees. Then we played some games."

"Well done, Wei Hua! Thank you," said Miss Zhao. "I think it's time for us to start the lesson now."

Lesson 11

1 Read and say

A: I think foreign languages are more interesting than science.
B: I really can't agree with you. I prefer science.

A: I think Chinese is more popular than any other subject.
B: I agree with you. / Maybe. But I prefer art.

2 Practise

A:				
I think	Chinese English Japanese science maths art music P.E.	is more is less	difficult important popular interesting useful	than ....

B:	
I agree with you. I don't agree. Maybe.	I prefer .... I think ... is much more .... But ....

3 Practise

A: I think foreign languages are as *difficult* as science subjects.
B: I agree. / I don't agree. I think languages are much *easier*

A: ... is not so *interesting* as ....
B: I agree. I prefer ... to .... / I don't agree. I think ... is much more *interesting*

useful	(more useful)
popular	(more popular)
important	(more important)

Lesson 12

1 **Listen** Turn to page 12 of your workbook.

2 **Practise**

A: Which is more difficult, science or English?
B: Science, maybe. But I don't know. They're both quite difficult.

A: Do you think that art is as interesting as music?
B: Yes, I do. / No, I don't. I prefer music.

A: I would like to drop maths. I find it very difficult.
B: You can't drop maths! It's very important!

3 **Practise**

You are the student on duty. Practise in English! Begin:
Today is .... Everyone is at school today except ... (and) ....
The weather today is .... Yesterday / Last Sunday, we ....

CHECKPOINT 3

● **Grammar**

1 Comparison of adjectives 形容词比较等级

Short adjectives	**Comparative 比较级**	**Superlative 最高级**
big	bigger	(the) biggest
strong	stronger	(the) strongest
Long adjectives:		
dangerous	more dangerous	(the) most dangerous
important	more important	(the) most important

2 用 as ... as 或 not as (so) ... as 做比较

English is *not so* important *as* maths.
I think science is *as* important *as* maths.

● **Useful expressions**

Say it like this. I agree / don't agree (with you). less useful than ...
I prefer ... to .... What do you mean by ...? as usual much more ...

Unit 4 What were they doing?

Lesson 13

1 Ask and answer

Today is Monday. The children are drawing some pictures on the blackboard. What are they drawing?

2 Read and act

Now the teacher comes into the classroom.

TEACHER: What are you doing, Li Lei?
LI LEI: I'm trying to draw a horse.
TEACHER: It's quite a nice horse! But please don't play with my chalk.
LI LEI: Sorry! I won't do it again.

Practise similar dialogues. Begin:

TEACHER: What are you drawing, Meimei?
MEIMEI: ....

3 Ask and answer

It is now Wednesday.

<table>
<tr><td>What was</td><td>Li Lei
Jim
Meimei</td><td rowspan="2">drawing when the teacher came in?</td></tr>
<tr><td>What were</td><td>the twins</td></tr>
</table>

What was he / she using? What was he / she drawing on?
What were they using? What were they drawing on?

Read

Here is a Russian story.
Read it quickly and find out: "Why couldn't the man downstairs sleep?"

Then read the story again and answer the questions on page 14 in your workbook.

THE MAN UPSTAIRS

A man lived in a tall building in the city of Moscow. He liked living there. It was usually very quiet, and he could see the park from his window. There was only one problem: the man upstairs.

Every night, the man upstairs came back late. He always took off his shoes and threw them on the floor. At this time, the man downstairs was trying to sleep. But every night he heard the noise upstairs. Bang! One shoe. Bang! The other shoe. It was too bad. He found it very difficult to get to sleep and he was rather angry with the man upstairs.

One day, the man downstairs went to talk to the man. He went upstairs and knocked at the door. The man opened it. With a smile the man from downstairs said: "I'm sorry to trouble you, comrade."

"What is it?" asked the man.

"Well, every time you get back at night, you drop your shoes on the floor. It happens every night. The noise wakes me up! Would you please not do this?"

"I'm very sorry, comrade," said the man. "I won't do it again."

The next evening the man upstairs came home from work late as usual. He was feeling very tired. He took off the first shoe and threw it on the floor. Then he remembered his comrade downstairs. So he took off the second shoe and put it under his bed very quietly. He had his supper, listened to the radio, read a newspaper and then went to bed. He was just falling asleep when there was a loud knock at the door. He opened it and saw the man from downstairs.

"Please!" said the man from downstairs. "Please drop the other shoe! I was waiting for the sound of the other shoe! I can't get to sleep!"

Lesson 15

1 Ask and answer

What were you doing	last night? last Saturday? at ten o'clock yesterday morning? at noon yesterday? yesterday afternoon?	I was	cooking a meal. playing football. working in class. watching TV. riding a horse. mending my bike. sweeping the floor. cleaning the classroom. ....

2 Ask and answer

One day the man upstairs heard the sound of children playing in the park. He looked out of his window. What could he see? What were the children and other people doing?

Examples: A man was selling ....
The boys were ....

Lesson 16

1 **Listen** Turn to page 16 in your workbook.

2 **Read and say**

A policeman wants to know:
"What were you doing at ten o'clock yesterday morning?"

1 Choose the best answers:

If you are	*a doctor* *a driver* *a League member* *a maths teacher* *an English teacher* *a student* *a farmer* *a policeman* *a cleaner*	*you may say* I was	growing my vegetables. helping Granny Ma with her housework. working in the hospital. teaching maths. studying in class. teaching English. driving a truck. watching the traffic. sweeping the road.

2 Practise dialogues like this:

A: What was the driver doing? **B:** He was driving a truck.

CHECKPOINT 4

- **Grammar**

The Past Continuous Tense (1) 过去进行时态（一）

动词的过去进行时表示在过去某一时刻或某一段时间内正在进行或发生的动作，由"was(were) + 动词 -ing"构成。

Statement forms 陈述句形式	**Question forms** 疑问句形式
I / He / She / It was working.	What was I / he / she / it doing?
You / We / They were working.	What were we / you / they doing?

- **Useful expressions**

It's quite a nice .... try to ... get to sleep come / get back at noon
I'm sorry to trouble you. be angry with help ... with ...

Unit 5 The accident

Lesson 17

1 Ask and answer

Questions / **Short answers**

Was / Were	you Lin Tao Wei Hua Polly the Blacks the twins your parents	watching TV washing clothes making a dress riding a motorbike writing a letter doing homework learning Russian	last night?	Yes, I was. No, I wasn't. Yes, he / she was. No, he / she wasn't. Yes, they were. No, they weren't.

2 Practise dialogues like these

A: Hello. You look tired today.
B: Yes. I went to bed too late last night. I was *doing my homework* and forgot the time.
A: You'd better go to bed earlier tonight, if you can.
B: Yes, you're right.

drawing a picture
listening to the radio
reading a story-book
watching TV
helping my parents with the housework

A: I had a little accident last Sunday.
B: Oh? What happened?
A: My pen dropped on the ground when I was *walking in the park*.
B: Did you lose it?
A: A woman saw it happen when she was *walking past*. She picked it up and gave it back to me.
B: How kind! You were lucky.

flying my kite
riding my bike
playing football

riding along the road
playing with her baby
walking with her child

 **Read**

Read the story below and find out: "What happened?"
Do NOT worry about any new words. Put your hand up when you've found out the answer.

A TRAFFIC ACCIDENT

The children were leaving school on Tuesday when they saw a truck. The truck was coming round the corner near the school. It was carrying some large bags of rice. Suddenly one of the bags fell off the truck. It landed in the middle of the road.

The children shouted to the driver, but he did not hear them.

"Let's move that bag, or there may be an accident," said Li Lei.

The children were running to move the bag of rice when they heard the sound of a motorbike. It was coming round the corner. The man on the motorbike was travelling too fast. He did not see the bag until it was too late. His bike hit the bag of rice and he fell off. The man lay on the road. Luckily, he was not badly hurt. But he could not move.

"Quick!" said Li Lei. "Lucy and Wei Hua, go round that corner and stop the traffic."

The two boys carried the man to the school gate keeper's room. "It's really nice of you. Thank you very much," said the man.

"It's nothing. Don't worry. You'll be OK," said Li Lei. "But you'd better not talk."

"Don't crowd round him," said the gate keeper. "Li Lei, go and find a teacher. I'll go and move away the bag of rice with Lin Tao."

After they moved the bag away, the girls let the traffic go again.

Li Lei went into the school and found Miss Zhao in the school library. She was choosing a book. He told her about the accident. As quickly as she could, Miss Zhao got a medicine box.

"I'll go and look after the man," she said. "You go to the school office and telephone the police. Please hurry up!"

With the medicine box under her arm, Miss Zhao hurried off to look after the man.

Answer the questions on page 18 of your workbook.

Lesson 19

1 Read and answer

Luckily a car soon came and took the man to hospital. Two policemen came too. You are one of the children. The policemen's questions are in the workbook. Try to answer them.

2 Tell the story

Here is the policemen's report. Choose the best words for the blanks:

	A	B
1	was falling	fell
2	went	was going
3	want	wanted
4	came	was coming
5	was travelling	travelled
6	hit	was hitting
7	was falling	fell
8	were stopping	stopped
9	were carrying	carried
10	were moving	moved
11	ran	was running
12	hurried	was hurrying

ACCIDENT REPORT

A large bag of rice ...(1)... off a truck when it ...(2)... round a corner of the road near No. 14 Middle School. Some students ...(3)... to move the bag, but a man on a motorbike ...(4)... round the corner. He ...(5)... too fast, and his bike ...(6)... the bag. The man ...(7)... off his bike and lay on the ground.

While some of the students ...(8)... the traffic, the boys ...(9)... the man to the gate keeper's room. The gate keeper and Lin Tao ...(10)... away the bag. Li Lei ...(11)... to get help from the school, and a teacher ...(12)... over with a box of medicine.

3 Listen Turn to page 19 in your workbook.

Lesson 20

1 Ask and answer

Give short answers to these questions.

Were / Was	you they the twins Jim Han Meimei Li Lei	writing listening carefully standing up talking sweeping the floor drawing a picture	when the teacher came in?

2 Practise   Make up similar sentences.

While	we were talking, they were sweeping the floor, Jim was mending his bike, Meimei was making a cake, the girls were eating supper,	the teacher came in. the bell rang. Lin Tao came to see him. Lucy called to see her. their father came home.

CHECKPOINT 5

- **Grammar   The Past Continuous Tense (2) 过去进行时态（二）**

Statement forms 陈述句形式

I
He/She/It } was (not) } travelling too fast.
We/You
They } were (not)

Question forms 疑问句形式

Was I
Was he/she/it
Were you/we
Were they } travelling too fast?

- **Useful expressions**

You'd better go to bed earlier.
Go as quickly as you can.
It's nice of you.
You'd better not talk.
Don't crowd round him.
Hurry up.   give back

Unit 6 In the library

Lesson 21

1 Read and act

A: Excuse me. Have you got ...?
B: I think I've got one. Yes, here you are.

A: Excuse me. Have you got ...?
B: Sorry. I haven't got one. Ask Lucy.

a ruler a red pencil an eraser
a science book a dictionary

2 Ask and answer In the school library

A: Excuse me, have you got any books about ...?
B: Yes, we've got several. They're on that shelf. /
Sorry. We haven't got any at the moment.

maths art
science music
travel sports
foreign countries

3 Read and act

1

A: I've lost my science book. Have you seen it anywhere?
B: Yes, I think I have. Look at that book on the desk. Maybe it's yours.
A: Oh yes, it's mine! Thanks a lot.
B: You're welcome.

2

A: I've lost my ruler. Have you seen it anywhere?
B: Sorry, I haven't. Why don't you ask Jim?
A: Thanks. I will.

B: Hello! Have you found your ruler yet?
A: Yes, I have. I found it in my bag five minutes ago.
B: I'm so glad.

Lesson 22

Read

Read this story and find out the answer to this question: "What was the name of Meimei's library book?" Then read the story again and answer the questions on page 22 of your workbook.

THE LOST BOOK

Miss Yang works in the school library. She loves her work because she loves books. In the library she has got books on many different subjects. She works very hard and is very helpful. She likes the children to read newspapers and books in the reading room. She also likes them to borrow the books. But she is very strict. You must always return your library book on time!

One morning she was working at her desk in the library when a boy came in. He asked very politely:

"Excuse me, have you got any books about the moon and the stars?"

"Yes," said Miss Yang, "they're on that shelf over there."

Then Han Meimei came in.

"Excuse me, Miss Yang," she said. "I'm very sorry. I borrowed a book from the library two weeks ago. But I can't find it. I think I've lost it."

"Oh dear!" said Miss Yang. "Are you sure you've lost it?"

"Yes, I've looked for it everywhere," said Han Meimei. "I've looked round the whole school. I can't find it anywhere."

"What was the name of the book?" asked Miss Yang.

" 'Red Star over China'."

"What a pity! I'm afraid that if you've lost it, you must pay for it," said Miss Yang.

Read the end of the story in the next lesson for homework.

Lesson 23

1 **Read** Read the end of the story. Then act the whole story.

We must both thank Lucy!
You're welcome!

At that moment Lucy came into the library.

"Excuse me, Miss Yang. I've just found this library book."

"Oh, that's mine!" said Han Meimei. "Thank goodness!"

"No, it isn't yours!" said Miss Yang. "It's the library's. Please be more careful from now on!"

"Yes, Miss Yang," said Meimei. "I'm very sorry. Usually I'm very careful. I have never lost a book before. It won't happen again."

"OK!" said Miss Yang kindly. "Let's forget the whole thing."

"Thank you," said Meimei.

"Don't thank me," said Miss Yang. "We must both thank Lucy!"

"Not at all," smiled Lucy. "You're welcome!"

2 **Ask and answer**

Have you / they ever	made dumplings?	Yes, I have.
	eaten fish and chips?	Yes, we have often.
	spoken to a foreigner?	Yes, they have.
	listened to foreign music?	No, I/we/they haven't.
	travelled on a train?	No, never.

3 **Practise**

BRUCE:

I've just done my homework.
I've just washed my clothes.
I've just cleaned my shoes.
I've just washed the plates.

MR KNOW-ALL:

Really? I did mine hours ago!

Lesson 24

1 **Listen** Turn to page 24 in your workbook.

2 **Practise**

A: Have you got any books about science, please?
B: Yes, we have. They're on the shelves. / No, we haven't.
But we've got some books about history.

A: Has she / he returned her / his library book yet?
B: Yes, she / he returned it yesterday.

CHECKPOINT 6

● **Grammar**

The Present Perfect Tense (1) **现在完成时态 (一)**

现在完成时由"助动词 have(has) + 过去分词"构成。

Statement forms 陈述句形式	**Question forms 疑问句形式**
I/You have just seen	Have you/I seen ... yet?
She/He/It has just seen	Has he/she/it seen ... yet?
We have just seen	Have we seen ... yet?
They have just seen	Have they seen ... yet?

Short answers 简略答语

Yes, I/you/we/they have.	No, I/you/we/they haven't.
Yes, he/she/it has.	No, he/she/it hasn't.

	Verbs 动词（原形）	**Past tense 过去式**	**Past participle 过去分词**
Regular forms	ask	asked	asked
规则形式	travel	travelled	travelled
Irregular forms	lose	lost	lost
不 规 则 形 式	eat	ate	eaten
	find	found	found

● **Useful expressions**

I have got a book. Have you got a book? (Yes, I have./No, I haven't.)
I'm so glad. What a pity! pay for on time from now on

Unit 7 Mainly revision

Lesson 25

1 Ask and answer

What were	you your parents your friends the twins the boys	doing	yesterday afternoon? yesterday evening? at noon last Sunday? last Saturday evening? at this time yesterday?

2 Practise Give short answers like this: (Liu Mei) is.

What is the most popular subject Who is the youngest person Who is the best in Chinese	in your class?

Who is the most popular TV / film star What is the most popular piece of music Who is the best football player	at the moment?

3 Practise What do you think?

(Science)	is	not so	popular	as	(Chinese).
(Maths)	is	as	interesting	as	(English).

Lesson 26

Read Read this story and answer the questions on page 26 of your workbook.

MISS FORGETFUL

One day, Mrs King asked Lucy to go shopping for her.

"Here is a shopping list so you won't forget anything," she said.

"OK, Mom!" said Lucy.

When she got to the shop, she bought all the things on the list.

"I haven't forgotten anything," she said to herself. But then it was time to pay for them.

"Sorry!" she said to the shopkeeper. "I've forgotten my money!"

"I'll keep the things on this shelf for you," said the shopkeeper.

Lucy ran home at once. Her mother saw her when she arrived.

"That was quick!" she said. "Have you finished already?"

"No, Mom," said Lucy. "I forgot the money!"

"That wasn't very clever! And you'd better take the shopping basket with you, too!" said Mother.

In the shop, Lucy got all the things on her shopping list, and took them home. When she reached home, her mother asked:

"Have you got everything?"

"Yes, Mom," said Lucy. "I haven't forgotten anything."

She quickly put the basket on the table. She was taking the things out of the basket when she dropped a bag of sweets. The bag fell on the floor and broke open. The sweets went everywhere! "Oh dear!" she said.

"Bad luck!" said Mother. "It doesn't matter!"

They both started to pick them up again.

"How much did you pay for all these things?" asked her mother.

"Not too much," said Lucy. "I didn't spend all the money. I brought some of it back again."

"Where is it?" asked her mother.

"Here it is, Mom! That's one thing I haven't forgotten today!"

Use your dictionary

Look up these words in a dictionary: list sweet spend break

Lesson 27

1 Ask and answer

A: Have you started *your homework*?
B: Yes, but I haven't finished it/them yet.

A: Have you finished *your homework*?
B: Yes, I've already finished it/them.

the maths problems
your library book

2 Practise

Choose the best words

A: What have you done with the library book?
B: I've just ... to the library.

A: What have you done with the nuts?
B: We've just ....

A: What has she done with the milk?
B: She's just ....

A: What has he done with the meat?
B: He's just ....

A: What have they done with the eggs?
B: They've just .... Would you like one? Help yourself.

eaten it

cooked them

drunk it

given them to Polly

returned it

3 Read and say

MRS READ: Excuse me. I've lost my cat. Have you seen it anywhere?
LI LEI: Is it a black cat with one white ear and two white legs?
MRS READ: Yes, that's right! Where did you see it?
LI LEI: Sorry. I haven't seen it anywhere.

Lesson 28

1 Word study

What's another way of saying	bike? TV? phone?

Bicycle	Bike is short for ....
Television	TV is short for ....
Telephone	Phone is short for ....

2 Making words

Nouns →	Adjectives	Verbs →	Nouns	Compounds
help	helpful	run	runner	playground
care	careful	win	winner	afternoon
sun	sunny	play	player	everywhere
cloud	cloudy	speak	speaker	loudspeaker
rain	rainy	farm	farmer	newspaper

Adjectives →	Adverbs	Adjectives →	Adverbs
lucky	luckily	polite	politely
usual	usually	happy	happily
bad	badly	careful	carefully
loud	loudly	quiet	quietly
heavy	heavily	noisy	noisily

3 Listen and answer

How is the weather in Picture 1? Ask the same question about the other pictures. Is the weather the same in different parts of China? Turn to page 28 in your workbook. Listen to the weather report and fill in the form.

CHECKPOINT 7

Revise Checkpoints 1 - 6.

Unit 8 On the farm

Lesson 29

1 Listen, read and learn

Look at West Hill Farm. There are several kinds of animals on the farm. What kinds of animals have they got? What other things can you see?

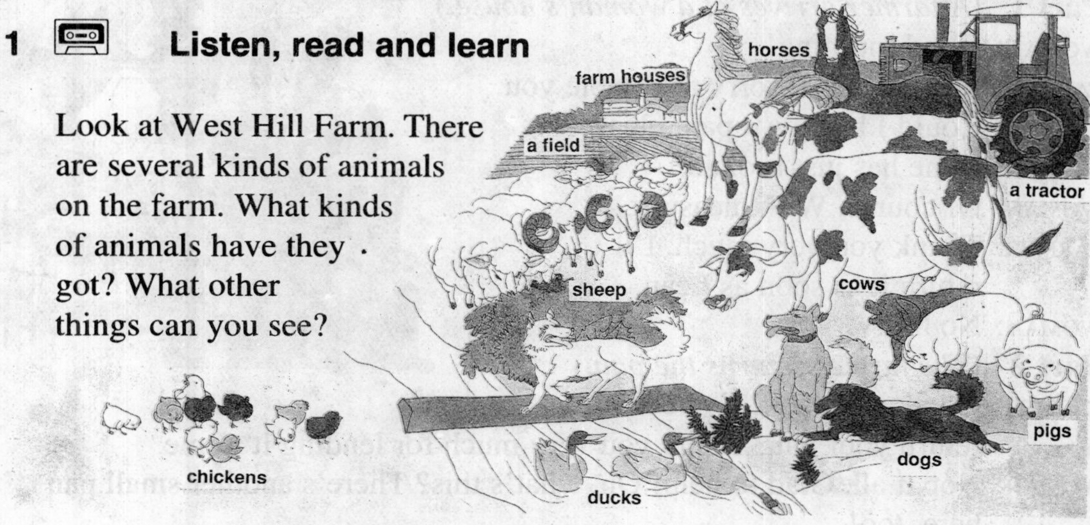

2 Ask and answer

How many	pigs cows sheep horses dogs fields tractors	have they got?	Only one. Two / Five / Ten. Several. Many. I'm not sure.

3 Read and act

A: Have you ever been to West Hill Farm?
B: No. I've never been to that farm before. What kinds of animals have they got?
A: They've got some beautiful *pigs*
B: Really? Are *pigs* beautiful? I've seen them before, but they weren't beautiful at all!

sheep
cows
dogs
horses
chickens

Lesson 30

Read

THE PAN (A PLAY)

Part 1 (*A farmer arrives at a woman's house.*)

WOMAN: Good morning!

FARMER: Morning! I'm sorry to trouble you. Could I borrow a pan, please? Mine has just broken.

WOMAN: Of course. With pleasure.

FARMER: Thank you very much. I'll return it as soon as I can.

WOMAN: No hurry.

Part 2 (*The farmer returns the pan.*)

FARMER: Good afternoon! I've come to return your pan. Thank you very much for lending it to me.

WOMAN: Not at all. Glad to help! Oh, what's this? There's another small pan here, too!

FARMER: Yes, that's right. It's just had a baby!

WOMAN: (*laughing*) Really? I've never heard of that before! Thank you very much! Goodbye!

Part 3 (*The farmer arrives at the woman's house again.*)

FARMER: Hello! Is there anyone at home?

WOMAN: Yes. What is it?

FARMER: I'm sorry to trouble you. Could I borrow your pan again?

WOMAN: Certainly! What happened? Has your pan broken again?

FARMER: No. Two visitors have just arrived and I want to give them something nice to eat.

WOMAN: I see. I hope everything goes well. Bye!

FARMER: Thank you. Goodbye.

Part 4 (*Two weeks later. The woman arrives at the farmer's house.*)

FARMER: Good morning! What can I do for you?

WOMAN: I lent a pan to you two weeks ago. I've come to get it back again.

FARMER: Your pan? Oh, I'm very sorry. It's dead.

WOMAN: Dead? Pans can't die! How can a pan die? I've never heard of that before!

FARMER: Well, have you forgotten already? Two weeks ago it had a baby. If a pan can have a baby, it can die, too! (*He starts to laugh.*) Here you are. It was only a joke! Thanks a lot!

Lesson 31

1 Ask and answer

What do you get from	cows? sheep? pigs? chickens?	Eggs and meat. Wool and mutton. Pork. Milk and beef.

2 Ask and answer

A: Have you ever *milked a cow*?
B: No, I haven't. / No, never.
Yes, I have, but only once.
Yes, twice.
Yes, several times.
Yes, many times.

ridden a horse
driven a tractor
seen a sheep
eaten chicken/mutton
cleaned a pigsty

3 Read and practise

Lucy and Lily have arrived at West Hill Farm. They are helping the farmer. Practise these dialogues:

FARMER: Have you *milked the cows* yet?

THE TWINS: Yes, we've done that already.

taken the sheep to the field
cleaned the pigsty
given the horses their food

FARMER: Well done! When did you do that?

THE TWINS: We did it an hour ago.

Lesson 32

1 **Listen** Turn to page 32 of your workbook.

2 **Read and say**

Put these sentences in the right order. Then read the dialogue:

( ) FARMER: What do you want?
( ) MAN: It's very clever and very strong. It can do half the work on the farm.
( ) FARMER: No. I've never heard of it! What can it do?
(1) MAN: Good morning. I'm sorry to trouble you. Have you got a moment? I'd like to talk to you.
( ) FARMER: Really? Well, we'll have two of them. Then they'll do the whole of the work!
( ) MAN: I'd like to tell you about this new kind of tractor — the Strongman Tractor. Have you ever heard of it?

CHECKPOINT 8

● **Grammar The Present Perfect Tense (2) 现在完成时态 (二)**

现在完成时的用法

1 表示过去发生或已经完成的某一动作对现在造成的影响或结果。

a) 常与 *already, just* 和 *yet* 等连用。例如:

Have you finished your work *yet*?
Yes, I have. I've *just* finished it.
I've *already* finished it. No, I haven't finished it *yet*.

b) 也可以和 *ever* 和 *never* 等连用。例如:

Have you *ever* been to a chicken farm?
Yes, I have. / No, I've *never* been to a chicken farm.

● **Useful expressions:**

With pleasure. as soon as I can
No hurry. I hope everything goes well.

Unit 9 A visit to a factory

Lesson 33

1 Listen, read and act

LI LEI: Jim, how long have you been at this school?
JIM: Let me see. Er, I've been here for just over two years.
LI LEI: What about your sister Kate? You didn't come together, did you?
JIM: No, she's much younger than I am. She only started here this term.
LI LEI: So she's been at this school since September?
JIM: That's right.

2 Read and learn

A: How long have you been at this school?
B: I've been here for about two years. I've been here since 19__.
A: How long has Jim been at his school?
B: He's been there for over two years. He's been there since two years ago.
A: How long has Kate been at her school?
B: She's been there for two months. She's been there since September.

3 Ask and answer

Ask questions about the teachers in the pictures like this:

A: How long has the *English* teacher been at this school?
B: *She* has been here *for four years*.
A: How long has the *P.E.* teacher been at this school?
B: He has been here *since September 1991*.

Now ask the same questions about your own teachers.

Lesson 34

 **Read**

Read this story as quickly as you can and find out "What does the factory make?" Then read it again more carefully and answer the questions on page 34 of your workbook.

UNCLE WANG'S FACTORY

There is a factory near No. 14 Middle School. The factory has been there for several years. Uncle Wang works in the factory. He has worked there since it opened in 1989.

Every year, several classes visit the factory. Last November it was Class 3's turn. They arrived early on a Tuesday morning. Uncle Wang was waiting for them outside the factory gate.

When they arrived, he said: "Welcome to our factory! Please come this way. Don't rush."

The students walked through the gates with Uncle Wang.

"Now, everyone. Listen, please. First, I'd like to tell you a few things about this factory. This factory opened in 1989. We make many kinds of useful things here. For example, we make bicycle parts and tractor parts. Any questions?

"OK. Let's go to Number 1 Machine Shop. Come up these steps with me, please, and be careful. The steps are rather narrow."

They all went up some narrow steps into a large room.

"This is No. 1 Machine Shop. Keep together, please!" said Uncle Wang.

"Please don't touch the machines. They're dangerous! If you touch them you may break something or have an accident and hurt yourselves."

"What do the machines do?" asked Jim.

"That's a good question," smiled Uncle Wang. "The ones in this corner are cutting machines. They cut big pieces of metal into small pieces. Can you see the machine in that corner?"

They all looked at a big and noisy machine in another corner of the machine shop. It was making a lot of noise.

"That machine joins these different pieces of metal together. Let's go and take a look at it."

Read the end of the story in the next lesson for homework.

Lesson 35

1 Read

Find out: What are the workers making?

"Come straight along here, please. Oh, and please keep together. We don't want any of you to get lost!"

The students followed Uncle Wang to see the other machine.

"This machine joins the metal pieces together," he said. "The workers all wear thick clothes and glasses over their eyes. The glasses keep their eyes safe."

"What are they making?" asked Li Lei. Uncle Wang laughed. "Guess!" he said.

"I know!" smiled Lucy. "They have steps, and they begin with L!"

2 Read and act

JIM: Uncle Wang, may I ask you some questions, please?
UNCLE WANG: Of course.
JIM: How long has this factory been open?
UNCLE WANG: It's been open for several years.
JIM: How long have you worked in this factory?
UNCLE WANG: I've worked here since 1989.
JIM: Do you live near the factory?
UNCLE WANG: Not far. My house is about twenty minutes by bike.
JIM: How long have you lived there?
UNCLE WANG: I've lived there all my life.
JIM: Thank you very much.

3 Ask and answer

A: Where does your ... work?
B: She / He works ....

father mother uncle aunt
in a factory / shop in an office
on a boat on a train on a farm

A: How long has she / he worked there?

B: He's worked there ....

all his / her life for three years / for ...
since last year / since 19_ _ / ...

Lesson 36

1 **Listen** Turn to page 36 of your workbook.

2 Play this game "I spy!"

"I spy,
With my little eye
Something beginning with ...!"
What is it?

3 **Read**

Read this passage written by Jim. Make up some questions about him.

My name is Jim Green. I live at 152 Jianguo Street, not far from the centre of the city. I have lived there since 1990. I go to No. 14 Middle School. I've been a student there for nearly two and a half years.

4 **Write** Now write about yourself in the same way.

CHECKPOINT 9

● **Grammar The Present Perfect Tense (3) 现在完成时态 (三)**

2 表示过去已经开始，持续到现在的动作或状态，可以和表示从过去某一时刻延续到现在（包括"现在"在内）的一段时间的状语连用。例如：

I'*ve known* Li Lei *for three years*. I'*ve lived* here *since 1990*.
I'*ve been* at this school *for over two years*.

• *for* 和表示一段时间的词组连用。例如：*for* three minutes *for* six hours *for* nine days *for* twelve weeks *for* fifteen months *for* thirty years

• *since* 和表示过去某一时刻的词或词组连用。例如：*since* nine o'clock this morning *since* last Friday *since* three weeks ago *since* September

● **Useful expressions**

Don't rush. keep ... safe It's about twenty minutes by bike. all one's life

Unit 10 Mr Green's problem

Lesson 37

1 Listen, read and act

TELEPHONE MESSAGE

FROM: *Mr Green*
TO: *The headmaster*
DATE: *Nov. 15* TIME: *9:12*
MESSAGE: *He would like to meet you between 8:00 – 9:00 tomorrow morning.*

MR GREEN: Hello! Could I speak to the headmaster, please?

TEACHER: Hold on for a moment, please. I'm sorry he isn't here right now. May I help you?

MR GREEN: That's very kind of you, but I want to speak to him about my son, Jim Green. I would like to see him as soon as possible, please.

TEACHER: Are you free later today, Mr Green?

MR GREEN: Sorry. I'm free every day except today.

TEACHER: Are you able to come tomorrow?

MR GREEN: I think so. What time?

TEACHER: Between 8:00 and 9:00.

MR GREEN: Yes, that would be fine.

TEACHER: I'll leave a message on his desk.

MR GREEN: Thank you very much. Goodbye!

TEACHER: Goodbye!

2 Practise Talk about the dialogue.

Example:

A: What does the teacher say?
B: She says that she will leave a message on the headmaster's desk.
A: What does Mr Green say?

TELEPHONE MESSAGE

FROM: *Mr Green*
TO: *The headmaster*
DATE: *Nov.15* TIME: *9:12*
MESSAGE: *He wants to see you as soon as possible.*

B: He says that
- he wants to speak to the headmaster.
- he wants to see him as soon as possible.
- he won't be free until tomorrow.
- he can come between 8:00 and 9:00 on Wednesday.

Lesson 38

Read

Read this dialogue between Mr Green and Mr Zhang. Find out:

1 Where is Mr Green going to travel next month?

2 Why is Mr Green worried?

Put your hand up when you've found the answers. Then read it again and answer the questions on page 38 of the workbook.

MR GREEN'S PROBLEM

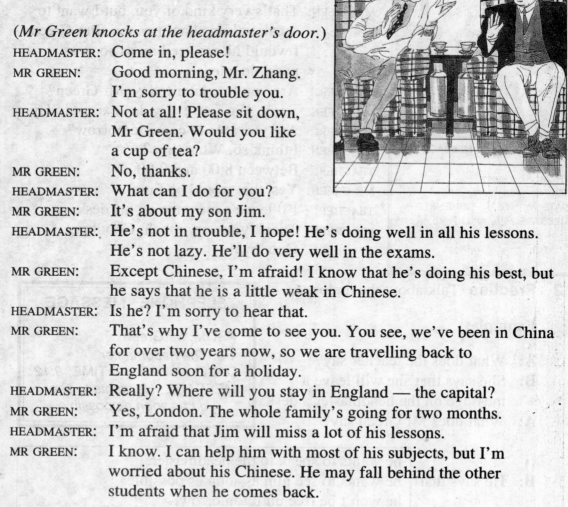

(*Mr Green knocks at the headmaster's door.*)

HEADMASTER: Come in, please!

MR GREEN: Good morning, Mr. Zhang. I'm sorry to trouble you.

HEADMASTER: Not at all! Please sit down, Mr Green. Would you like a cup of tea?

MR GREEN: No, thanks.

HEADMASTER: What can I do for you?

MR GREEN: It's about my son Jim.

HEADMASTER: He's not in trouble, I hope! He's doing well in all his lessons. He's not lazy. He'll do very well in the exams.

MR GREEN: Except Chinese, I'm afraid! I know that he's doing his best, but he says that he is a little weak in Chinese.

HEADMASTER: Is he? I'm sorry to hear that.

MR GREEN: That's why I've come to see you. You see, we've been in China for over two years now, so we are travelling back to England soon for a holiday.

HEADMASTER: Really? Where will you stay in England — the capital?

MR GREEN: Yes, London. The whole family's going for two months.

HEADMASTER: I'm afraid that Jim will miss a lot of his lessons.

MR GREEN: I know. I can help him with most of his subjects, but I'm worried about his Chinese. He may fall behind the other students when he comes back.

Read the end of the dialogue in the next lesson for homework.

Lesson 39

1 Read

Read the end of the dialogue. Find out: What does Mr Green want?

MR GREEN: He's already a little weak in Chinese. I'm afraid that he'll forget it if he misses so many lessons. He may even fail his Chinese exam.

HEADMASTER: It's possible. Two months is quite a long time. It's true that he may fall behind the other students. But of course, he can learn by himself. He has a book and a dictionary.

MR GREEN: I know. But even that is not enough. I think that maybe his Chinese teacher will give Jim some work to do during the holiday.

HEADMASTER: Yes, that's possible. I'll ask Mr Hu. I'm sure that he won't mind. We may talk again next week.

MR GREEN: All right! Thank you very much. I'll give you a call.

2 Practise Talk about the dialogue.

Find the right answers from the second box:

What does Mr Green say about travelling to England?
What does he say about his wife and children?
Why is he worried about Jim?
What does he say about Jim's Chinese exam?
What does he say about Mr Hu?
What does the headmaster say about next week?

He says that
- they may talk about it next week.
- he may fail it.
- he wants to take them with him.
- he will go back to England soon for a holiday.
- Jim is a little weak in Chinese.
- he wants Mr Hu to give Jim some work to do during the holiday.

Lesson 40

1 **Listen** Answer the questions on page 40 of the workbook.

2 **Ask and answer**

Find the right answers:

What does the headmaster say about Jim's lessons?
What does he say about Jim's work?
What does he say about Jim's two-month holiday?
Why is he worried about Jim?
What does he say about Mr Hu?

He says that
- he will ask Mr Hu to give Jim some work.
- Jim isn't lazy.
- Jim is doing very well in his lessons.
- Jim will miss a lot of lessons.
- Jim may fall behind the other students.

CHECKPOINT 10

● **Grammar** **The Object Clause (1) 宾语从句（一）**

宾语从句在复合句中作主句的宾语。

1 宾语从句常由 that 引导。that 在口语中常省略。

She says (that) she will leave a message on his desk.
He says (that) Jim may fail the Chinese exam.
He knows (that) Jim will work hard.
He is afraid (that) Jim will forget his Chinese.

● **Useful expressions**

Hold on for a moment, please.
as soon as possible
May I help you?
He may fail .... do one's best
Yes, that would be fine.
I'm sorry he isn't here right now.
I'm sure he won't mind.
go back be able to ... do well in ...

Unit 11 A great inventor

Lesson 41

1 Read, say and learn

Here are some important inventions. They are all very useful, and they have all changed the world. What do you call them in English?

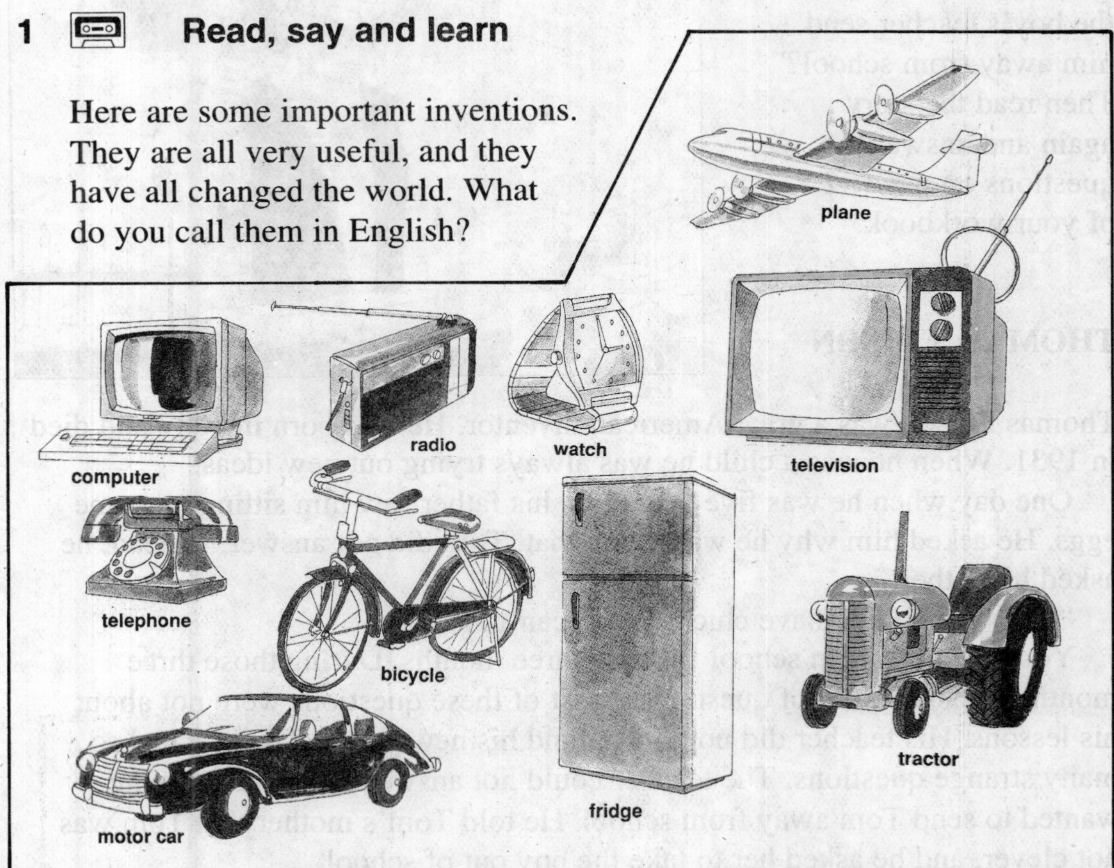

2 Ask and answer

Some of these inventions have changed the world more than others. Ask two friends these questions and write down their answers:

1 Which of these do you think is
- the most useful invention?
- the second most useful invention?
- the third most useful invention?

2 Which of these would you most like to own?

Answer 1
Answer 2

Lesson 42

 **Read**

Read the story quickly and find out: "Why did the boy's teacher send him away from school?" Then read the story again and answer the questions on page 42 of your workbook.

THOMAS EDISON

Thomas Edison was a great American inventor. He was born in 1847 and died in 1931. When he was a child he was always trying out new ideas.

One day when he was five years old, his father saw him sitting on some eggs. He asked him why he was doing that. Tom did not answer. Instead, he asked his father:

"Hens are able to have chicks. Why can't I?"

Young Tom was in school for only three months. During those three months he asked a lot of questions. Most of these questions were not about his lessons. His teacher did not understand his new pupil. The boy had so many strange questions. The teacher could not answer all of them. So he wanted to send Tom away from school. He told Tom's mother that Tom was not clever, and he asked her to take the boy out of school.

So Tom's mother took him out of school, and taught him herself. She taught him to read and write, and she found him a very good pupil. He learnt very fast. Even before he was ten he became very interested in science.

"Mom, I want a science lab," he said one day.

"Why, Tom? What do you want a science lab for?"

"I want to try out some of my ideas."

"Well, you'll have to build it yourself. We haven't got enough money for that kind of thing," said his mother.

So he built a science lab himself. He grew vegetables in his garden and sold them. With the money he bought things for his lab.

Read the end of the text in the next lesson for homework.

Lesson 43

1 Read

Look at the picture. You can see Thomas putting a mirror and some lights on a table. Read the second part of the story and find out why.

THOMAS EDISON

One day his mother was ill. She sent for a doctor.

"Ask him to come quickly," she said. The doctor came as soon as possible. When he saw her, he said that she needed an operation at once. But it was night, and the light in the room was very bad. The doctor wanted to operate, but he wasn't able to.

"I can't see clearly enough!" he said.

Edison thought hard. At last he had an idea. His father owned a large mirror. Edison took all the lights in the house and put them on a long table. Then he put the big mirror behind them. Now there was enough light, so the doctor was able to see clearly. He operated on her at once, and Edison's mother was saved.

2 Listen and read

A: Don't you think his radio is too noisy?
B: Yes, I do. Ask him to turn it down, please.
A: OK. Excuse me. Could you turn your radio down, please?
C: Certainly. Sorry!

3 Practise

A: Don't you think	B: Yes, I do.
her radio is too loud?	Tell her to turn it down.
his fridge is making a strange noise?	Ask him to turn it down.
Jim is speaking too quickly?	Ask him to speak more slowly.
the twins speak too quietly?	Ask them to speak more loudly.

Lesson 44

1 **Listen** Turn to page 44 in your workbook.

2 **Read and act**

A: Hello!
B: Hello, Ann. Could I borrow your *radio* tomorrow, please? (*watch*)
A: Sorry! It's not a very good line. Could you speak more *clearly*, please? (*slowly / loudly*)
B: Yes. I said, could I borrow your *radio*, please? Mine's broken.
A: Sure! When do you want it?
B: Tomorrow if possible.
A: OK. I'll bring it to school in the morning.
B: Thanks. Bye!
C: Who was that?
A: It was Lucy.
C: Why were you shouting?
A: She asked me to speak more *loudly*. The line was bad.
C: What did she want?
A: She wanted to borrow my *radio*.
C: Why didn't you tell her to use her own?
A: She said hers was broken.

CHECKPOINT 11

- **Grammar**

The Infinitive (1) 动词不定式(一)

1 用作宾语

The doctor wanted *to operate*.
She wanted *to borrow* my radio.

2 用作宾语补足语

Tell her *to turn it down*.
Ask him *to come* quickly.

- **Useful expressions**

It's a bad line. to send away/for to turn down

Unit 12 Have a good time, Jim!

Lesson 45

1 Read and act

JIM: Ling Feng, could you do something for me, please?

LING FENG: Certainly! What would you like me to do?

JIM: Well, you know I'm going to England next week for a holiday?

LING FENG: Yes.

JIM: Well, we can't take Polly with us. Could you look after her for me while we're away?

LING FENG: With pleasure!

JIM: Are you sure you don't mind?

LING FENG: Yes, of course I'm sure. I would love to look after her. Glad to help! What do I have to do?

JIM: I've written it all down on this list.

LING FENG: Good. Don't worry. I'll take good care of her.

JIM: I'm sure you will!

2 Ask and answer

Read the list of instructions below. Practise like this:

A: How often does Ling Feng have to speak to Polly in English?
B: Jim told him to do it every day.

Looking after Polly — instructions

1 *Give her some bird food every day.*
2 *Make sure she has clean water every day. Don't fill her pan too full!*
3 *Give her a clean cabbage leaf twice a week.*
4 *Cover her cage every night to help her to sleep.*
5 *Polly is trying to learn English. Please speak to her in English as much as possible every day!*
6 *Please clean the floor of her cage once a week.*

Lesson 46

Read

Read this story as quickly as possible, and find out "Why does Mrs Green hate travelling?" Then read it again more carefully, and answer the questions on page 46 of your workbook.

GETTING READY TO GO

It was Friday evening. Mr and Mrs Green were getting ready to fly to England for their holiday. They and the children were filling their bags with clothes and other things.

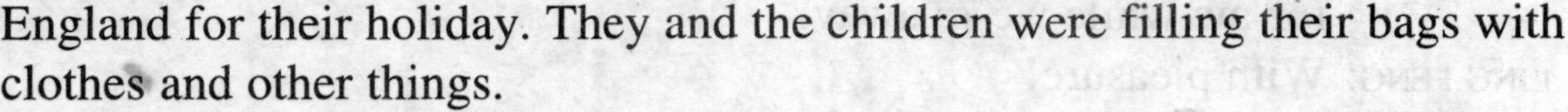

"You can have one bag each, children," said Mrs Green. "Put them beside mine when they're ready."

Mrs Green was worried about their journey. She liked to stay safely in the same place. She hated travelling by air: the seats were too narrow, and the journey was always too long. She tried to sleep, but she was never able to sleep very well. She tried not to worry, but she found it difficult.

"Make sure you've got the air tickets, Jack!" said Mrs Green.

"Don't worry! I have them here in my jacket," said Mr Green.

"Do we have enough money for the journey?" his wife asked.

"Yes, that's in my jacket, too. Don't worry!" said Mr Green.

"Oh, I nearly forgot! What about Polly?" said Mrs Green. "She's not coming with us, I hope. She hates travelling, too."

"Don't worry, Mum," said Jim. "I've asked Ling Feng to take care of her while we are away."

"That's very kind of him. Are you sure he doesn't mind?"

"Yes, I'm quite sure."

"Are you going to take Polly to his house?"

"No, Mum. He's coming round to get her quite soon. He'll be here in a minute," answered Jim.

Just then there was a knock on the door.

"Oh, that must be Ling Feng now!" said Jim.

He was right. It was Ling Feng.

Read the end of the story in the next lesson for homework.

Lesson 47

1 Read

Read the end of the story:

"Hi, Ling Feng!" said Jim. "Have you come to get Polly? Oh, you haven't changed your mind, have you?"

"Of course I haven't!" laughed Ling Feng. "Yes, I've come to get her. Oh, you look busy! Can I do anything to help?"

"No, thanks, Ling Feng," said Jim. "Here's Polly, and here's her food, in these bags. They're both full. There's enough bird food here to last for two months."

"Great!" said Ling Feng. "I hope that you have a good holiday."

"Thanks a lot," said Jim. "See you in February! Goodbye, Polly!"

"*Zai jian*!" said Polly.

2 Ask and answer

Look at the instructions for Jim's journey. These instructions use the 24 hour clock. For example, 0700 hours means seven o'clock in the morning. 1900 hours means seven o'clock in the evening.

The Green family
Date: 14 December
Flight No. CA 907
Leave Beijing 0745
Arrive in Moscow 1130
Flight No. BA 347
Leave Moscow 1610
Arrive in London 2230

1. What is the flight number of their plane leaving Beijing?
2 Do you know what time their plane leaves Beijing?
3 Where do the Greens stop on the way?
4 Do you know what time the plane arrives in Moscow?
5 Do they have to change planes in Moscow?

3 Practise

Mr Green needs help.

MR GREEN: Excuse me! ...

WOMAN: Certainly. ...

Could you tell me	where we show our tickets?	Go straight along here.
	how we can get to the plane?	Please go to Gate 12.
	which gate we have to go to?	It leaves at seven.
	what time the plane leaves?	That man over there.
	who we have to see?	Please come this way.

Lesson 48

1 **Listen** Turn to page 48 of your workbook.

2 **Find the words** Then act the dialogue. The Green family are just starting their flight. The plane is nearly full.

narrow	seat	moment	beside	won't
furthest	sit	quickly	better	course

FATHER: Where are our seats?
JIM: Along here, I think. They're a bit ..., aren't they? What row are we in?
FATHER: Row 14. Our ... numbers are 14A, B, C and D.
JIM: Ah, here they are!
FATHER: Right. Who wants to ... next to the window? What about you, Mother?
MOTHER: No, thanks. I'll have the seat ... from the window, please. I just want to close my eyes and go to sleep as ... as possible.
JIM: Can I have the window seat please, Dad?
FATHER: Sure, Jim. But you ... see much. We'll be above the clouds most of the time.
KATE: Can I sit ... you please, Mum?
MOTHER: Of ... you can, dear.
JIM: We'd ... sit down. I think the plane's going to take off in a ....

CHECKPOINT 12

● **Grammar** **The Object Clause (2) 宾语从句 (二)**

2 宾语从句常由连接代词或连接副词引导。
Do you know *what* time the ship leaves? We don't know *when* we arrive.
Could you tell me *where* the nearest post office is?
Can you tell me *who* we have to see?
Could you tell me *how* we get to the plane?

● **Useful expressions**

Have you changed your mind? I don't mind. as much as possible
Could you do something for me, please? make sure take (good) care of

Unit 13 Merry Christmas!

Lesson 49

1 Read and act

MR HU: Good afternoon, class! Who's on duty today?
LILY: Good afternoon! I am. Today is (day and date). Everybody is here except Jim Green.
MR HU: Where's Jim Green?
LILY: He's gone to England with his family. He won't be back until January.
MR HU: That's right. I remember now.

2 Read and act

A: Have you received a letter from Jim yet?
B: No, I haven't.
A: Really? Oh well, no news is good news.

3 Ask and answer

Find the right answers, then practise in pairs.

1 Where's Jim?	A Sorry, I don't know.
2 Where was his seat?	B He's gone to England.
3 When did he go?	C He went by plane.
4 How did he travel?	D He went with his family.
5 Whom did he travel with?	E He'll be away for about eight weeks.
6 How many bags did he and Kate have on the plane?	F He went last week.
7 How long will he be away?	G His seat was beside Ling Feng's, in the centre of the classroom.
8 Why did he go?	H He went for a holiday.
9 When is he coming back?	I He's coming back at the end of January.
10 Has Ling Feng received a letter from him yet?	J One each.

Lesson 50

Read Ling Feng has just received this letter from Jim. Read it and answer the questions on page 50 of your workbook.

---

115 Park Road
London SE3 7SD

December 23rd, 19__

Dear Ling Feng,

How time flies! More than a week has passed already!

I hope that you and everybody at school are all well. Please give them all my best wishes. I hope Polly is well, too. Is she very unhappy without me? Don't forget to give her some food and change her water, will you? Please tell Mr Hu that I am working hard on my Chinese.

We had a very good journey home. I had a seat beside the window, but I didn't see much during the flight because there was too much cloud. Mum slept almost the whole way. We stopped in Moscow on the way, but only for an hour or two, so there was no time to go into the centre of the city. I didn't mind, because it was really cold in Moscow. There was thick snow everywhere!

We've seen several members of the family since we arrived — my grandfather and my aunt and uncle. But we won't have our big family get-together until Christmas. Everybody here is busy getting ready for it and buying Christmas presents. I will have to choose presents for all the family soon, but I haven't chosen any yet!

Tomorrow is Christmas Eve, and my father and I went to choose a Christmas tree today. We chose a big one. It is almost as tall as the room. It is now standing in the corner of our sitting room. Kate has covered it with Christmas lights. The sitting room looks really beautiful at the moment. There is a fire burning in the fireplace, and the Christmas tree lights are shining brightly. Well, I must stop now. Please write soon and tell me all your news.

Merry Christmas and best wishes for the New Year!

Yours,

Jim

Lesson 51

1 Ask and answer

Look at these sentences:

Jim asked Ling Feng to look after Polly.
Jim asked him not to forget her.
Now make similar sentences:

Jim told Ling Feng Jim asked Ling Feng	to write soon. to give his best wishes to everybody. to tell Mr Hu he was doing a lot of Chinese. to say Merry Christmas to everybody. not to forget to give Polly her food. not to forget to change her water.

2 Ask and answer

Find the right answers.

1 Did Jim have a good journey home?
2 Did they stop on the way?
3 Did he go into the centre of Moscow?
4 Was it warm in Moscow?
5 Has he bought any presents yet?
6 Is Jim doing any work?

Yes, he said that	he was working hard on his Chinese. he had a very good journey home. they stopped in Moscow on the way.
No, he said that	he hadn't bought any yet. it was very cold in Moscow. there wasn't time to go to the centre.

3 Practise

A: Where's Jim?
B: He's gone to England.
A: Has he ever been there before?
B: Of course! He lived there before he came to China.
A: Have you heard from him?
B: Oh, didn't I tell you? I've just had a letter from him! Have a look.

Lesson 52

1 **Listen** Turn to page 52 in the workbook.

2 **Find the right words** Then act the dialogue.

once	given	often	changed	care
enough	gave	about	cleaning	think

MOTHER: I hope that you are taking ... of Polly. Have you ... her some food today?
LING FENG: Yes, I ... her some this morning.
MOTHER: Glad to hear it. What ... her water?
LING FENG: Yes, I ... her water, too.
MOTHER: Are you ... her cage?
LING FENG: Yes, I am.
MOTHER: How ... do you do that?
LING FENG: ... a week.
MOTHER: Is that often ...?
LING FENG: Yes, I ... so.

CHECKPOINT 13

● **Grammar**

1 The Infinitive (2) **动词不定式（二）**

3 用作状语

I went *to choose a Christmas tree today*.

2 The Object Clause (3) 宾语从句（三）

He *said* (that) they *had* a very good journey home.

He *said* (that) it *was* very cold in Moscow.

3 been to 和 gone to 的区别

She's *gone to* England. 意思是 She hasn't returned yet.

She's *been to* England. 意思是 She went there once.

● **Useful expressions**

Everybody is here except ....

How time flies!

No news is good news.

Merry Christmas!

Unit 14 Mainly revision

Lesson 53

1 Ask and answer

A: What has happened? B: They've had an accident.
A: When did it happen? B: Five minutes ago.
A: Has anyone called the police? B: Yes, they have.
A: Is anyone hurt? B: Yes, a man is hurt, but not badly.

2 Puzzle dialogues Find the right answers!

1 Has Mr Li ever been to a foreign country?
2 Have you ever spoken to an Englishman?
3 Has Linda ever been to Beijing?
4 Have you ever ridden a horse?
5 Has Lucy ever been to the USA ?
6 Have you ever run in a relay race?
7 Have they ever been to the moon?

A Beijing? Yes, she's been there several times.
B No, I haven't. But I've ridden a motorbike.
C Of course! She comes from America!
D No, I've never met a foreigner.
E Yes. I was the first runner, but we came last!
F Not yet!
G No, but they'd like to go, one day!

Now make up some similar questions, and ask your friends.

3 Read and act

A: Where have Jim and Kate gone?
B: They've gone to London.
A: Have they ever been there before?
B: Of course. They lived there.
A: When did they live there?
B: They lived there before they came to China.
A: Are they going to return soon?
B: Yes, I think they'll return next month.

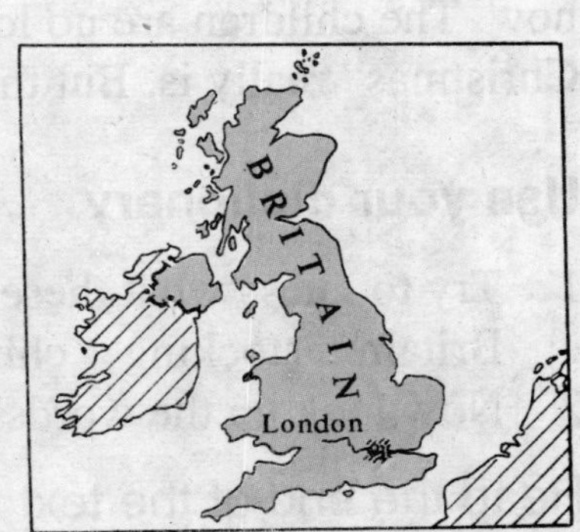

Lesson 54

Read

Christmas is an important festival in Britain and many other parts of the world. Read the passage below very quickly and find out "Who is Father Christmas?" Then read it again and answer the questions on page 54 of your workbook.

CHRISTMAS DAY

On Christmas Eve — the night before Christmas Day — children all over Britain put a stocking at the end of their beds before they go to sleep. Their parents usually tell them that Father Christmas will come during the night.

Father Christmas is very kind-hearted. He lands on top of each house and climbs down the chimney into the fireplace. He fills each of the stockings with Christmas presents.

Of course, Father Christmas isn't real. In Jim and Kate's house, "Father Christmas" is really Mr Green. Mr Green doesn't climb down the chimney. He waits until the children are asleep. Then he quietly goes into their bedrooms, and fills their stockings with small presents. When they were very young, Mr Green sometimes dressed up in a red coat. But he doesn't do that now. The children are no longer young, and they know who "Father Christmas" really is. But they still put their stockings at the end of their beds.

Use your dictionary

1 Try to guess what these words mean:
Britain stocking chimney kind-hearted top

2 Now look up the words in a dictionary.

Read the end of the text in the next lesson for homework.

Lesson 55

1 Read

Read the end of the reading passage. Find out: "What does Christmas Day mean?"

Mr and Mrs Green have stockings, too. They put small presents in each other's stockings. "You're never too old to enjoy a Christmas stocking," they say. So they still have them.

Christmas Day always begins before breakfast. The children wake up very early, and can't wait to open the presents in their stockings. Then they wake up their parents, calling: "Merry Christmas!" They help their parents to open their stockings, too.

What does Christmas mean? Christmas Day is the birthday of Jesus Christ. When Christ was born nearly two thousand years ago, many people, rich and poor, gave him presents. So today, people still do the same thing to each other. Of course, everyone likes presents. But Mr Green says: "It is better to give than to receive."

What do you think?

2 Practise

Make up sentences:

1 The small children did not know	who filled their stockings. who Father Christmas was. that their father was Father Christmas. that Father Christmas wasn't real.
2 Now they are older, they know that	Father Christmas isn't real. their parents fill their stockings with presents. Father Christmas is really their father.
3 But they don't know	what is in their stockings. what time their father fills their stockings. what their presents are.

Lesson 56

1 **Dictation** Follow your teacher's instructions.

2 **Practise** Make sentences, beginning:
(a) The children ... (b) The parents ...

	Father Christmas	to give them a present.
asked	their parents	not to wake them up in the night.
told	the children	not to wake them up too early.
	each other	to try not to sleep on Christmas Eve.

3 **Read and act**

LILY: Oh, you've got a letter! Why haven't you opened it?
LI LEI: I've only just received it. I don't even know who it's from.
LILY: It's from England, isn't it?
LI LEI: Yes. It must be from Jim. Yes! It's a Christmas card!
LILY: Really? What does it say?
LI LEI: "Best wishes for Christmas and the New Year!"

CHECKPOINT 14

Revise Checkpoints 8-13.

Unit 15 At home with the twins

Lesson 57

1 Read and act

1 FATHER: Do we need some more tea?

MOTHER: Yes, I think we do. Lucy, we need some more tea. Can you get some, please?

LUCY: Sure, Mom. I'll get some at once.

2 FATHER: Do we need some more hot water?

MOTHER: Yes, I think we do. Lucy, we need some more hot water. Can you go and get some, please?

LUCY: Mom, can't Lily do it? It's her turn!

MOTHER: So it is! Lily, did you hear what I said?

LILY: Yes, Mom! I'll do it right away.

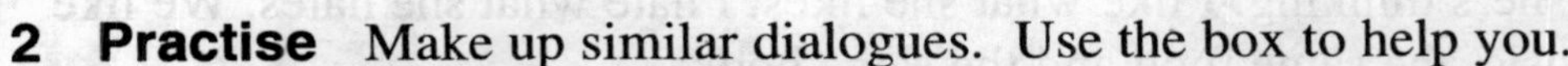

2 Practise Make up similar dialogues. Use the box to help you.

A: We need some more .... **B:** Can you go ...

A	B
bread	and get some, please?
potatoes	and buy some, please?
rice	and cook some, please?
...	...

3 Ask and answer Ask and answer these questions about Dialogue 1:

What did father/mother ask? What did Lucy say?

He asked whether	they needed some more tea.
She asked Lucy if	she could go and get some.
Lucy said that	she could get some at once.

Ask and answer similar questions about Dialogue 2.

Lesson 58

 **Read**

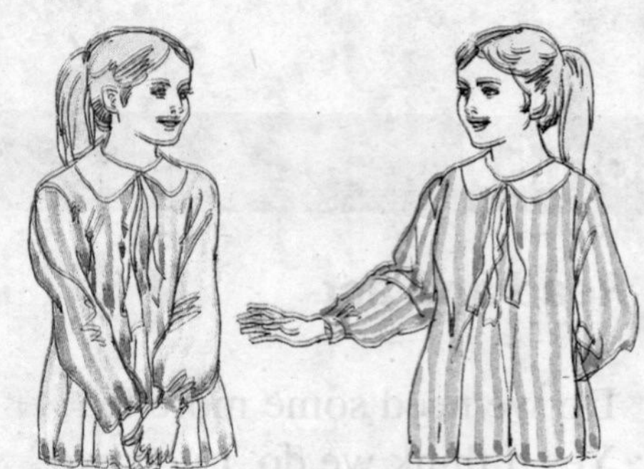

Lucy and Lily are twins. Read the passage below, and find out: "Who is speaking, Lucy or Lily?"

I'M A TWIN

People often ask me whether I like being a twin. Well, it feels strange to have a twin sister. But it's great! We're together most of the time. So we never feel lonely. Of course, sometimes we're together too often, and we fight. But we never fight for long. We always make friends with each other again. Usually we get on very well with each other.

People think we look the same, but I can see that we're different. But people still mistake us for each other. They call me Lily sometimes, and I don't always tell them that they've made a mistake.

I like having a twin sister. When she's happy, I'm happy. When she feels unhappy, I feel the same. Often, I know what she's going to say. Sometimes, I know what she's thinking. I like what she likes. I hate what she hates. We like the same music, the same food and the same books.

But we have a few small differences, too. For example, Lily likes to dance, but I like to sing. We don't like the same colours, either. On our birthday, we often get the same presents. One year for our birthday Mom gave us both a T-shirt — two green T-shirts!

"Why did you give us two T-shirts, both the same colour?" we asked. "Can't we be different from each other sometimes?"

So now, if Mom buys us new clothes, she chooses different colours, and it's better. I like light green, but Lily prefers dark blue.

Sometimes, my grandma decides to buy one big birthday present for both of us. I hate this. It always makes problems. We can't decide who should open it first. Lily was born ten minutes before me, so she says:

"I'm older than you! So I must open the present!"

Then, when it's open, we fight about who plays with it first.

But we don't fight very often. We love each other and we are both very happy that we are twins.

Answer the questions on page 58 in your workbook.

Lesson 59

1 Read and act

SHOPKEEPER: Good morning! What can I do for you?

MOTHER: I'd like two sweaters for my daughters.

SHOPKEEPER: Certainly. The woolen ones are hanging here, and the cotton ones are hanging there. Which would you like?

MOTHER: We'll have a look at the woolen ones, thank you.

SHOPKEEPER: No hurry! Please take your time!

2 Practise

A: I can't decide which *sweater* to buy!
B: Let me help!
Do you like this one / these ones?
A: I like the colour, but it's / they're too ....
/ No, the colour's too ....
B: Maybe you're right.
What about this one / these ones?
A: It's great, but it's not ... enough. /
They're great, but they're not ... enough.
B: What about this one/these ones?
A: I like it, but it costs too much. You decide! /
I like them, but they cost too much. You decide!

blouse	shirt
trousers	socks

large	expensive
dark	light

strong	long	soft
warm	thick	cheap

3 Practise

Lily asked Lucy asked Mother asked The shopkeeper asked	if / whether	they were too expensive. they had a dark blue one. they had any lighter ones. they had a cheaper one. she could help them. there were any cheaper ones.

Lesson 60

1 **Listen** Turn to page 60 in your workbook.

2 **Ask and answer**

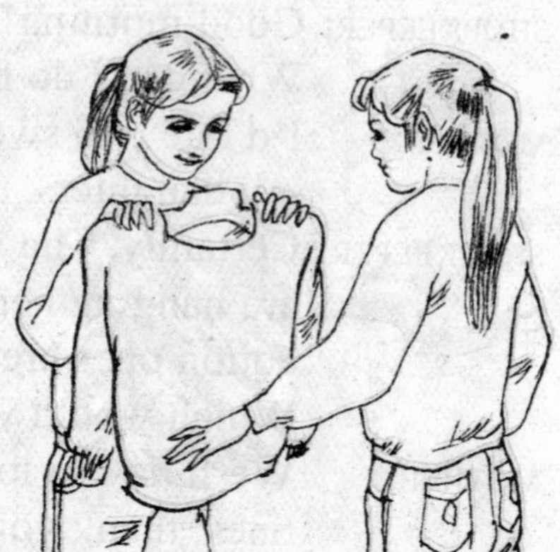

LUCY: Which sweater do you like?
LILY: I can't decide!
LUCY: Well, which colour do you like?
LILY: I prefer blue, but this blue is too dark!
LUCY: What about this one?
LILY: That's too light!
LUCY: Is this one better?
LILY: Yes. That's just right. It's nice and soft, too. Shall I ask the shopkeeper if I can try it on?
LUCY: OK. And we'd better ask Mom whether it's cheap enough!

Now make a similar dialogue. Begin:

A: Which trousers do you like?
B: I can't decide!
A: Well, which colour ...?
B: I prefer ..., but ....
A: ....

CHECKPOINT 15

- **Grammar**

The Object Clause (4) 宾语从句（四）

3 由连词 whether 或 if 引导。
Lily asked *if / whether* she liked it.
She asked *if / whether* they had a cotton one.

- **Useful expressions**

What can I do for you?	make friends with	make a mistake
I can't decide which one to buy.	try on	(not) cheap /large enough
Please take your time!	get on well with	right away

Unit 16 What's it made of?

Lesson 61

1 Read and say

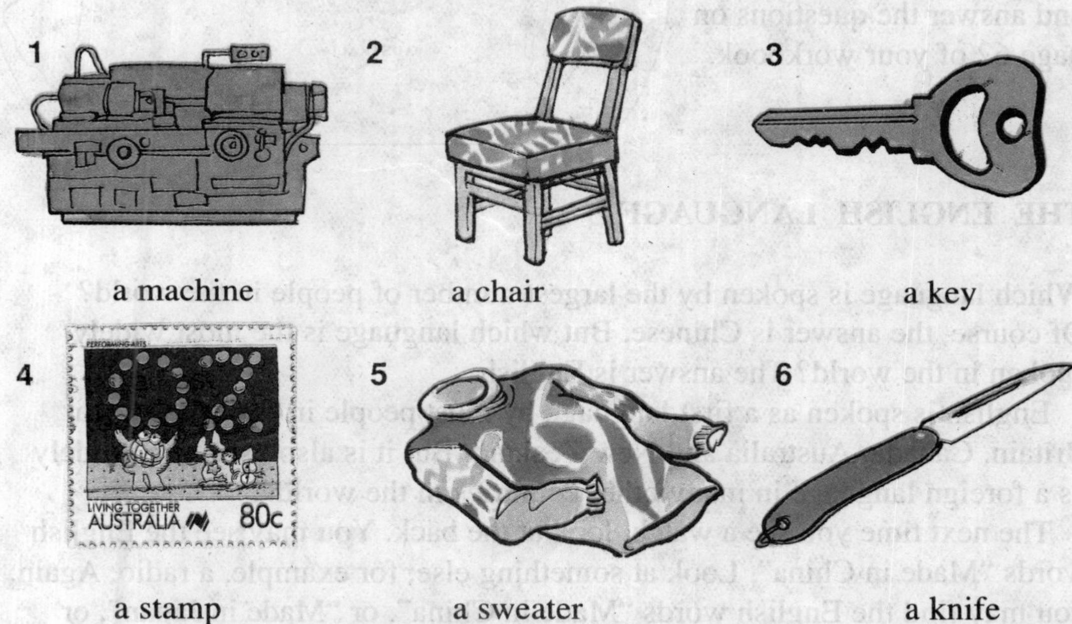

1 a machine 2 a chair 3 a key

4 a stamp 5 a sweater 6 a knife

2 Ask and answer

A: What's this in English? **B:** It's a *knife*.
A: What's it made of? **B:** It's made of *metal and wood*.
A: What's it used for? **B:** It's used for *cutting*.

What's this?	What's it made of?	What's it used for?
pan	metal	cooking
glass	glass	drinking
sweater	wool	keeping warm
stamp	paper	sending letters
knife	metal and wood	cutting things
key	metal	locking doors

Lesson 62

Read

Read the following passage and find the names of the five countries where English is spoken as the first language. Then read the passage again and answer the questions on page 62 of your workbook.

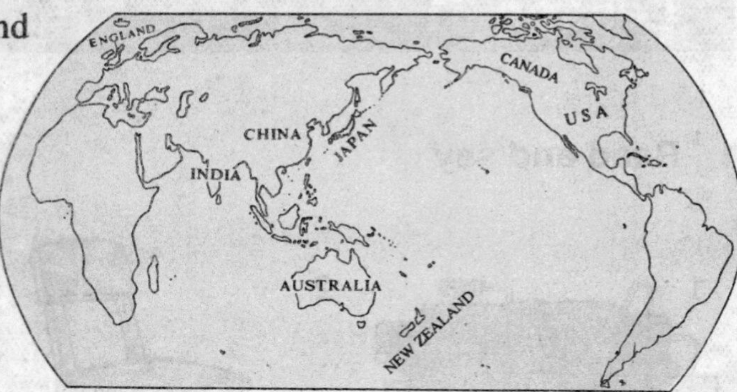

THE ENGLISH LANGUAGE

Which language is spoken by the largest number of people in the world? Of course, the answer is Chinese. But which language is the most widely spoken in the world? The answer is English.

English is spoken as a first language by most people in the USA, Great Britain, Canada, Australia and New Zealand. But it is also used very widely as a foreign language in many other countries in the world.

The next time you see a watch, look at the back. You may see the English words "Made in China". Look at something else, for example, a radio. Again, you may find the English words "Made in China", or "Made in Japan", or even "Made in Germany".

Why? English is the first language in none of these countries. So why are the English words "Made in ..." written on these things? It is because in the modern world, English is very widely used for business between different countries. So when a German buys something from a Japanese, or an Indian sells something to a Frenchman, they may all use English. Most business letters around the world are written in English. Half the world's telephone calls are made in English. Three quarters of the world's books and newspapers are written in English.

If you travel in India, or France, or Germany, or almost any other country in the world, you will still be able to use English. It is used by travellers and business people all over the world. That is why we are learning English in China. It is one of the world's most important languages because it is so widely used. If you learn even a little English, you will find it useful after you leave school.

Lesson 63

1 Ask and answer

A: What's this *jacket* made of?
B: I think it's made of *cotton*.

A: What're these *coats* made of?
B: I think they're made of *wool*.

sweater	trousers	pens
blouse	socks	rulers

cotton	silk
wood	metal

2 Ask and answer

Where's tea grown? It's grown in the southeast of China.
Where's salt produced? It's produced in East and South China.
Where're trains made? They're made in Zhuzhou.

Now ask and answer similar questions. Use the map below.

Where's paper/glass made? Where's rice/cotton grown?
Where're bananas grown? Where's silk produced?
Where's salt/sugar produced? Where're trains/cars made?

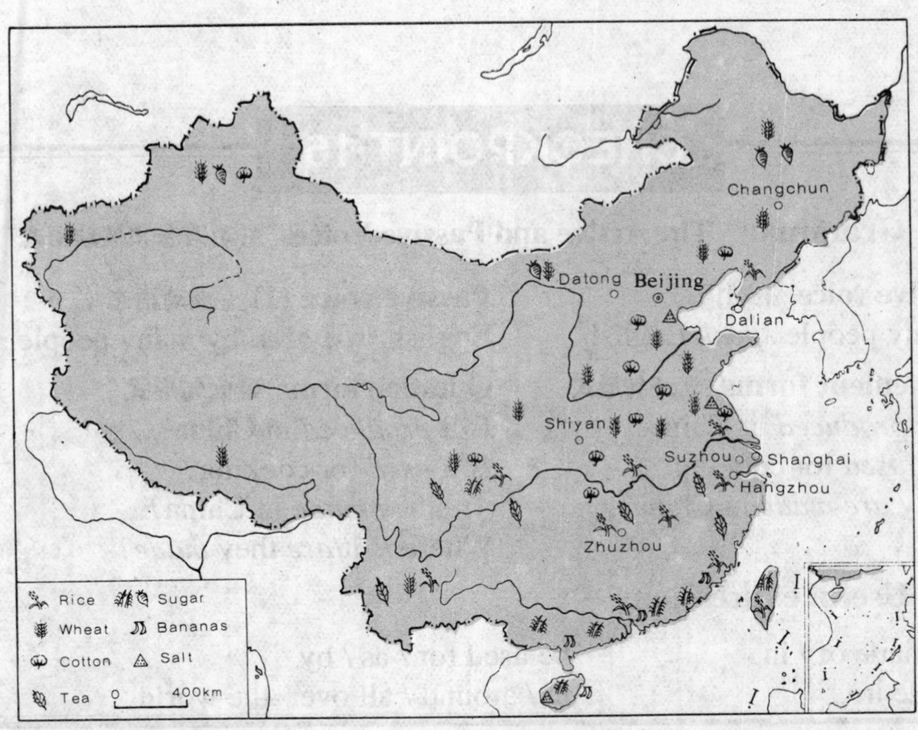

Lesson 64

1 **Dictation** Follow your teacher's instructions.

2 **Crossword** Complete the puzzle:

1 Bikes are made of ....
2 Jim's jacket is made of ....
3 That beautiful blouse is made of ....
4 This chair is made of ....
5 This dress is made of ....
6 Windows are made of ....

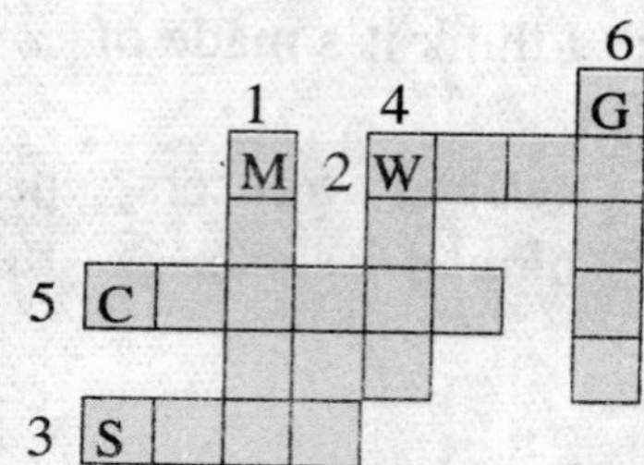

3 **Write** Rewrite these sentences:

Model: They *make* trains in Zhuzhou. → Trains *are made* in Zhuzhou.

1 People use knives for cutting things. (Knives ...)
2 People use metal for making machines.
3 They produce silk in Suzhou.
4 They use this key for locking the classroom door.
5 They speak English in Canada.

CHECKPOINT 16

● **Grammar** **The Active and Passive Voices 主动语态和被动语态**

Active voice 主动语态	**Passive voice (1) 被动语态（一）**
Many people *speak* English.	English *is spoken* by many people.
Statement forms 陈述句形式	**Question forms 疑问句形式**
It *is produced* in China.	*Is* it *produced* in China?
It *is used* for cooking.	*Is* it *used* for cooking?
They *are made* in China.	*Are* they *made* in China?
	Where *is* it/*are* they *made*?

● **Useful expressions**

be made of / in	be used for / as / by
Made in ...	in / around / all over the world

Unit 17 What was it used for?

Lesson 65

1 Look and say

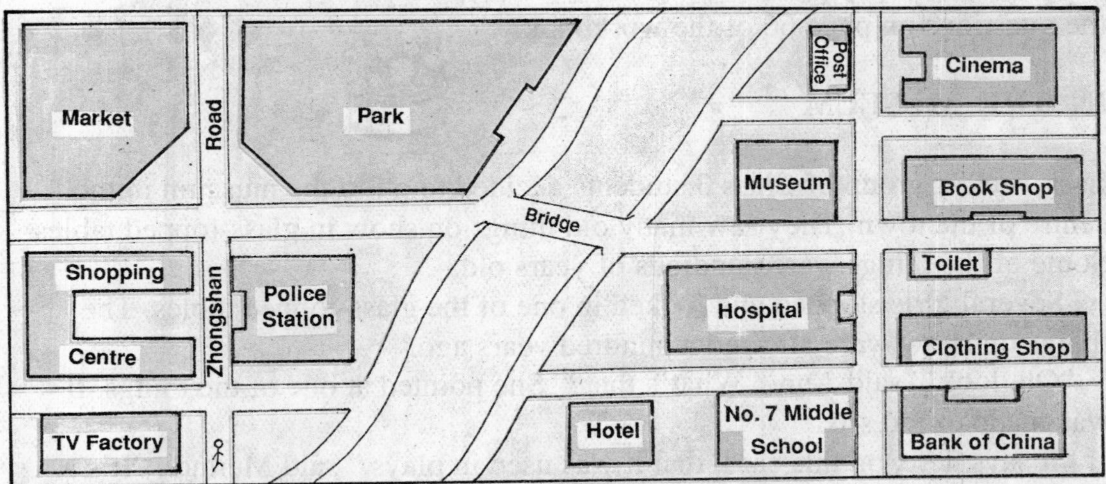

2 Read and act

A: Excuse me! Can you tell me the way to the *museum*, please?

B: Yes. Go along Zhongshan Road, and turn right at the second crossing. Go across the bridge. You'll find the museum on the left. It's between the post office and the hospital. You can't miss it.

A: Thanks very much.

3 Practise

Use the words on the right to help you practise similar dialogues. Ask the way to

the police station.
the bookshop.
the hospital.
the market.
...

Go along this road and ....
Go up this road to the end.
Turn (left) at the third crossing.
Take the second turning on the left.
Go across the bridge.
It's between the ... and the ....
You can't miss it!

Lesson 66

 **Read**

Here are four pictures. Read the story below and find out: "Which of these things is modern, and which is old?" Then read the story again and answer the questions on page 66 of the workbook.

IN THE MUSEUM

Last week, a group of Class 3 students decided to go to the museum in the centre of the town. They saw many old things on show in glass-topped tables. Some of the things were hundreds of years old.

Several girls stopped and looked in one of the glass-topped tables. The things on show were all used a hundred years ago.

"Oh, look!" said Ann. "What's that?" She pointed at one of the things. It was made of red silk.

"It says here, on this card, that it was used in plays," said Meimei. "It's a king's hat!"

"Is that true?" said Lucy. She was surprised. "Is it a real king's hat?"

"No. It isn't real," said Meimei. "It was used in plays."

"There's an old teapot over there. Isn't it beautiful!" said Ann. "Look! It's inside another pot. What was that pot used for?"

"It was used for keeping tea hot after it was made," said Wei Hua. "It was filled with hot water."

"These days we use a thermos," said Li Lei.

"I know. That's a good idea!" said Ann. "But in England we still make tea in teapots."

"That's what we did in China in the old days, before thermoses were invented," said Wei Hua.

"What's that?" asked Lucy. She pointed at a strange thing with three legs and a strange top. It was made of metal.

"That was used for drinking," said Wei Hua.

"How interesting!" said Ann. "It makes me feel thirsty!"

"I'm feeling thirsty, too!" said Meimei. "Look, it's noon already! Let's go and have a drink!"

The group of girls all moved on and had a good drink of tea together, from a modern thermos!

Lesson 67

1 Ask and answer Find the right answers.

When was the	League PLA PRC Party	founded?	It was founded on / in ....

A July 1, 1921 B October 1, 1949 C August 1, 1927 D May, 1922

2 Read and learn

You can see these signs in a museum. Where else can you see them? What do they mean? Look up the new words in a dictionary.

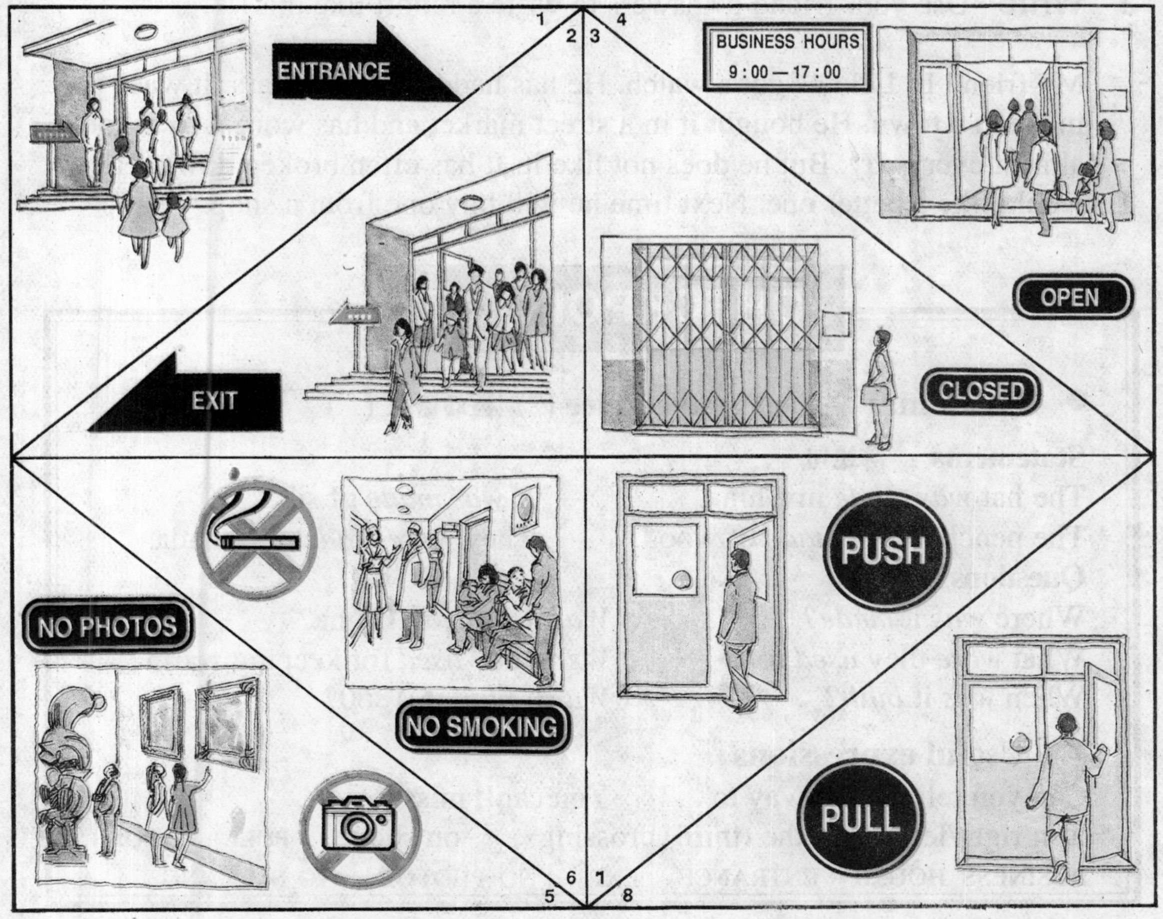

Lesson 68

1 Listen Turn to page 68 of your workbook.

2 Ask and answer

Choose one of the words from the box. Ask other students questions about it. Write down their answers, and report to the class.

Questions:

1 Have you got a ...?
2 How long have you had it?
3 Where was it made?
4 Where did you buy it?
5 Has it ever broken (down)?
6 Have you used / worn it a lot?
7 Do you like it, or would you like a better one?

a watch	a radio
a mirror	a thermos
a bicycle	a lock
a key	a jacket

3 Write Use your friend's answers to write a report like this:

My friend Li Lei has got a watch. He has had it for two years. It was made in a town. He bought it in a street market and has worn it to school almost every day. But he does not like it. It has often broken down. He would like a better one. Next time he will buy one from a shop.

CHECKPOINT 17

● **Grammar The Passive Voice (2) 被动语态（二）**

Statements 陈述句

The hat *was made* in China. It *was made* of silk.
The pencils *were made* of wood. They *were made* in Canada.

Questions 疑问句

Where *was* it *made*? *Was* it *made* in China?
What *were* they *used* for? *Were* they *used* for keeping warm?
When *was* it *built*? *Was* it *built* in 1860?

● **Useful expressions**

Can you tell me the way to ...? You can't miss it.
turn right/left at the (third) crossing on show PULL PUSH
BUSINESS HOURS ENTRANCE EXIT NO PHOTOS NO SMOKING

Unit 18 Planting trees

Lesson 69

1 Read and act

A: Come to school in your old clothes tomorrow!
B: Why? What's happening?
A: It's Tree Planting Day. We're going to plant trees in the park / along the lake.
B: Really? Wonderful!

2 Read

Read these instructions. Then answer the questions.

HOW TO PLANT A TREE

1 The ground must be just right — neither too wet nor too dry. It's best to plant trees in spring because it's warmer.
2 Dig a hole large enough for the tree. But the hole should not be too deep.
3 Knock a long, strong stick into the earth next to the hole. Make sure that it is straight.
4 Put the tree in the hole so that it is straight.
5 Put the earth back in the hole again. Push it down hard with your foot several times.
6 Tie the tree to the top of the stick to keep it straight.
7 Water it well, as often as possible.

	True or untrue?
1 Summer is the best time for planting trees.	/ / / /
2 The earth should be wet.	/ / / /
3 The hole must be very big.	/ / / /
4 The ground must not be too hard.	/ / / /
5 The hole must not be too deep.	/ / / /
6 The ground should be hot.	/ / / /
7 The tree must be straight.	/ / / /

Lesson 70

Read

Read the following passage and find out "Why was the Great Green Wall built?" Then read the passage again more carefully, and answer the questions on page 70 of your workbook.

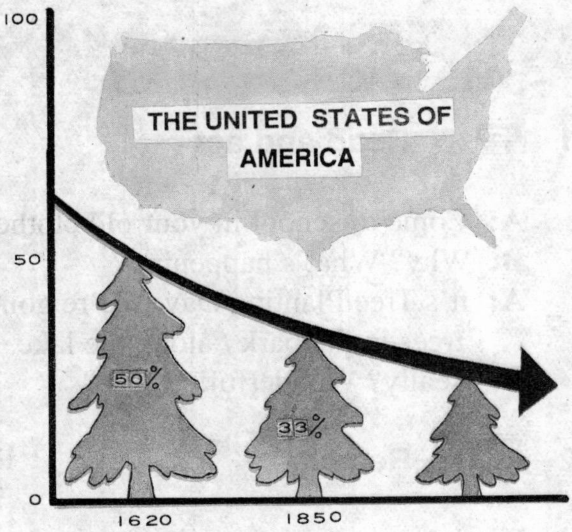

THE GREAT GREEN WALL

Look at the diagram on the right. It shows what has happened to the forests of the USA in the last 350 years. In 1620, about half the USA was covered by forests. In 1850, about a third was covered by forests. Today, the forests have almost gone. A lot of good land has gone with them, leaving only sand. Today, too many trees are still being cut down in the USA.

China does not want to copy the USA's example. So China has built a new Great Wall across the northern part of the country. This time, it is a "Great Green Wall" of trees, millions of trees.

The Great Green Wall is 7,000 kilometres long, and between 400 and 1,700 kilometres wide. The Great Green Wall will stop the wind from blowing the earth away. It will stop the sand from moving towards the rich farmland in the south. It has already saved a lot of land. But more "Great Green Walls" are still needed, and not only in China. They must be built all over the world.

Wang Feng is a worker at Yulin in Shaanxi. He works on the Great Green Wall with many other people. We visited him at his workplace among the young trees and asked him about his work. "Many thousands of trees must be planted every year," he said. "The more, the better. This year alone, we've already planted ten thousand trees. You see all those small trees over there on that hill? That was sand five years ago. Now it's a young forest! In a few years' time, those mountains will be covered with trees, too!" He pointed to the high mountains far away.

Was it difficult to work on the Great Green Wall?

"Yes. It's hard work, but it's very important. The only problem is you can't eat trees! So we grow our own food, too. But we're growing a lot more now, thanks to the Green Wall."

Lesson 71

1 Practise

Make true sentences from the table.

The Great Green Wall is	between 400 and 1,700 kilometres wide.
Australia is	half a metre deep.
Mr Green is nearly	twelve metres long.
The river near here is	over four metres deep.
Our classroom is about	thousands of metres high.
The Great Wall is	over six thousand kilometres long.
The hole must be	thousands of kilometres away.
Those mountains are	two metres tall.

2 Read and say

We asked Wang Feng how trees should be planted. Find his answers in this table:

Trees		pushed down hard.
A large hole	must be	watered well.
A long stick		dug.
The earth	should be	tied to the stick.
The tree		planted in spring.
The young tree		knocked into the earth.

3 Practise Make sentences.

Many more trees		picked in the autumn.
Young trees		looked after.
All trees	must be	watered well when it is dry.
Fruit		harvested at the right time.
Rice	should be	dug in winter.
The ground		planted.

Lesson 72

1 Listen Turn to page 72 in your workbook.

2 Read and act

1 **A:** Will you help me plant this tree, please?
B: Of course! What do you want me to do?
A: Well, I've dug this hole. Hold this stick, while I knock it in.
B: OK! Is it straight?
A: More or less!

2 **B:** What's next?
A: The tree must be put in the hole now.
B: OK! I've done that!
A: Right! Hold it straight! I'll fill in the hole with earth.

3 **B:** Good! That's done. Now the tree must be tied to the stick.
A: OK. While you're doing that I'll go and get some water.
B: OK.
A: Can we go and have a drink after that?
B: A drink? We've only just started! There are twenty more trees to be planted!

CHECKPOINT 18

● Grammar

1 The Passive Voice (3) 被动语态 (三) 含有情态动词的被动语态

More trees *must be planted.*
They *may be planted* at other times of the year.
The trees *should be watered* often.
They *can be planted* at the side of a road.

2 Measurement 计量

It is (ten) metres/kilometres long/wide/deep/high.

● Useful expressions

Just right. The more, the better. Thanks to .... more or less far away
stop ... from ... be covered with neither ... nor in a few years' time

Unit 19 Mainly revision

Lesson 73

1 Ask and answer Look at the table. Practise like this.

A: How many kilometres by train is it from Nanjing to Wuhan?
B: 1229 (one thousand two hundred and twenty-nine). How many ...?

TRAINS BETWEEN IMPORTANT CITIES IN CHINA (in kilometres)

	Beijing					
Shanghai	1462	Shanghai				
Guangzhou	2313	1811	Guangzhou			
Changsha	1587	1187	726	Changsha		
Wuhan	1229	1534	1084	358	Wuhan	
Nanjing	1157	305	2116	1492	1229	Nanjing
Kunming	3179	2677	2216	1592	1950	2982

2 Practise Change these sentences:

Model: People produce salt in Jiangxi. →
Salt is produced (by people) in Jiangxi.

1 Farmers grow cotton in Shandong. (Cotton ...)
2 People grow bananas in Hainan.
3 Workers make cars in Shanghai.
4 Workers make glass in Qingdao.
5 Farmers grow rice and many other things in Sichuan.

3 Write Make sentences.

Satellites are used by people	for sending and receiving messages.
Radios are used by policemen	for studying the universe.
Keys are used by people	for learning more about the earth.
Stamps are used by people	for locking doors.
Sheep are kept by farmers	for making many different things.
Machines are used by workers	for producing wool and meat.
Computers are used by people	for doing problems.

Lesson 74

Read

Read this passage and find out: "What is a satellite?"

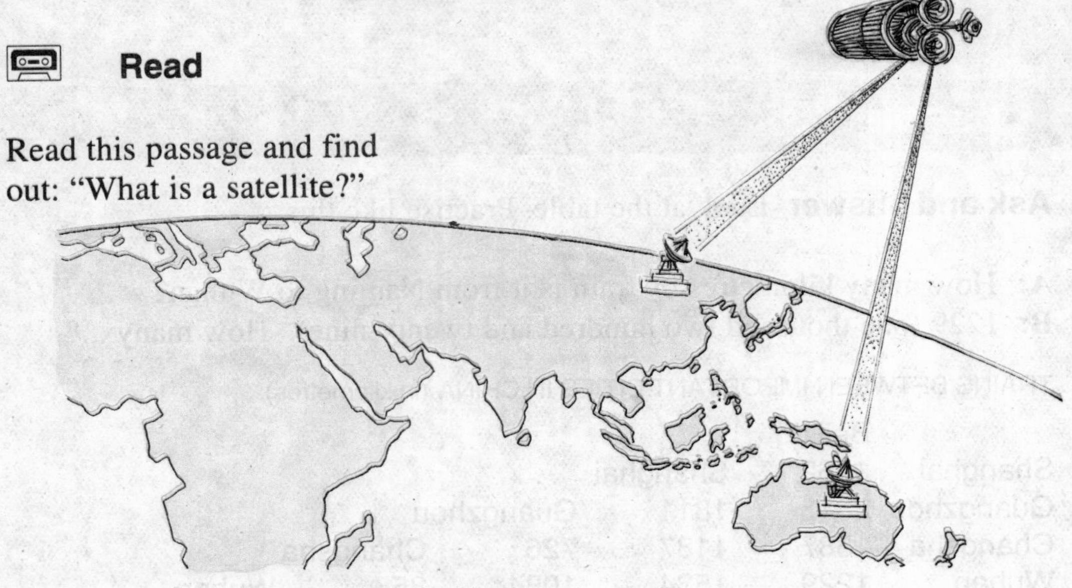

THE UNIVERSE AND MAN-MADE SATELLITES

When we talk about the universe, we mean the earth, the sun, the moon and the stars, and the space between them. Many of the stars cannot be seen because they are too far away.

The moon travels round the earth. It is our satellite. It is quite near us in space. It is only 380,000 kilometres away, and it has been visited by man already. So far, no man has travelled farther than the moon, but spaceships without people have reached other parts of the universe.

Man-made satellites have been sent up into space by many countries. These satellites go round the earth and help us to learn more about the earth, the weather and other things. Most countries use these satellites to send and receive messages. For example, with their help China can send its TV and radio programmes to the other side of the world. Foreign countries can send their programmes to China. We can also use satellites to help us make telephone calls to foreign countries.

Our knowledge of the universe is growing all the time. Our knowledge grows and the universe develops. Thanks to space satellites, the world itself is becoming a much smaller place and people from different countries now understand each other better.

Read the passage again and answer the questions on page 74 of your workbook.

Lesson 75

1 Ask and answer

Ask questions like: How far away is *Sydney* from *Beijing*?

Man-made satellites are	about 8,000 kilometres away from the earth.
New York is	14,800 kilometres away from Beijing.
The moon is	380,000 kilometres away from the earth.
Britain is only	30 kilometres away from France.
Sydney is	10,400 kilometres away from Beijing.

2 Practise

A: Which *TV* programme shall we *watch*?
I can't decide.
B: Which do you think is more *interesting*?
A: Well, I don't think any of them is *interesting*.
B: I think I shall *read a book* instead.
A: Good idea! That is much better than *watching* a bad *TV* programme!

radio listen to

enjoyable

do my homework

listening to radio

3 Choose the right words

find	anything	may	still	take
found	something	must	them	mend

LUCY: I'm trying to ... our favourite TV programme.
WEI HUA: Which channel is it on?
LUCY: It is usually ... on Channel 1. But I can't get ....
WEI HUA: It ... be on Channel 2. Try that.
LUCY: I've tried that, too. I ... can't get anything.
WEI HUA: What about the other channels?
LUCY: I've tried ..., too.
WEI HUA: There must be ... wrong with the TV.
LUCY: I'm afraid you ... be right.
I'd better ... it to Uncle Wang.
WEI HUA: Good idea. If he can't ... it, nobody can!

Lesson 76

1 **Listen** Turn to page 76 in your workbook.

2 Word building

1 Nouns

home + work	=	homework	class + room	=	classroom
house + work	=	housework	bed + room	=	bedroom
farm + work	=	farmwork	birth + day	=	birthday
space + ship	=	spaceship	hand + bag	=	handbag
loud + speaker	=	loudspeaker	play + ground	=	playground
grand + parent	=	grandparent	police + man	=	policeman

2 Nouns → Adjectives

interest - interesting   surprise - surprising   wool - woollen

3 Verb → noun

drive - driver   teach - teacher   keep - keeper

farm - farmer   travel - traveller   invent - inventor

3 Practise Make true sentences.

1	The playground must be ...	A	spoken to politely.
2	The flowers must be ...	B	watered often.
3	Older people must be ...	C	kept clean.
4	Your teacher must be ...	D	kept clean and tidy.
5	Homework may be ...	E	listened to carefully.
6	Your clothes should always be ...	F	done on time.

4 Write Read this passage. Then write a similar passage.

My penfriend lives in the USA. Last week she sent me a letter. She said that she heard a very interesting programme on the radio. It was sent to the USA from China by satellite. The programme was about the Great Green Wall. She enjoyed it very much.

CHECKPOINT 19

Revise Checkpoints 15 - 18.

Unit 20 The world's population

Lesson 77

1 Listen, read and learn

100	500	1,000	10,000
a hundred	five hundred	a thousand	ten thousand
100,000	1,000,000	1,000,000,000	
a hundred thousand	a million	a thousand million (a billion)	

2 Listen, read and say Can you say these numbers?

Model: 3,333,333,333
three billion, three hundred and thirty-three million, three hundred and thirty-three thousand, three hundred and thirty-three

A 597	E 5,829	I 19,581	M 5,789,211
B 976	F 9,784	J 24,783	N 444,444,000
C 1,234	G 10,000	K 198,679	O 5,555,555,000
D 4,978	H 12,648	L 1,678,000	

3 Ask and answer

Look at the table. Practise like this:

A: What's the population of *Germany*? Do you think it will grow?
B: About *eighty-one million* I don't know if it will grow. What's the population of *France*?
C: About *fifty-seven million*. I don't know if it will grow. What about the population of ...?
D: ....

COUNTRY	POPULATION (*1993*)
Australia	17,800,000
Canada	28,100,000
China	1,160,000,000
France	57,000,000
Germany	81,100,000
Great Britain	58,000,000
India	897,400,000
The U S A	258,300,000
The world	5,506,000,000

Lesson 78

Read

Read the following passage as quickly as you can and find out the answers to these questions:

1 What does 'standing room only' mean?
2 By what year will the world's population reach 6 billion?

STANDING ROOM ONLY

Look at your watch for just one minute. During that time, 174 babies were born in the world. Maybe you think that isn't many. During the next hour, over 10,440 more babies will be born on the earth.

So it goes on, hour after hour. In one day, people have to find food for over 250,000 mouths more. Just think how many more there will be in one year! What will happen in a hundred years?

The population problem may be the greatest one of the world today. The world's population is growing faster and faster. Two thousand years ago, there were only 250 million people on the earth. Four hundred years ago, the number was over 500 million. But at the beginning of the twentieth century, the world's population was about 1,700 million. In 1970, this number was over 3,600 million. In 1990, the number was over five billion. A UN report says that the world population will pass six billion by the end of the twentieth century. This is just ten years after it reached five billion. People say that by the year 2010, it may be seven billion. That means that in about 600 years, there will be standing room only on the earth. There will not be enough space for anybody else.

Turn to page 78 of your workbook and answer the questions.

Lesson 79

1 Read and learn

year	the population of the world	the population of the more developed countries	the population of the less developed countries
1950	2,525,000,000	832,000,000	1,693,000,000
1990	5,321,000,000	1,214,000,000	4,107,000,000
2000	6,292,000,000	1,274,000,000	5,018,000,000

2 Ask and answer

Look at the table above.

1 What was the population of the world in 1950?
2 What will be the population of the world in the year 2000?
3 What was the population of the more developed countries in 1950 / 1990?
4 What will be the population of these countries by the end of the twentieth century?
5 What was the population of the less developed countries in 1950 / 1990?
6 What will be the population of these countries in the year 2000?
7 Is the population of the world still growing?

3 Make sentences

I didn't know that My uncle never knew if They never asked what My grandparents didn't know if They never knew that My parents couldn't decide if They couldn't find out whether	he was going to have a boy. China's population would grow so fast. they would have another child. would happen in a hundred years. population would be a big problem. it would be a girl or a boy. they would have a grandson.

Lesson 80

1 **Listen** Turn to page 80 of your workbook.

2 **Write**

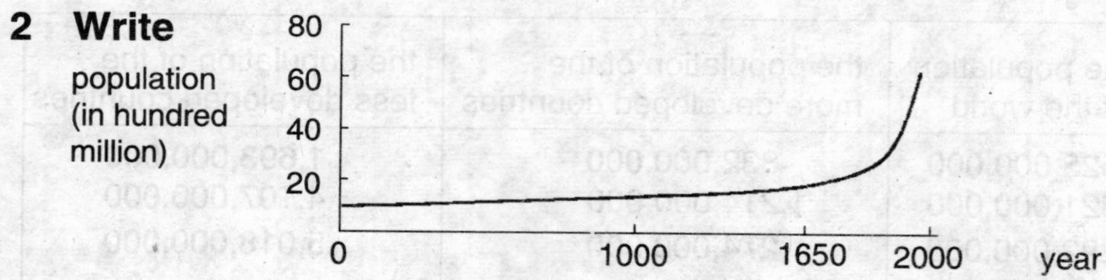

Look at the diagram and choose the right words:

10,000 years ago, the world's population was very .... For several thousand years it grew quite .... But during the last three or four hundred years it has grown very .... Today, it is still growing ... than ever before. This means we must grow ... food, and have ... families with ..., but ..., children. If we don't do these things, the results will be very .... There will not be enough space even to stand in on the earth.	slowly quickly faster bad small smaller more healthier fewer

CHECKPOINT 20

● **Grammar** *** The Future-in-the-Past Tense 过去将来时态**

I didn't know if he *would come*.
We didn't know whether she *was going to speak* at the meeting.
I wasn't sure if it *would rain*.
They never knew that population *would become* a big problem.
They never asked what *would happen* to the world.
She didn't tell me where she *would go*.
He didn't say when she *was coming*.

● **Useful expressions**

So it goes on, hour after hour. grow faster and faster
Standing room only! at the beginning of on (the) earth

Unit 21 Shopping

Lesson 81

1 Read and act

MAN: My shoes are worn out.
WOMAN: Can't they be mended?
MAN: No! Look at these holes.
WOMAN: You'd better buy a new pair.
MAN: Yes, I'm afraid you're right.
I'll go tomorrow afternoon.

2 Read and act

A: What can I do for you?
B: I'm looking for a pair of black shoes.
A: What size do you want?
B: Size eight.
A: I'm afraid we haven't got any black shoes in that size at the moment. But we've got some brown ones.
B: Hmm. Have you got any other kind?
A: What about those shoes over there?
B: Well, that pair looks nice. How much do they cost?
A: Fifty-five *yuan*.
B: Hmm! That's a bit expensive. Can I try them on, please?
A: Certainly.

Make similar dialogues about: *dark blue suits; light green dresses*.
Use some of the sentences in the box to help you.

> Have you got any other colour / size / kind?
> How much does it cost?
> That's too expensive. Have you got anything cheaper?
> That's cheap. I'll have it, please.
> That's a bit expensive. I'll think about it. / I don't think I'll take it.

Lesson 82

 **Read**

Look at the picture. John is trying on a pair of shoes in a shop. Read this passage and find out: "What did John buy?" Then read it again, and answer the questions on page 82 of your workbook.

SHOPPING

It was a Saturday afternoon. A young man named John had just left school for the last time. He was going to start work the following week, so he decided to buy some new clothes and a new pair of shoes. There was quite a nice shop near his home. The shop was quite new, for it had opened only the week before. It sold men's shoes and clothes. John decided to go and see what they had.

The shoes in the shop were quite good and were not very expensive. But none of them were the right size. They were either too big or too small.

"I'm sorry," said the shopkeeper. "We've sold out the shoes in your size."

"Never mind! Let me look at your suits. May I try this one on, please?" John asked the shopkeeper.

"Certainly, sir!" said the shopkeeper. "This way, please!"

John put the suit on, and then went to look at himself in a mirror. He had never worn a suit before, and it looked very nice.

"It looks great," he said. "How much does it cost?"

"239 dollars," said the shopkeeper. John was very surprised.

"That's much too expensive! Have you got anything cheaper?"

"That's the cheapest suit we have, I'm afraid," said the shopkeeper. "But we have some nice jackets over there."

"Perhaps I'll just buy a jacket," said the young man. John tried on several jackets, and at last chose a very nice one. It was quite cheap.

"I'll have this one, please!" he said.

The shopkeeper put the jacket in a bag.

Close your books. Retell the story.
Perhaps some of you would like to act the story though it isn't finished yet.

Read the end of the story in the next lesson for homework.

Lesson 83

1 **Read** Read the second part of the story and find out: "Who did John meet?" Then close your books and retell the end of the story.

At that moment another young man came into the shop. It was John's old friend Ron.

"Ron!" John said. "I haven't seen you for months!"

The two friends were very pleased to see each other again. They were so pleased to see each other that they forgot everything else. Soon they were very busy talking. They talked on and on very happily.

"Look at the time!" said Ron. "It's nearly six o'clock. Let's go and have dinner together."

"What a good idea!" said John. He picked up the bag, and they walked towards the door of the shop.

"Just a moment, please!" said the shopkeeper. "Haven't you forgotten something?"

John turned round and looked at him in surprise. "Pardon?" he said.

"The jacket!" said the shopkeeper. "You haven't paid for it yet!" Then John remembered: he had chosen a new jacket, but he hadn't paid for it!

"I'm really very sorry," he said. "We were so busy talking that I forgot to pay!"

He took out his money and paid for the jacket. His friend laughed.

"That was nearly the cheapest jacket in town!" he said.

2 **Read and learn**

The suit was so expensive that he could not buy it.
The jacket was so cheap that he decided to buy it.
His shoes were so dirty that he must brush them.

3 **Practise** How many different sentences can you make?

The jacket The shoes The socks The shirt The sweater The suit	cost so much cost so little	that he bought it. that we didn't buy any. that we bought several (pairs). that he didn't buy it.

Lesson 84

1 **Listen** Turn to page 84 of the workbook.

2 **Study and practise**

Some verbs do not change in the Simple Past form:

How much do these shoes *cost*?	How much did those shoes *cost* last year?
They *cost* twenty *yuan*.	They *cost* fifteen *yuan*.

The same is true for these verbs: *hit* *hurt* *let* *cut*

How many different sentences can you make?

			had to see the doctor.
He hurt her so badly		he	cried.
She hit him so hard	that	she	fell over.
He cut his finger so badly		it	had to go to hospital.
The truck hit the tree so hard			had to go home.
			fell down.

CHECKPOINT 21

● Grammar

1 The Past Perfect Tense (1) 过去完成时态 （一）

过去完成时由 “助动词 had（用于各种人称和数） + 过去分词” 构成。例如：

I/You/He/She/It/We/You/They had left .... Had you/I/he/she/it/we/you/they left ...?

Yes, I/you/he/she/it/we/you/they had. No, I/you/he/she/it/we/you/they hadn't.

2 由 so ... that 引导的状语从句中，如果 so 前面是系动词 be, become, feel 等，那么 so 后面一般跟形容词。例如：

He became *so* angry *that* he couldn't speak.

She was *so* happy *that* she danced.

如果 so前面是其它动词，那么 so 后面跟副词。例如：

He ran *so* quickly *that* he won the race.

She worked *so* quietly *that* no one knew she was there.

● Useful expressions

Just a moment, please! worn out a pair of on and on a bit

Pardon? Never mind. think about be busy doing sth.

in surprise either ... or sell out fall over

Unit 22 At the doctor's

Lesson 85

1 Read and act

(*In Kate's bedroom*)

KATE: Mum, I don't feel very well.

MOTHER: Oh dear! What's wrong?

KATE: I don't know. I've got a headache and a cough.

MOTHER: You'd better stay in bed till tomorrow. If you're not better by then, I'll take you to see the doctor.

(*At breakfast*)

MOTHER: There's something wrong with Kate.

FATHER: Really? What's the trouble?

MOTHER: She's not feeling well. I told her to stay in bed till tomorrow.

FATHER: Nothing serious, I hope.

MOTHER: I hope not. She says she's got a headache and a cough. Perhaps she's caught a cold.

2 Practise

Make similar dialogues and act one in front of the class.

CHILD:	MOTHER:
I'm not feeling well.	You'd better stay in bed.
I'm feeling very ill.	You'd better see a doctor at once.
I think I've caught a cold.	You'd better not go to school.
I've got a headache.	Here, try this medicine.
I've got a cough.	Bad luck. Drink this.
I don't know what to do.	Lie down and have a rest.
I don't know what to eat.	Have some noodles or porridge.

Lesson 86

Read

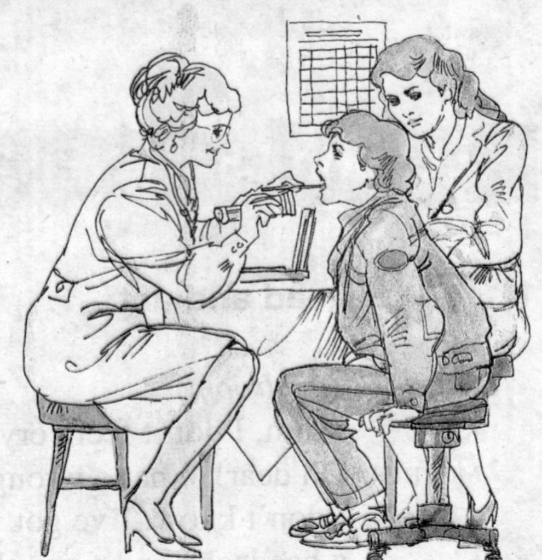

Read this dialogue and find out what is wrong with Tom. Then read it again and answer the questions on page 86 of your workbook.

WHAT'S WRONG WITH TOM?

(*At the doctor's*)

MOTHER: Good morning, doctor.

DOCTOR: Good morning, Mrs Brown. Well, what's your trouble, young man?

TOM: I ... I've got a headache and ... (*He begins to cough.*)

MOTHER: Oh dear! What a terrible cough!

TOM: I feel terrible!

DOCTOR: Have you taken his temperature?

MOTHER: Yes, I have. His temperature seems to be all right.

DOCTOR: Open your mouth and say "Ah".

TOM: Aahh!

DOCTOR: How long has he been like this?

MOTHER: Ever since last night.

DOCTOR: Did he sleep well?

MOTHER: I think so. But he seemed rather tired last night.

TOM: Yes, I feel tired all the time.

DOCTOR: Has he had anything to eat this morning?

MOTHER: Yes, for breakfast he had some bread, two eggs, some fruit and a glass of milk.

DOCTOR: Well, Mrs Brown, maybe he has caught a bit of a cold.

MOTHER: Is that all? It seems worse than a cold.

DOCTOR: Don't worry. But you'd better take him to the nurse, and she'll give him some pills.

MOTHER: Shall I keep him away from school?

DOCTOR: No, I think it'll be all right for him to go to school.

TOM: Oh, I'm feeling even worse! I think I'm going to die!

MOTHER: Oh, doctor. He seems terribly ill. Are you sure it's nothing serious?

DOCTOR: Yes, he'll be all right soon. I'm sure of that!

Read the end of the dialogue in the next lesson for homework.

Lesson 87

1 **Read** Find out what's wrong with Tom.

MOTHER: So it's not serious, doctor?
DOCTOR: No, Mrs Brown. Your son's trouble is very common these days. It happens all the time. It comes and goes very quickly. He'll get well soon.
MOTHER: But I don't understand.
DOCTOR: This afternoon the biggest football match of the year will be on TV. Tom won't feel well till it's over. You wait. After the game he'll be fine!
MOTHER: Thank you, doctor. Come along, Tom.
DOCTOR: Goodbye!

2 **Practise**

Kate is in hospital. She is rather ill. Practise these dialogues:

NURSE: Have you slept well?
KATE: Yes, I slept very well all night, thanks.
NURSE: Have you taken your medicine today?
KATE: Yes, I took it after breakfast.
NURSE: Have you had a wash yet?
KATE: Yes, I washed before breakfast.
NURSE: You haven't finished your lunch!
KATE: Sorry. I had a little, but I don't feel like eating.

3 **Puzzle dialogues**

1 You need something to drink, don't you?	A Yes, please, nurse.
2 Do you want anything to eat?	B Yes, I understand. Thanks.
3 Take this medicine twice a day. Do you understand?	C Yes, thank you.
4 Open your mouth, please. I want to take your temperature.	D No, thanks. I'm not hungry.
5 Are you feeling better today?	E Yes, a little better, thanks.
6 How are you feeling today?	F I've got a pain here.
7 What's wrong?	G I'm feeling even worse.

Lesson 88

1 **Listen** Turn to page 88 of your workbook.

2 **Practise** Make up sentences about Mr Know-all and Mr Know-little.

Mr Know-all knows	how to make a key,	but I don't.
Mr Know-little doesn't know	how to mend a lock,	but I do.
	how to ride a motor-bike,	
	how to use a computer,	
	how to do maths problems,	

CHECKPOINT 22

● **Grammar**

1 The Present Perfect Tense (4) 现在完成时态 (四)

动词的现在完成时不能和表示过去的时间状语，如 *at ten this morning, before lunch, two days ago* 等连用。例如:

Have you *had* your medicine? Yes, I *had* it at ten.

2 The Infinitive (3) 动词不定式 (三)

4 和疑问词连用

I don't know *where to go*.
She doesn't know *what to do*.
We didn't know *who(m) to ask*.
They didn't know *when to go*.
He didn't know *how to do* it.

*5 用作定语

Do you want anything *to eat*?
No, thanks. I had something *to eat* this morning.

● **Useful expressions**

I don't feel very well.
I've got a headache and a cough.
I feel terrible.
There's something wrong with ....
It's nothing serious.
You'll be all right / well soon.
Take this medicine twice a day.

Unit 23 The football match

Lesson 89

1 Read and act

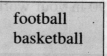

LI LEI: Hi, Jim! It's a long time since we met last!
JIM: Hi, Li Lei! Nice to see you again!
LI LEI: Did you have a good journey?
JIM: Yes, wonderful, thanks.
LI LEI: You're just in time for the ... match.
JIM: Great. Am I playing?
LI LEI: Of course, you are.
Or: I'm afraid not. The team has already been chosen.
Or: Perhaps. You'd better ask the P.E. teacher.

football
basketball

2 Study

1 Wei Hua may be on the team, or Ann may.
Either Wei Hua or Ann may be on the team. (But not both!)
2 Wei Hua isn't on the team, and Ann isn't (either).
Neither Wei Hua nor Ann is on the team.
Or: Neither of them is on the team.
3 Who is on the team, John or Bill?
Neither. / Neither of them is on the team.

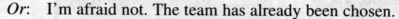

3 Practise

1 **A:** Which would you like, a cup of tea or a glass of milk?
B: Neither, thanks. I think I'll just have a glass of water.
2 **A:** When shall we meet, this evening or tomorrow morning?
B: I don't mind. Either time is OK.
A: Well, which would you prefer?
B: Oh, I don't know. You decide!
3 **A:** What are you doing tomorrow?
B: I'm watching the league match, of course!
A: I thought you wanted to visit your friends.
B: Yes. But it's such an important match, we can't miss it.

Lesson 90

 **Read**

Here is a page from a student's diary. Read it as quickly as you can and find out: "What was No. 64 Middle School's football team like?" Then read it again and answer the questions on page 90 in your workbook.

Saturday June 22nd, 19_ _ cloudy

Today was a very important day. We had the last match in the league. Our school had played very well during the past year, and before this match we were almost top of the league. If we won this match, we would be top!

I woke up early this morning. I had a quick breakfast, and got all my football clothes ready. At school I found it a bit difficult to work in class because I kept on thinking about the match in the afternoon.

School ended a little earlier. We all went to the football field, and soon the game started. We were playing against No. 64 Middle School. It was a draw when we played against them last time. They were all very big and strong, and we felt a little afraid of them. Though we were neither very big nor very strong, we were a good team. We played together very well. But still we weren't sure we could beat them.

"Don't worry," said Mr Hu, our P.E. teacher. "Playas well as you can, and we're sure to beat them! Just remember — TEAMWORK! Keep passing the ball to each other, and you'll be OK!"

That's what we found. The other team had some very good players, and some of them were very hard to stop when they got the ball. But they were a weak team. They didn't pass the ball often enough, and they didn't play together very well.

Read the second part of the diary in the next lesson for homework.

Lesson 91

1 **Read** Read Part 2 of the diary.

One of their players was a big boy called Wu Yong. He thought he was "King of the match", and he was really rather good. Early in the first half of the match he kicked a goal, but we soon got one ourselves. We were playing so well together that they couldn't get the ball. We kept passing it to each other, and they began to get angry. This didn't help them at all, and soon we kicked another goal. At the end of the first half we were winning 2 - 1.

In the second half of the match, Wu Yong kicked another goal; but one player does not make a team. By the end of the match, they had kicked two goals and we had kicked four.

"Congratulations to everybody!" said Mr Hu. "You played very well! Ours is the best team in the league."

We were all very pleased.

2 **Practise**

A: I had never *seen such a good match* before that day!
B: Yes, it was great, wasn't it?

heard such a wonderful piece of music
eaten such a wonderful meal
heard such a beautiful song

3 **Read and act**

HUIMING: Hi, Bill! Congratulations!
BILL: Thank you. You watched the match, didn't you?
HUIMING: Of course. When I got there, you had already started playing. So you didn't see me.
BILL: It wasn't easy to win the match. No. 64 Middle School is really a strong team.
HUIMING: But your team is even stronger. I knew you would beat them because you had played so well in the league.
BILL: We must thank Mr Hu. He kept asking us to remember TEAMWORK. We did as he told us and we won the first place in the league at last!

Lesson 92

1 **Dictation** Follow your teacher's instructions.

2 **Read and act**

FATHER: Was it a good match?
WANG LEI: Yes, it was a very good match.
FATHER: Who were you playing against?
WANG LEI: Number 64 Middle School.
FATHER: Really? They're rather a strong team, aren't they?
WANG LEI: Strong players, but a weak team.
FATHER: Who won?
WANG LEI: We did, 4 - 2.
FATHER: Well done! Does that mean that your team is top of the league?
WANG LEI: Yes, that's right.
FATHER: CONGRATULATIONS!

CHECKPOINT 23

● **Grammar** ***The Past Perfect Tense (2) 过去完成时 （二）**

过去完成时表示在过去某一时间或动作之前已经发生或完成的动作。过去完成时由“助动词 had（用于各种人称和数）+过去分词”构成。

He said that he *had* never *seen* such a beautiful bird before.
He remembered he *had chosen* a new jacket, but he *hadn't paid* for it!
When I got there, the train *had* already *left*.
By the end of the match, they *had kicked* two goals and we *had kicked* four.

● **Useful expressions**

Did you have a good journey? keep on doing in time
Play as well as you can. feel afraid of on the team

Unit 24 Mainly revision

Lesson 93

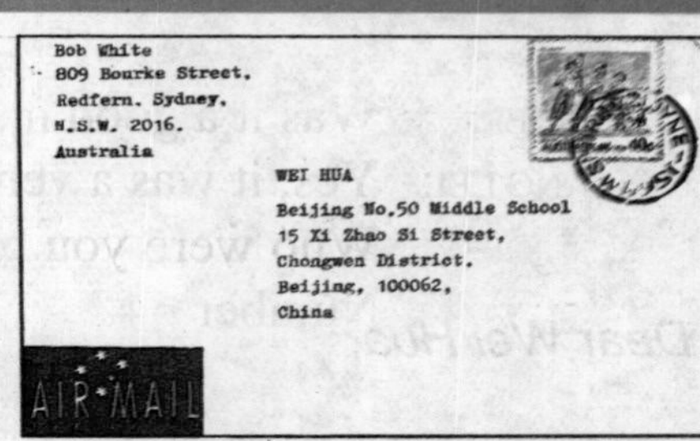

Bob White
809 Bourke Street,
Redfern. Sydney.
N.S.W. 2016.
Australia
WEI HUA
Beijing No.50 Middle School
15 Xi Zhao Si Street,
Chongwen District,
Beijing, 100062,
China
AIR MAIL

1 Read and say

A: Have you got a penfriend?
B: No, I haven't. Why? Have you?
A: Yes, I have. He's in Sydney, Australia.
B: How often do you write?
A: About once a month. Not too often, because neither of us has much time. We both have too much work to do.

2 Study

1 John has got a penfriend. Ann has got a penfriend.
This means: John and Ann have got penfriends.
or Both John and Ann have got penfriends.

2 John has got a penfriend. Ann hasn't.
This means: John has got a penfriend, but Ann hasn't.

3 Practise

I like writing to my penfriend,	but it takes a lot of time.
I like reading English books,	but they're sometimes rather hard.
I like listening to the radio,	but I can't spend much time on it.
He doesn't like writing letters,	but he likes receiving them.
I like looking after my sister's baby,	but my sister doesn't let me do it.

4 Practise

Read this sentence:
Though I like writing to my penfriend, it takes a lot of time.

Make similar sentences, using the table above.

Lesson 94

 **Read** Read this letter from Wei Hua's penfriend:

29 King Street,
New Town 2042,
Sydney, Australia
April 14th, l9_ _

Dear Wei Hua,

We've just returned from a short holiday at Ayers Rock. Ayers Rock is right in the centre of Australia. It's nearly two thousand kilometres from Sydney, so we flew most of the way. From Sydney we flew over a line of mountains in the southeast. It was rather cloudy at first. But after we left the mountains behind us, there was hardly a cloud in the sky. Most of the land below looked like sand, though Dad told me it is greener than you think. "There are a lot of sheep down there," he said, "but hardly any people!"

Ayers Rock is a large, low mountain. The day after we arrived, we got up early in the morning before the sun rose. We started climbing up before it was light. It gets too hot for climbing later. Lower down, at the foot of Ayers Rock, most of the ground is covered with forest and grass, and there are even a few small rivers. But when you climb higher, you will find nothing grows there at all. We didn't reach the top because it was too hot. All around it is sand. In the evening, when the sun goes down, the sand is almost red. The sky is red too, so it is very, very beautiful. Though we only stayed there for a few days, we had a great time.

Thank you very much for your last letter. It arrived three days ago. You asked me how many sheep there are in Australia. Well, there are a lot! The population of Australia is about seventeen million, and they say that there are ten sheep for every person, so you can count them yourself!

Please send me some Chinese stamps. I must stop writing now, as I have rather a lot of work to do.

Yours,
Bob White

Lesson 95

1 Ask and answer

Ayers Rock is very famous. Look at the picture.
Choose the right answers to the questions:

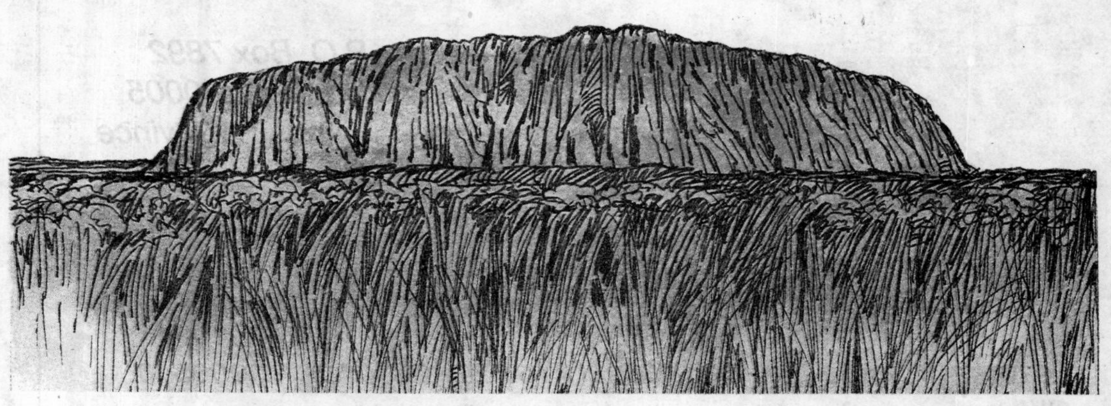

1 How many people are there 2 How many trees are there 3 How many sheep are there 4 How many cows can you see 5 Can you see any birds 6 Can you see much grass	on top of the rock?	Hardly any. None at all.

2 Practise Make sentences like this:

Though there are about seventeen million people in Australia, there are more than a hundred and seventy million sheep.

Though	Ayers Rock is difficult to reach, Bob has never been to China, Australia is very large, Australia is very rich, it is a very young country, much of its land is sand,	Australia is very rich. the population is quite small. he is very interested in it. much of the land is sand. it grows a lot of fruit. it is very famous.

Lesson 96

1 **Listen** Turn to page 96 in your workbook.

2 **Read and write**

Liu Zhong has just written a letter to her new penfriend. Read it, then write a similar letter about yourself:

P.O. Box 7892
Nanjing 210005
Jiangsu Province
China
21st. May 19_ _

Dear Linda,

I saw your name in a newspaper. You asked for penfriends in China.

I am fifteen years old, and I live in the city of Nanjing. I am in my third year at Number 1 Middle School. You can see from my photograph that I have a big smile and long black hair.

My father is a factory worker. My mother is a cook. She works in a hospital. I am very interested in stamps, watching films, listening to music and reading. I enjoy dancing and helping my uncle on the farm, too. I am also very interested in your country. Please write soon.

Yours,
Liu Zhong

GOODBYE, EVERYBODY! *GOOD LUCK!*

Notes to the texts 课文注释

Lesson 1

1. Teachers' Day 教师节
2. And your parents? = And how're your parents? 还有，你父母好吗？（或你父母身体怎样？）
3. Everyone is going into class. 大家都去上课了（或到班上去了）。
4. with our best wishes 致以我们良好的祝愿。又如:

   Please accept this little present with our best wishes. 请接受这件小小的礼物，并向你致意。

5. 英语贺卡的写法

   1) 称呼: 指祝贺人对受贺人的称呼，如 To dear teacher, To my dearest Father and Mother 等。但前面也有不加 to 的，如 Mr and Mrs Read（里德先生、夫人）。称呼一般写在卡片的左上方。

   2) 贺词: 通常写一些固定的贺节用语，如 Happy Teachers' Day, With Best Wishes for a Happy New Year（敬祝新年快乐！），但也有预先印制好的。这一部分内容也可根据实际情况写一些简短的表示感谢和良好祝愿的话。

   3) 祝贺人签名: 写在贺卡的右下方。姓名前常加 from, 如 From your student Li Lei, From Mr and Mrs Clarke, 但前面也有不加 from 的。

   4) 格式

To my dear Uncle and Aunt,	亲爱的叔叔、婶婶:
With Best Wishes for A Happy New Year	敬祝 新年快乐
From your loving nephew Lei	您亲爱的侄子雷 敬贺

Lesson 2

1. Nothing difficult! = There's nothing difficult. 没有什么困难的（东西）。

   这是省略句，省略了谓语部分。注意修饰 nothing 的形容词 (difficult) 习惯上放在后面。

2. What subject should I talk about? 我能讲什么题目呢？

   should作为情态动词和疑问词连用时，常常表示意外、惊奇、不能理解等，有“竟会”的意思。又如:

How *should* I know? 我怎么知道？

"Give me that photo." "Why *should* I?" "把那张照片给我。" "为什么（要）给你？"

3. Maybe I could talk about English names. 也许我可以讲讲英国人的名字（问题）。

could 是情态动词 can 的过去形式，但也可以用于现在时间，表示委婉地提出问题，可以译作"可以"。又如: I could get you a ticket. 我可以给你弄张票。

4. ... do please. ……，就讲这个。相当于 Do please talk about English names. 就请讲讲英国人的名字问题吧。

do 在这里作加强祈使的语气用，发强音[du:]。常常译作 "一定"、"务必"等。又如: Do tell me. 一定要告诉我。 Do be careful. 务必小心。

5. family name 姓。

6. So "John Henry Brown" is usually called "John Brown". 所以"约翰·亨利·布朗"通常叫作"约翰·布朗"。

这个句子中的谓语 is called 是被动语态，意思是"被（人们）称作 ……"。

7. given name 名字（不包括姓）；教名。

8. ... people usually call me Jim for short. …… 人家通常简称我为吉姆。

for short 简称。

Lesson 5

1. Which sport are you in today? 你今天参加哪一项运动？

Lesson 6

1. a team race 团体赛跑。

2. Ready? Go! 预备 — 跑！

3. Come on! 快！快呀！

4. neck and neck 齐头并进（一般快）。

5. They both passed on their sticks at the same time. 他们两人同时传出接力棒。

both 表示 "两个都"，只能用于两个人或两件事物。又如:

They both want to come. 他们俩都想来。

You may take them both. 你可以把两个都拿去。

6. ... and went on running. …… 继续跑了下去。

Lesson 7

1. ... but not fast enough. …… 但还不够快。

当 enough 修饰形容词或副词时，一般位于被修饰的词之后。又如:

That room is not big enough. 那间屋子不够大。

He didn't speak loudly enough. 他说话声音不够响。

2. Class 3 were the winners! 三班获胜了！（或三班是优胜者！）

集体名词 class 在这里根据意思作复数看待，所以动词要用 were。

3. Well done, everyone! 个个干得好！

4. Congratulations, Lin Tao! 祝贺你，林涛！

5. She did rather badly. 她表现得相当糟。

6. the girls' 400 metres 女子400米（赛跑）。

7. It was difficult to see. 很难看清楚。

Lesson 9

1. In English, *qu* makes a [kw] sound. 在英语里，*qu* 发 [kw] 音。

2. Hands up, please! = Put up your hands, please! 请举手！

3. It's another way of saying *fast*. 那是“快”的另一种说法。

4. Will you please say it again more slowly? 请你慢一点儿再说一遍好吗？

5. What do you mean by ..., please? 请问 …… 是什么意思？

6. Look, there's a picture of one. 瞧，有一张 …… 的图片（照片）。

one 在这里用作代词，代表照片上所照的（即上文所提到的）实物。

Lesson 10

1. There was a big smile on her face. 她脸上充满笑容。

2. ... and it was not as clean as usual. …… 它（教室）不像往常那样干净。

not as ... as ... 与 …… 不一样 ……。

3. The radio says that it may stop raining later. 广播说一会儿雨可能会停止。

stop doing 在动词 stop 后面跟另一动词的 ing 形式，表示停止这一动作。

4. Luckily the weather was not so wet as it is today. 幸亏那天不像今天这样下雨。

not so (as) ... as ... 和 …… 不一样 ……。

5. We had a long walk along the wall. 我们沿着城墙走了很长一段路。

Lesson 11

1. less difficult (useful, ...) than ... 没有 …… 难（有用，……）。

Lesson 12

1. I find it very difficult. 我发现它（数学）很难。

Lesson 13

1. I'm trying to draw a horse. 我在试着画一匹马。

2. quite a nice horse 一匹相当好的马。

注意: a 在 quite 的后面。

Lesson 14

1. He found it very difficult to get to sleep .... 他发现很难入睡 ……。

   it 在这里用作形式宾语，而真正的宾语是后面的不定式 to get to sleep。

   get to sleep 中的 get to 有"开始"的意思。

2. With a smile, the man from downstairs said: "...." 这位楼下人笑着说:"……。"
3. He was just falling asleep when there was a loud knock at the door. 他刚要入睡，就有人大声敲门。

   这里，when = and then （那时）。又如:

   I was just going to speak when the bell rang. 我刚要讲，铃就响了。

4. I was waiting for the sound of the other shoe! 我一直在等待另一只鞋（落地）的响声！

Lesson 15

1. One day the man upstairs heard the sound of children playing in the park. 一天楼上那个人听到了孩子们在公园玩耍的声音。

Lesson 16

1. I was watching the traffic. 我在监管交通。

Lesson 17

1. What happened? 出了什么事儿？
2. A woman saw it happen when she was walking past. 一位妇女走过的时候，看到了事情的发生。

   注意: 表示感觉的动词 see 后面的动词不定式（happen） 不带 to。

Lesson 18

1. Luckily, he was not badly hurt. 幸好他伤得不重。
2. It's really nice of you. 你们真好。
3. But you'd better not talk. 不过你最好不要说话。

   注意: 短语 had better （还是 …… 好；最好还是 ……） 后面的动词不定式 (talk) 不带 to; 不定式的否定形式是"not + 动词不定式", 所以这里就成为 not talk。又如:

   You had better go at once. 你最好马上去。

   You had better not go. 你最好不去。

4. As quickly as she could, Miss Zhao got a medicine box. 赵小姐尽快取来药箱。

   注意代词 she 和名词 Miss Zhao 在句中出现的先后顺序，英语的和汉语不同。正常语序为 Miss Zhao got a medicine box as quickly as she could. 句中 as quickly as she could 后省略 get a medicine box, 汉语的意思“她尽可能快地（取来药箱）”。

Lesson 21

1. Have you got ...? 你有 …… 吗？

现在完成时 have got 在口语中往往相当于一般现在时 have 的意思。例如:

Have you *got* a ruler? 你有直尺吗？

Yes, I'*ve got* a new one. = I *have* a new one. 是的，我有一把新的。

但有时则不然，试比较:

I'*ve got* two letters from my father this month. 这个月我已经收到两封爸爸的来信了。另外， have got 表示“有”的意思常见于英国英语，而美国英语常用 have。例如: 美国人通常问 Do you have ...? 而英国人却爱问 Have you got ...?

2. I think I've got one. 我想我有一把。

I've = I have。

3. I'm so glad. 我真高兴。

so在口语中用以加重语气，带有惊叹的口吻。意思相当于very。

Lesson 22

1. library book 图书馆藏书。

2. Red Star over China 《西行漫记》。原文意思是“红星照耀中国”,为埃德加·帕克斯·斯诺 (Edgar ['edgə] Parks Snow) 所著。埃德加·斯诺（1905-1972)是美国著名作家和记者，1936年到中国陕北革命根据地采访，受到毛泽东、周恩来等领导同志的接见，后写成《西行漫记》一书，最早向美国和全世界介绍了中国人民革命斗争和红军二万五千里长征的英雄业绩，成为举世名著。

Lesson 23

1. Mr Know-all 无所不知先生; 百事通先生。

know-all 自称无所不知的人。

Lesson 26

1. Miss Forgetful 健忘小姐。

2. That's one thing I haven't forgotten today! 这是我今天唯一没有忘记的事情！

Lesson 28

1. Bike is short for bicycle. Bike 是 bicycle 的缩写。

2. Making words 构词。

Lesson 29

1. several kinds of animal(s) 几种动物。
2. Have you ever been to West Hill Farm? 你曾到过西山农场吗？

   动词 be 的现在完成时 have (has) been (to) 是 "曾到过某地"的意思。又如:

   Where have you been? 你到哪儿去了？（我已经回来。）

   I have been to the library. 我到图书馆去了。（去过图书馆。）

Lesson 30

1. A farmer arrives at a woman's house. 一位农民来到一位妇女的家里。

   注意:剧情介绍、舞台说明中使用的动词用一般现在时态。
2. With pleasure. 十分愿意;高兴地。
3. I'll return it as soon as I can. 我尽快归还。
4. No hurry. 不必忙。（为 There's no hurry. 的省略。）
5. It's just had a baby! = It has just had a baby. 它刚生了个孩子。

   have a baby 意思是 "生孩子"。 have / has had 是 have / has 的现在完成时。
6. I hope everything goes well. 希望一切顺利。
7. I've never heard of that before! 我以往从来没有听说过这种事。

   hear of 听到. 又如: I've never heard of him. 我从来没有听到过他。

Lesson 33

1. I've been here for just about two years. 我来这里刚两年。

   for 表示一段时间。
2. since 19_ _ 自19_ _以来。

   since two years ago 从两年前到现在。

   since September 从九月起。

Lesson 34

1. They arrived early on a Tuesday morning. 他们是在一个星期二的清早到达的。

   当 morning / afternoon / evening 有定语修饰时，介词用 on, 不用 in。 又如:

   on Friday afternoon on Sunday evening
2. Don't rush! 别跑！别急！
3. ... a few things about this factory. …… 这个工厂的一些情况。
4. Number 1 Machine Shop; No. 1 Machine Shop 第一机械车间, 第一金工车间。

5. Come up these steps .... ……（走）上这些台阶。

6. Keep together, please. 请靠拢点; 请保持在一起。

7. cutting machines 切削机。

Lesson 35

1. Come straight along here. please. 请直接从这里走过来。

2. get lost 丢失; 迷路。

3. keep ... safe 保持……安全。

4. My house is about twenty minutes by bike. 骑自行车到我家大概得20分钟

5. I've lived there all my life. 我住在那儿已经一辈子了

   all one's life 终身，一生。

Lesson 36

1. two and a half years 也可以说作 two years and a half 两年半。

   同样: one and a half years = one (a) year and a half 一年半。

   但应注意整数部分是1时，两种说法中的名词 (year) 有单、复数的区别。

Lesson 37

1. Could I speak to ..., please? 我能和 …… 通话吗？（打电话用语）

   speak to somebody 同某人说话。

2. Hold on for a moment, please! 请稍等一下。（打电话用语）

3. That's very kind of you. 您真好;谢谢您。

4. I would like to see him as soon as possible, please. 我想能尽快看到他。

Lesson 38

1. The whole family's going for two months. 全家要去两个月。

   注意: 这里 family 指整个家庭，所以动词用单数 is going。试比较:

   My family are very well. 我全家都很健康。这里指家庭成员，动词用复数 (are)。

   其次，现在进行时可以用来表示按计划或安排最近要进行或即将发生的动作，所以这句话的动词用 is going。同样，前段还有:

   ... we are travelling back to England soon for a holiday. …… 我们就要回英国度假。

Lesson 39

1. He may even fail his Chinese exam. 他的语文考试甚至会不及格。

2. I think that maybe his Chinese teacher will give Jim some work to do during the holiday. 我想吉姆的汉语老师也许会给他一些假期作业。

注意代词 his 和名词 Jim 在句中出现的先后顺序，英语的习惯和汉语不同。

3. I'm sure that he won't mind. 我肯定他不会介意。

Lesson 40

1. Jim's two-month holiday 或写作: Jim's two months' holiday 吉姆的两个月假期。

   two-month 作定语用，加连字符，名词用单数。

Lesson 41

1. Which of these do you think is the most useful invention? 这些发明中你认为哪一种是最有用的？

   这里 do you think 用作插入语，即与句子的其他成分没有语法上的关系，只是作为一种附加的解释。

2. the second most useful invention 第二项最有用的发明。

3. Which of these would you most like to own? 这些（东西）你最想要（拥有）哪一种？

Lesson 42

1. Thomas Edison ['tɔməs 'edisn] 全名为 Thomas Alva ['ælvə] Edison (1847—1931)。

   托马斯·阿尔瓦·爱迪生是美国发明家、企业家，发明有留声机、电灯等。在电影技术、矿业、建筑、化工等方面也有不少著名的发明。

2. ... he was always trying out new ideas. …… 他总是试验一些新的设想。

   这里过去进行时和 always 连用，表示过去经常反复的动作，含有赞扬的情感。又如:

   She was always doing things for other people. 她总是为别人做事。

   try out （彻底）试验。

3. ... his father saw him sitting on some eggs. 爱迪生的父亲见他坐在一些鸡蛋上。

   see ... doing something 看到某人正在干某事。

4. ... to send Tom away from school. 把汤姆赶出学校去。

   send away 驱逐; 把 …… 送到远处去。

5. ... to take the boy out of school. …… 把孩子从学校接出来。

6. ... she found him a very good pupil. 她发现他是个好学生。

7. What do you want a science lab for? 你要科学实验室做什么？

   what for 为何目的; 为什么。又如:

   What did you do that *for*? 你干那件事为了什么？

Lesson 43

1. Edison thought hard. 爱迪生苦苦地思索。

2. ... Edison's mother was saved. …… 爱迪生的母亲得救了。

Lesson 44

1. It's not a very good line. 线路不太好。

2. The line was bad. 线路很糟。

3. It's a bad line. 线路不好;这是条很糟的线路。

Lesson 45

1. Could you do something for me, please? 你能为我做件事，行吗？

2. as much as possible 尽可能多地。

3. the floor of her cage 她的笼底。

4. once a week 一星期一次。

Lesson 46

1. You can have one bag each, ... 你们每人可以带一个手提包 …… 。

2. the air tickets 飞机票。

3. He's coming round to get her quite soon. 他很快就会过来取（她）的。

   come round 来; 前来。

4. Oh, that must be Ling Feng now! 噢，这一定是凌峰！

Lesson 47

1. Oh, you haven't changed your mind, have you? 嗨，你没有改变主意，是吧？

2. Can I do anything to help? 我能帮你做点什么吗？

3. Flight No. CA907 中国民航 907 班机 。 Flight No. BA347 英航 347 班机。

4. arrive in 到达。

   到达大城市等较大的地方，arrive 后面的介词用 in。如到达城镇、乡村等较小的地方，介词用at。

5. What is the flight number of their plane leaving Beijing? 他们离京的航班号是多少？

   leaving Beijing 为现在分词结构, 放在名词后面, 起定语作用。

6. Gate 12 第 12 登机口。

Lesson 48

1. What about you, Mother? 你怎么样，孩子妈？

   Father 跟着孩子，把妻子叫作 Mother。

Lesson 49

1. He won't be back until January. 不到元月，他不会回来。

2. ... no news is good news. …… 没有消息就是好消息。

3. Whom did he travel with? 他和谁一起旅行？

whom 是 who 的宾格，用于正式文体中，在一般口语中经常用 who 代替，这句话也可以说作: Who did he travel with? 介词可以置于句末，也可以置于句首。例如:

With whom did you travel?

Of whom are you speaking? = *Who(m)* are you speaking *of*? 你说的是谁？

Lesson 50

1. How time flies! 光阴似箭！（或时间过得好快！）
2. ... I am working hard on my Chinese. …… 我正在努力学习汉语。
3. We had a very good journey home. 我们回家的旅行很顺利。

Lesson 51

1. No, he said that he hadn't bought any yet. 没有,他说他现在还没有买什么礼物。

主句的动词 said 是过去时，宾语从句中的动词用过去完成时。表示在 said 以前尚未买什么礼物。

Lesson 54

1. Father Christmas 圣诞老人（英国说法）。
2. Christmas Day 圣诞节。
3. Christmas Eve 圣诞节前夕。

Lesson 55

1. So today, people still do the same thing to each other. 所以，今天人们还在互相做同样的事情（指上文所提到的互送礼物）。
2. It is better to give than to receive. 给予比接受好。

本句也可写作 To give is better than to receive.

Lesson 57

1. — It's her turn ! 轮到她了。

— So it is! 是呀！

so 常用来代替上文中的形容词、名词或动词，表示赞同。又如:

— It was hot yesterday. 昨天很热。

— So it was. 对。（或: 是这样的。）

Lesson 58

1. People often ask me whether I like being a twin. 人们常常问我是否喜欢是双胞胎。
2. Well, it feels strange to have a twin sister. 是呀，有个孪生姐姐是觉得奇怪。

3. ... I can see that we're different. …… 我能看出我们是有差别的。

4. T-shirt 短袖圆领汗衫。

5. Then, when it's open, we fight about who plays with it first. 然后,当礼物打开时，我们就争着谁先来玩。

Lesson 59

1. I can't decide which sweater to buy! 我不能决定买哪种毛衣！

动词不定式 to buy 作定语，放在它所修饰的名词短语 which sweater 后面。

Lesson 62

1. ... find the names of the five countries where English is spoken as the first language. 找出以英语为第一语言的五个国家的名字。

where English is spoken ... 是定语从句，用以修饰 countries。

2. English is spoken as a first language by most people in the USA, ... 在美国，……大多数人都把英语作为第一语言。

3. The next time you see a watch, look at the back. 下次你看一块手表时，瞧瞧它的背面。

4. That is why we are learning English in China. 这就是我们在中国学英语的原因。

5. If you learn even a little English, you will find ... school. 假如你那怕只学一点英语，在你离开学校（毕业）后，会发现它是有用的。

Lesson 66

1. the museum in the centre of the town 城镇中心的博物馆。

many old things on show in glass-topped tables 在带玻璃桌面的桌子里展览的许多古老的东西。

介词短语作定语时，放在它所修饰的名词后面。如不只一个介词短语，语序与汉语的相反。

2. It says here, on this card, that it was used in plays. 这儿，这张卡片上说，那是演戏用的。

3. Isn't it beautiful! 它不美丽吗？=它真美丽！

用否定疑问句表示惊叹，标点符号用感叹号。

4. It was used for keeping tea hot after it was made. 那是在茶煮好后用来保温的。

make tea 沏茶，泡茶。

5. That's what we did in China in the old days, ... 那是我们中国从前 …… 的作法。

in the old days 从前，以往。 day 在这里常用复数，意思是“日子”; “时代”。

6. The group of girls all moved on and ... thermos! 这一群女生全都继续往前走去，从现代的保温瓶里倒了茶，一起痛痛快快地喝了下去！

move on 继续前进。

have a drink of tea 喝茶。

Lesson 69

1. Tree Planting Day 植树节。
2. Make sure that it is straight. 一定要把它立直。

   make sure 查明，弄确实。
3. Put the tree in the hole so that it is straight. 把树放在穴内，让它立直。

   so that 意思是 “以便”；“为了”。
4. Push it down hard with your foot several times. 用脚踩几下，把土压实。
5. Tie the tree to the top of the stick to keep it straight. 把树和木棍的顶端捆好，以保持直立。

Lesson 70

1. In 1850, about a third was covered by forest. 1850年，大约有三分之一（土地）被森林覆盖着。

   a third = one third 三分之一; two thirds 三分之二。
2. A lot of good land has gone with them, leaving only sand. 许多好地和森林一起消失了，留下来的只有沙漠。
3. Today, too many trees are still being cut down in the USA. 今天，在美国仍有大量的树木在继续被砍伐。

   are being cut 是现在进行时的被动语态。
4. China does not want to copy the USA's example. 中国不愿仿照美国的样子。
5. The Great Green Wall will stop the wind from blowing the earth away. 绿色长城将阻止风刮走土。

   stop ... from doing something 是“阻止 …… 以免（或防止）作某事”的意思。又如:

   She stopped the child from listening. 她阻止孩子，不让听了（她不让孩子再听了）
6. Many thousands of trees must be planted every year. 每年都得种成千上万株树。

   many thousands of 数千; 成千上万。
7. The more, the better. 越多越好。

   the ..., the ... 愈 …… 愈 ……；越是 ……，越是 …… 。
8. In a few years' time, those mountains will be covered with trees, too. 过几年以后，那些山上也会长满了树。
9. The only problem is you can't eat trees! 唯一的难题是你不能吃树呀！

Lesson 74

1. Man-made satellites have been sent up into space by many countries. 许多国家都向太空发射了人造卫星。

   注意这句话使用的时态是现在完成时的被动语态。send up 在这里是"射出，发送"的意思。

2. Our knowledge of the universe is growing all the time. Our knowledge grows and the universe develops. 我们对宇宙的认识一直在增长。我们的认识在增长，宇宙也在发展。

   all the time 一直; 始终。

Lesson 77

1. 3,333,333,333　　33亿3千3百33万3千3百33。

   读多位大数要注意以下各点:

   1) 1,000 以上的大数，要使用计数逗点",", 即从个位开始，每隔三位加一逗点，第一个逗点前是 thousand（千），第二个逗点前是 million（百万），第三个逗点前是 thousand million（英国读法）或 billion（美国读法）（十亿）。

   2) 分段以后,各段就都成了 101-999 等三位数了。读的时候十位数（或个位数）的前面一般要加 and（也可不加）。因此，333,333,333 就可以读作:

      333,000,000　　three hundred (and) thirty-three million,
      333,000　　three hundred (and) thirty-three thousand,
      333　　three hundred and thirty-three

   3) 英语没有单独表示"万"和"亿"的词，以"ten thousand"表示"一万","几十 thousand"表示"几万","几百 thousand"表示"几十万"。以"ten million"表示"一千万","几十 million"表示"几千万"，以"a hundred million"表示"一亿","几百 million"表示"几亿"。

Lesson 78

1. Standing room only 只有立足之地。

   room 在这里是"空间; 地方"的意思。

2. A UN report ... 一份联合国报告 ……

   UN = (the) United Nations 联合国。

3. by the end of the twentieth century 到 20世纪末。

   by 到…… 之前; 不迟于。

4. That means that in about 600 years, there will be ... earth.　那就是说，大约过 600 年以后，地球上只有立足之地了。

   in ... years / months / weeks / days 在 …… 年（月、周、日）以后。

Lesson 79

1. the more developed countries 比较发达国家。
2. the less developed counries 不太发达国家。

Lesson 80

1. There will not be enough space even to stand in on the earth. 就是在地球上站着，也不会有足够的地方了。

Lesson 81

1. My shoes are worn out. 我的鞋穿破了。

   wear out 穿破; 磨破; 用坏。

   当 shoes 作主语时，谓语要用被动语态 be worn out。

Lesson 82

1. A young man named John had just left school for the last time. 一个名叫约翰的青年刚刚从学校毕业。

   leave school for the last time 最后一次离开学校（指毕业）。
2. The shop was quite new, for it had opened only the week before. 这家商店相当新，因为在一星期前它才开业。
3. That's the cheapest suit we have, I'm afraid. 恐怕那是我们最便宜的西服了。

   I'm afraid 在这里是插入语。也就是说，与句子的其它成分没有语法关系。如果移到句子前面，就成为整个句子的主要部分，而原来的句子变成全句的一个从句了。

Lesson 83

1. They were so pleased to see each other that they forgot everything else. 他们彼此见到面，高兴得连别的什么事情都忘了。
2. John turned round and looked at him in surprise. 约翰转过身来，惊奇地望着他。

   turn round 转身。 in surprise 惊异地。
3. ... he had chosen a new jacket, but he hadn't paid for it! …… 他曾经挑了一件夹克，但是还没有交款！
4. That was nearly the cheapest jacket in town! 这件夹克几乎成了城里最便宜的夹克了！

   因不是事实，动词用过去时 was。

Lesson 85

1. At the doctor's 在医务室。 在提到住宅、商店等地时，名词所有格所修饰的名词往往省略。又如:

   at Jack's (house) 在杰克家。

at my uncle's (house) 在我叔叔家。

He went to the barber's (shop). 他到理发店去了。

2. I've got a headache and a cough. 我有点头痛，还咳嗽。

3. There's something wrong with Kate. 凯特有点不舒服。

4. FATHER: Nothing serious, I hope! 父亲：我希望不严重！

MOTHER: I hope not. 母亲：（我）希望不严重。

5. You'd better not go to school. 你最好不要去上学了。

Lesson 86

1. His temperature seems to be all right. 他的体温好像完全正常。

2. Has he had anything to eat this morning? 今天早晨他吃过什么东西了吗？

3. ... he has caught a bit of a cold. …… 他着了点凉；他有点感冒。

a bit of 有点，有些。

4. Shall I keep him away from school? 我是否要不让他去上学？

5. ... I think it'll be all right for him to go to school. …… 我想他上学没关系。

it 在这里用作形式主语，而后面的 for him to go to school 则是真正的主语。

6. ... he'll be all right soon. I'm sure of that! …… 他很快就没事了。我肯定！

Lesson 87

1. Your son's trouble is very common these days. 你儿子的毛病现在是极常见的。

these days 现在，现时，这几天。

2. Tom won't feel well till it's over. 等到它（足球赛）结束后，汤姆才会好。

3. Have you had a wash yet? 你已经洗过脸了吗？

have a wash 洗一洗脸。

4. ... but I don't feel like eating. …… 但是我不想吃。

feel like (doing) （指人）想要。后面常接动词 -ing 形式。又如：

I feel like taking a walk. 我想散散步。

Lesson 89

1. It's a long time since we met last! 从我们上次见面以后，已经很久了。

2. Did you have a good journey? 你旅途愉快吗？

3. Am I playing? 我参加吗？

这里用现在进行时表示即将发生的动作。

4. A: What are you doing tomorrow? 明天你干什么？

B: I'm watching the league match, of course! 我当然要看联赛！

league match 联赛。在英国，指参加足球、篮球等竞赛联合会的各队之间的比赛。

5. But it's such an important match, we can't miss it. 不过这是一场如此重要的球赛，我们不能不观看（不能错过）。

Lesson 90

1. ... and before this match we were almost top of the league. …… 在这次比赛以前，我们差一点就是联赛的冠军了。

2. ... I found it a bit difficult to work in class because I kept on thinking about the match in the afternoon. ……我发现在班上有点难以学习，因为我一直在想下午的比赛。

   a bit 少许， 在这里用作状语。 又如: I'm feeling *a bit* tired. 我感觉有点累。

3. Keep passing the ball to each other, and you'll be OK! 坚持互相传球，你们就行！

4. That's what we found. 那是我们所发现的（指下文）。

5. ... some of them were very hard to stop when they got the ball. …… 他们有些人接到球后，很难拦阻。

6. They didn't pass the ball ... well. 他们传球不够，而且他们整体配合得不很好。

Lesson 91

1. At the end of the first half we were winning 2—1. 上半场结束时，我们以二比一领先。

2. ... but one player does not make a team. …… 但是一个队员组不成一个队。

3. By the end of the match, they *had kicked* two goals .... 比赛结束前，他们已踢进两球……。

   I *had* never *seen* such a good match before that day. 在那天之前，我从未见过这样精彩的比赛。

   When I got there, you *had* already *started* playing. 当我到那里时，你们已经开始踢球了。

   这三句中的谓语动词都用了过去完成时，表示过去某一时刻以前所发生的动作。

4. Ours is the best team in the league. 我们队在联赛中是最强的队。

Lesson 94

1. ... so we flew most of the way. …… 所以我们大部分旅途都是乘飞机。

2. From Sydney we flew over a line of mountains in the southeast. 从悉尼起飞，我们越过澳大利亚东南部的一系列山脉。

3. But after we left the mountains behind us, there was hardly a cloud in the sky. 然而当我们把群山峻岭甩在后面后，天空几乎万里无云。

4. hardly any people = there are hardly any people 简直没有什么人。

5. All around it is sand. 它（指艾尔斯山）的周围都是沙漠。

6. ... they say that ... = ... it is said that ... …… 据说 ……。

Lesson 96

1. P.O. Box 7892　　7892 信箱。

P.O. 为 Post Office 的缩写。

一般信件，信封上要把写信人的地址写在左上角。

Pronunciation and Spelling 发音和拼法

元音字母a及其字母组合在重读音节中的读音

a 在开音节中读 [ei]	
cage	45
hate	46
race	5
save	43
space	74
change	41
strange	42
a ble	37
fa mous	95
la zy	38

a 在闭音节中读 [æ]	
bang	14
glad	1
hang	59
lab	42
lap	6
match	87
maths	11
pan	30
sand	70
stamp	61
an gry	14
hap pen	14
jack et	46
lan guage	9
nar row	34
trav el	18
ex am	38
per haps	82
ac ci dent	17
cap i tal	38

a 在 n, s 和 th 等前读 [ɑ:]	
dance	58
fast	5
grass	94
plant	69
mas ter	37
rath er	7

ai 读 [ei]	
fail	39
pain	87
straight	35
a gainst	90

al 读 [ɔ:(l)]	
chalk	13
al most	50

ar 读 [ɑ:]	
art	1
card	1
star	58
hard ly	94
mar ket	65
par don	83

ay 读 [ei]	
pay	22
hoo ray	7

元音字母e及其字母组合在重读音节中的读音

e 在开音节中读 [i:]	
eve	50
e ven	39
re lay	6
re tell	83

e 在闭音节中读[e]	
hen	42
lend	30
neck	5
spend	26
step	34
yet	21
cen tre	36
mem ber	50
in vent	41
ev er	23
med i cine	18
sev er al	21

wheth er	57
cen tu ry	78
ex pen sive	59
ter ri ble	86
de vel op	74
to geth er	33

ea 读 **[i:]**	
beat	90
each	46
leaf	45
league	16
seat	46
weak	38
Zea land	65

ea 读 **[ei]**	
break	26
great	107 B2

ea 读 **[e]**	
dead	30
al read y	26
head ache	85

ee 读 **[i:]**	
deep	69
seem	86
sheep	29
sleep	14
sweep	10
sweet	26
a gree	11
be tween	37

ei 读 **[i:]**	
(ei ther)	58
(nei ther)	69
re ceive	49

er 读 **[ə:]**	
Ger man	62
per son	25
ther mos	66
pre fer	11

ew 读 **[ju:]**	
few	14 B2
news	49
news pa per	9

ear 读 **[ə:]**	
earth	69, 74
heard	23 B2
learn	102 B2

元音字母 i (y) 及其字母组合在重读音节中的读音

i 在开音节中读 **[ai]**	
life	35
rise	94
size	81
smile	10
twice	31
while	19
wide	71
ar rive	26
be side	46
de cide	58
po lite	22
sur prise	66
li bra ry	18

i 在闭音节中读 **[i]**	
dig	69
fill	45
film	25
miss	38
pig	29
silk	63
still	6
strict	22
till	85
win	5
wish	1
Christ mas	49
mir ror	43
win ner	7
pig sty	31
pit y	22
dic tion a ry	21
dif fi cult	2
his to ry	24
bridge	65

i 在 **gh** 和 **nd** 等前读 **[ai]**	
fight	58
flight	47
kind	54
mind	39

ie 读 [ai]	
die	30
lie	18
tie	69
ie 读 [i:]	
field	29

piece	1 B2
ir 读 [ə:]	
dirt y	83
thirst y	66

y 在开音节中读 [ai]	
sky	94
spy	36
try	13

元音字母o及其字母组合在重读音节中的读音

o 在开音节中读[əu]	
hole	69
joke	30
smoke	67
broke	26
chose	2
rose	94
lone ly	58
mo tor	18
pro gramme	74
o 在闭音节中读 [ɔ]	
cost	59
drop	6
knock	14
lock	61
mom	26
pot	66
rock	94
soft	59
song	91
top	54
a cross	65
com mon	87
com rade	14
dol lar	82
Mos cow	14
pos si ble	37
cop y	70

for eign	9
for est	70
mod ern	62
o 在 m, n 和 v 等前读 [ʌ]	
none	62
a mong	70
be come	42
cov er	45
won der ful	69
oa 读 [əu]	
coat	35 B1
goal	91
road	15 B2
oi / oy 读 [ɔi]	
join	34
noise	14
point	66
boy	22 B1
en joy	49 B2
oo 读 [u]	
cook	103 B1
wood	61
wool	31

oo 读 [u:]	
choose	2
noon	15
or 读 [ɔ:]	
horse	13
nor	69
or der	32
cor ner	18
im por tant	3
or 在[w]后读 [ə:]	
work	83 B1
world	41
worse	45 B2
ou 读 [au]	
found	67
ground	5
loud	6
mouth	78
sound	9
moun tain	70
thou sand	73
with out	50

ou 读 **[u:]**	
gr*ou*p	66
thr*ou*gh	34

ou 读 **[ʌ]**	
c*ou*n try	67 B2
tr*ou* ble	14

ow 读 **[əu]**	
l*ow*	94
*ow*n	41
sh*ow*	38 B2

ow 读 **[au]**	
c*ow*	29
cr*ow*d	18
d*ow*n stairs	14

our 读 **[ɔ:]**	
c*our*se	3
f*our*th	4 B2
y*our*	13 B1

元音字母u及其字母组合在重读音节中的读音

u 在开音节中读 **[(j)u:]**	
tr*ue*	39
m*u* seum	65
p*u* pil	42
pro d*u*ce	53
u ni verse	73
com p*u* ter	41

u 在闭音节中读 **[ʌ]**	
br*u*sh	83
c*u*t	34
j*u*st	14
l*u*ck	1
r*u*sh	34
s*u*ch	89
h*u*r ry	18
R*u*s sian	14
s*u*d den ly	18
s*u*b ject	2
*u*p stairs	14
in str*u*c tion	45

u 在闭音节中也读 **[u]**	
f*u*ll	11 B2
p*u*ll	99 B2
p*u*sh	99 B2
p*u*t	35 B1
s*u*g ar	79 B2

ur 读 **[ə:]**	
b*ur*n	50
n*ur*se	86
f*ur* ther	48
re t*ur*n	22

ur(e) 读 **[uə]**	
s*ure*	13 B2
d*ur* ing	39

Grammar 语法

I. 副词的比较级和最高级(The Comparative and Superlative Degrees of Adverbs)

副词和形容词一样，也有原级、比较级和最高级三个等级。

1. 副词比较级和最高级的构成

1) 规则变化

	构成方法	原级	比较级	最高级
单音节词和少数双音节词	一般在词尾加-er[ə]或-est[ist]	fast long near	faster longer nearer	fastest longest nearest
	以字母 e 结尾的副词，加 -r 或 -st	late	later	latest
	以“辅音字母+y”结尾的双音节词，先改“y”为 “i”，再加 -er 或-est	early	earlier	earliest
多音节词和部分双音节词	在词前加 more 或 most	quickly carefully	more quickly more carefully	most quickly most carefully

(2) 不规则变化

原级	比较级	最高级
well badly little much far	better worse less more farther ['fɑ:ðə] further ['fə:ðə]	best worst least most farthest ['fɑ:ðist] furthest ['fə:ðist]

2. 副词比较级和最高级的用法

级	用　　法	例　　句
比较级	副词比较级的用法与形容词相似。在"比较级+than"的句中，当than前后所使用的动词相同时，通常用助动词代替后面的动词。该动词或助动词可以省略。	Who runs **faster**, Lucy or Meimei? Li Lei jumped **farther than** Jim (did). He works much **harder than** I (do).
最高级	副词最高级的用法与形容词相似。（详见第二册教科书第127页。）副词最高级前可以不加定冠词the 。	Lin Tao jumped (the) **farthest** of all. Bob came to school the **latest** in his class yesterday.

3. 表示甲与乙在某一方面程度相同时用"as + 形容词或副词原形 + as" 的句型。如:

I think science is **as important as** maths.

Tom runs **as fast as** Jack.

表示甲在某一方面不及乙时用"not as (so) + 形容词或副词原形 + as" 的句型。如:

It is **not as (so) warm** today **as** yesterday.

He did **not** come **as (so) early as** Wang Lin.

II. 动词 (Verbs) (3)

1. 过去进行时 (The Past Continuous Tense)

1) 过去进行时的构成

过去进行时由 "was (were) + 动词 -ing" 构成。现以动词 work 为例，其肯定式、否定式和疑问式见下表:

肯　定　式	否　定　式
I / He / She / It was working. We / You / They were working.	I / He / She / It was not working. We / You / They were not working.

疑问式和简略答语		
Was I working? Yes, you were. No, you were not.	Were you working? Yes, I was. No, I was not.	Was he / she / it working? Yes, he / she / it was. No, he / she / it was not.
Were we / you / they working?	Yes, you / we / they were. No, you / we / they were not.	

注: was not 常简略为 wasn't ['wɔznt]; were not 常简略为 weren't [wə:nt]。

2) 过去进行时的用法: 表示在过去某一时刻或某一段时间正在进行的动作。这一特定的过去时间，除有上下文暗示以外，一般用时间状语来表示。如:

A: What **were** you **doing** *this time yesterday?*

B: We **were working** in class.

He **was mending** his bike *at ten o'clock yesterday*.

I **was drawing** a horse *when the teacher came in*.

3) 一般过去时与过去进行时用法的比较: 一般过去时表示在过去某个时间发生的动作或存在的状态，而过去进行时则表示在过去某一时刻或某一段时间正在进行的动作。如

Mary **wrote** a letter to her friend *last night*.

玛丽昨晚给她的朋友写了封信。（信写完了。）

Mary **was writing** a letter to her friend *last night*.

玛丽昨晚一直在给她的朋友写信。（信不一定写完。）

2. 现在完成时 (The Present Perfect Tense)

1) 现在完成时的构成

现在完成时由"助动词 have (has) + 过去分词"构成。现以动词 work 为例，将现在完成时的肯定式、否定式和疑问式以及简略答语列表如下:

肯定式	否定式
I / You have worked. He / She / It has worked. We / You / They have worked.	I / You have not worked. He / She / It has not worked. We / You / They have not worked.

疑问式和简略答语		
Have I / you worked? Has he / she / it worked? Have we / you / they worked?	Yes, you / I have. Yes, he / she / it has. Yes, you / we / they have.	No, you / I have not. No, he / she / it has not. No, you / we / they have not.

注: 1. 规则动词的过去分词的构成与动词过去式相同。不规则动词的过去分词见本书末《不规则动词表》。

2. have not 常简略为 haven't ['hævnt], has not 常简略为 hasn't ['hæznt]。

2) 现在完成时的用法

用　　法	例　　句
表示过去发生或已经完成的某一动作对现在造成的影响或结果。	— **Have** you **had** your lunch yet? — Yes, I **have**. I'**ve** just **had** it. （现在我不饿了。） I **have** already **posted** the photos. （这些照片已不在我这里了。）
表示过去已经开始，持续到现在的动作或状态，可以和表示从过去某一时刻延续到现在(包括“现在”在内)的一段时间的状语连用。	I **haven't seen** her *these days*. **Have** you **returned** the book *today*? I'**ve known** Li Lei *for three years*. I'**ve been** at this school *for over two years*. They **have lived** here *since 1989*.
现在完成时可以和 already, never, ever, just, before, yet 等状语连用。	**Have** you *ever* **eaten** fish and chips? I'**ve** *just* **lost** my science book. I'**ve** *never* **been** to that farm *before*. I **haven't learned** the word *yet*.
have (has) been 和 have (has) gone 的区别: 表示“曾到过某地”，要用have (has) been, 不能用have (has) gone。	Where **has** he **been**? 他刚才到哪儿去了？ （他已回来了。） Where **has** he **gone**? 他到哪儿去了？ （他现在不在这里。） She **has been** to Shanghai. 她到过上海。 （她已不在上海了。） She **has gone** to Shanghai. 她到上海去了。 （她可能在去上海的路上，或已到上海，总之，现在不在这里。）

3) 现在完成时和一般过去时的区别

现在完成时表示过去发生的某一动作对现在造成的影响或结果，强调的是现在的情况，所以它不能和表示过去的时间状语连用，如: yesterday, last night, three weeks ago, in 1990 等。而一般过去时只表示过去的动作或状态，和现在不发生关系，它可以和表示过去的时间状语连用。如:

I **have seen** the film. 我看过这部电影。（ 我了解这部电影的内容。）

I **saw** the film *last week*. 我上星期看了这个电影。（ 只说明上星期看了这个电影，不涉及现在的情况。）

He **has lived** here *since 1972*.　1972年以来他一直住在这里。（他现在还住在这里。）

He **lived** here in *1972*.　1972年他住在这里。（不涉及现在他是否还住在这里。）

*3 过去将来时 (The Future-in-the-Past Tense)

1) 过去将来时由“助动词 would + 动词原形”构成。would 常简缩为 'd, 如: I'd, you'd, he'd 等; would not 常简缩为 wouldn't ['wudnt]。

2) 过去将来时的用法

过去将来时表示从过去的某一时间看来将要发生的动作或存在的状态。过去将来时常用在宾语从句中。例如:

I didn't know if she **would come.**

I wasn't sure whether he **would do** it.

Lei Lei said that she **would visit** her uncle next Saturday.

过去将来时也可以用“was (were) going to + 动词原形”来表示。例如:

I didn't know if she **was going to come.**

Lei Lei said that she **was going to visit** her uncle next Saturday.

*4 过去完成时 (The Past Perfect Tense)

1) 过去完成时的构成

过去完成时由“助动词 had（用于各种人称和数）+ 过去分词”构成。

2) 过去完成时的用法

用　法	例　句
过去完成时表示在过去某一时间或动作之前已经发生或完成了的动作。它表示动作发生的时间是“过去的过去”。表示过去某一时间可用 by, before 等构成的短语，也可用 when, before 等引导的从句或者通过上下文表示。	By the end of the match, they **had kicked** two goals and we **had kicked** four. We **had reached** the station before ten o'clock. When I got there, you **had** already **started** playing. Wang Lin **had mended** the radio before his brother returned. We did as he **had told** us. He remembered he **had chosen** a new jacket, but he **hadn't paid** for it!

注: had not 常简略为 hadn't ['hædnt]。

5 动词不定式 (The Infinitive)

1) 动词不定式的基本形式是“to + 动词原形”，有时可以不带 to。动词不定式（或不定式短语）没有人称和数的变化，在句子中不能作谓语。动词不定式仍保留动词的特点，即可以有自己的宾语和状语。动词不定式同它的宾语或状语构成不定式短语。如: to read the newspaper, to speak at the meeting 等。

2) 动词不定式具有名词、形容词和副词的特征，因此在句中可以作主语、表语、宾语、宾语补足语、定语和状语。

句法作用	例　　句
作宾语	She wanted **to borrow my radio.** They began **to read and write.**
作状语	She went **to see her grandma** last Sunday. He came **to give us a talk** yesterday.
作宾语补足语	Lucy asked him **to turn down the radio.** She asked me **to speak more loudly.** Jim told Ling Feng **to give his best wishes to everybody.**
*作定语	Have you got anything **to say**? I had something **to eat** this morning.
*作主语	**To learn a foreign language** is not easy. **To play** in the street is dangerous.

注: 作主语用的动词不定式常常为 it 替代, 动词不定式（或短语）放在后面。例如:

It is not easy **to learn a foreign language.**

It is dangerous **to play in the street.**

3) 动词不定式的否定形式

由“not + 动词不定式”构成。如:

Tell him **not to be late.**

The policeman told the boys **not to play in the street.**

4) 动词不定式和疑问词连用

动词不定式可以和疑问词 what, which, how, where, when 等连用, 构成不定式短语。如:

The question is **when to start.**

I don't know **where to go**.

He showed me **how to use a computer**.

Nobody told us **what to do**.

6. 被动语态 (The Passive Voice)

1) 主动语态和被动语态

英语动词有两种语态，即主动语态 (The Active Voice) 和被动语态 (The Passive Voice)。主动语态表示主语是动作的执行者，被动语态表示主语是动作的承受者。例如:

Many people *speak* English. (主动语态)

English *is spoken* **by many people**. (被动语态)

2)被动语态的构成

被动语态由"助动词 be + 及物动词的过去分词"构成。助动词 be 有人称、数和时态的变化，其变化规则与 be 作为连系动词时完全一样。现以动词 ask 为例，将一般现在时和一般过去时被动语态的肯定式、否定式及疑问式列表如下:

	肯定式	否定式	疑问式
一般现在时	I am asked .... You are asked .... He is asked .... She is asked .... We are asked .... You are asked .... They are asked	I am not asked .... You are not asked .... He is not asked .... She is not asked .... We are not asked .... You are not asked .... They are not asked	Am I asked ...? Are you asked ...? Is he asked ...? Is she asked ...? Are we asked ...? Are you asked ...? Are they asked ...?
一般过去时	I was asked .... You were asked .... He was asked .... She was asked .... We were asked .... You were asked .... They were asked	I was not asked .... You were not asked .... He was not asked .... She was not asked .... We were not asked .... You were not asked .... They were not asked	Was I asked ...? Were you asked ...? Was he asked ...? Was she asked ...? Were we asked ...? Were you asked ...? Were they asked ...?

3) 含有情态动词的被动语态

含有情态动词的被动语态由"情态动词 + be + 及物动词的过去分词"构成。例如:

This bicycle **can be mended** in two hours.

The trees **may be planted** in spring.

The room **must be kept** clean.

The flowers **should be watered** often.

4) 被动语态的用法

当我们不知道谁是动作的执行者，或者没有必要指出谁是动作的执行者时，或者只需强调动作的承受者时，要用 被动语态。例如:

This jacket **is made** of cotton.

English **is spoken** in Canada.

III. 宾语从句 (The Object Clause)

宾语从句在复合句中作主句的宾语。宾语从句通常由下面一些词引导。

1. 由 that 引导 (that 在口语或非正式文体中常省略)。例如:

He said (that) he would like to see the headmaster.

She said (that) she would leave a message on his desk.

He knew (that) he should work hard.

He said (that) he might fall behind the other students.

He was afraid (that) he would forget his Chinese.

2. 由连接代词或连接副词引导。例如:

Do you know what time the train leaves?

I don't remember when we arrived.

I asked him where the tickets were.

Can you tell me which class you are in?

The children did not know who Father Christmas was.

3. 由连词 whether 或 if 引导（口语中常用 if)。 例如:

Lily wanted to know if / whether her grandma liked the handbag.

She asked if / whether they had white hats.

Words and expressions in each unit

各单元单词和习惯用语

注：不带标记的单词，要求学生会读，听得懂，会拼写，能说出词义和词类。凡带*号的单词只要求会读，听得懂，不要求拼写。标注Δ的单词只要求理解，不要求记住。不带音标的词为第一、二册出现的，转为四会或转词类、转词义。

Unit 1

glad [glæd] *adj.* 高兴的；乐意的 (1)
both [bəuθ] *adj.* & *pron.* 两个（人，……）都 (1)
*wish [wiʃ] *n.* & *vt.* 祝愿；希望；想要 (1)
*card [kɑ:d] *n.* 卡片；贺卡 (1)
*art [ɑ:t] *n.* 艺术；美术；艺术品 (1)
*luck [lʌk] *n.* 运气；好运 (1)
 *Good luck! 好运气！ (1)
talk *n.* 演讲；谈话 (2)
give a talk 做一次演讲 (2)
difficult ['difikəlt] *adj.* 难的；困难的 (2)
subject ['sʌbdʒikt] *n.* 题目；科目 (2)
should [ʃud, ʃəd] *v. aux.* （shall 的过去时态）会；应该 (2)
about *prep.* 关于 (2)
*choose [tʃu:z] (chose [tʃəuz]) *vt.* 选择 (2)
*for example 例如 (2)
full *adj.* 全部的 (2)
 full name 全名 (2)
given ['givn] (give的过去分词)
 given name = first / middle name 名字 (2)
important [im'pɔ:tənt] *adj.* 重要的 (3)
*course [kɔ:s] *n.* 过程；经过 (3)
 *of course 当然 (3)
How about ...? ……怎么样？ (4)

Unit 2

hold *vt.* 举行；进行 (5)
 hold a (sports) meeting 举行（运动）会 (5)
ground [graund] *n.* 地面 (5)
 playground ['pleigraund] *n.* （学校的）操场 (5)
*race [reis] *n.* 赛跑；竞赛 (5)
 *100-metre race 100米(赛跑) (5)
fast [fɑ:st] *adj.* & *adv.* 快的（地） (5)
*win [win] (won[wʌn]) *vt.* 获胜；赢得 (5)
jump *n.* 跳 (5)
 the high jump 跳高 (5)
 the long jump 跳远 (5)
*hurt [hə:t] (hurt, hurt) *vt.* 受伤；伤害 (5)
*neck [nek] *n.* 颈，脖子 (5)
*Bad luck! 倒霉！ (5)
Δ relay ['ri:lei] *n.* 接力 (6)
 relay race 接力赛 (6)
in front 在前方（面）；在正对面 (6)
*the starting line 起跑线 (6)
runner ['rʌnə] *n.* 赛跑的人 (6)
shout *vt.* & *vi.* 喊；呼喊 (6)
*loud [laud] *adj.* 大声的 (6)
 *loudly ['laudli] *adv.* 大声地 (6)
come on 赶快 (6)
Δ lap [læp] *n.* （跑道的）一圈 (6)
pass on 传递 (6)
*stick [stik] *n.* 木棒；木棍；枝条 (6)
catch up (with) 赶上 (6)
*neck and neck （赛跑时）齐头并进；不分上下 (6)
at the same time 同时 (6)
still [stil] *adv.* 还；仍旧 (6)
behind *adv.* 在后；在后面 (6)
*drop [drɔp] *vt.* & *vi.* （使）落下 (6)

a moment later 片刻之后 (6)
fall behind 落后; 跟不上 (7)
*winner ['winə] *n.* 获胜者 (7)
Δhooray [hu'rei] *interj.* 好哇！（欢呼声） (7)
*congratulation [kən ˌgrætju:'leiʃən] *n.* (常用复数)祝贺,庆贺 (7)
*rather ['rɑ:ðə] *adv.* 相当; 宁可 (7)
badly ['bædli] *adv.* 坏; 恶劣地 (7)
Δ take turns 替换; 轮流 (7)
*loudspeaker ['laud'spi:kə] *n.* 扬声器，喇叭 (7)
*result [ri'zʌlt] *n.* 结果; 效果 (7)
right now 现在; 刚刚 (7)
*headteacher [ˌhed'ti:tʃə] *n.* 中小学班主任 (8)

Unit 3

foreign ['fɔrin] *adj.* 外国的 (9)
*language ['læŋgwidʒ] *n.* 语言 (9)
*chick [tʃik] *n.* 小鸡 (9)
sound [saund] *n.* 声音 (9)
Hands up. 请举手。 (9)
letter ['letə] *n.* 字母 (9)
*newspaper ['nju:s ˌpeipə] *n.* 报纸 (9)
as [æz,əz] *adv., conj. & prep.* 像…… 一样; 同样地; 作为 (10)
*usual ['ju:ʒuəl] *adj.* 通常的 ;平常的(10)
*as usual 像平常一样 (10)
smile [smail] *n., vt. & vi.* 微笑 (10)
*sweep [swi:p] (swept [swept]) *vt. & vi.* 扫; 扫除 (10)
excuse [iks'kju:s] *n.* 借口; 托辞 (10)
*except [ik'sept] *prep.* 除 …… 之外 (10)
*lucky ['lʌki] *adj.* 运气好的; 侥幸的 (10)
*luckily ['lʌkili] *adv.* 运气 好地 (10)
*science ['saiəns] *n.* 科学; 自然科学 (11)
agree [ə'gri:] *vt. & vi.* 同意; 赞成 (11)
agree with 同意某人(或某人意见) (11)
*prefer [pri'fə:]*vt.* 宁愿(选择); 更喜欢(11)
*prefer ... to ... 比起 …… 来还是 …… 好;喜欢 ……（而不喜欢 ……） (11)
*maths [mæθs] *n.* (缩写词) 数学 (11)
*useful ['ju:sful] *adj.* 有用的; 有益的 (11)
* P. E. ['pi:'i:] *n.* 体育 = physical education ['fizikəl ˌedju:'keiʃən] (11)
*drop (maths) 放弃 (数学) (12)

Unit 4

draw (drew [dru:]) *vt. & vi.* 画; 绘制 (13)
try [trai] *vt. & vi.* 试(做); 试图; 努力 (13)
horse [hɔ:s] *n.* 马 (13)
play with 玩耍 (13)
*chalk [tʃɔ:k] *n.* 粉笔 (13)
*Russian ['rʌʃən] *adj. & n.* 俄国的; 俄国人(的); 俄语(的) (14)
*downstairs ['daun'stɛəz] *adv.* 在楼下; 到楼下 (14)
sleep [sli:p] (slept [slept]) *vi.* 睡; 睡觉 (14)
*upstairs ['ʌp'stɛəz] *adv.* 在楼上; 到楼上 (14)
ΔMoscow ['mɔskəu] *n.* 莫斯科 (14)
quiet ['kwaiət] *adj.* 安静的; 平静的 (14)
quietly ['kwaiətli] *adv.* 安静地; 平静地 (14)
come back 回来 (14)
*noise [nɔiz] *n.* 嘈杂声; 响声 (14)
Δbang [bæŋ] *interj.* 砰 (14)
angry ['æŋgri]*adj.* 生气的；发怒的 (14)
be angry with 生（某人的）气 (14)
*knock [nɔk] *vi.& n.* 敲; 击; 打 (14)
*knock at 敲(门,窗等) (14)
trouble ['trʌbl] *vt.* 麻烦; 使麻烦 (14)
*comrade ['kɔmrid] *n.* 同志 (14)
get back 回来 (14)
*happen ['hæpən] *vi.* (偶然) 发生 (14)
just [dʒʌst] *adv.* 正好; 恰好; 刚才 (14)
fall asleep 睡着; 入睡 (14)
noon [nu:n] *n.* 中午; 正午 (15)
at noon 在中午 (15)
*league [li:g] *n.* 联盟；社团 (16)
*member ['membə] *n.* 成员；会员 (16)
*League member 共青团员 (16)
help ... with 帮助(某人做某事) (16)

Unit 5

*accident ['æksidənt] *n.* 事故; 意外的事 (17)
*motor ['məutə] *n.* 发动机; 马达 (17)
*motorbike 摩托车 (17)
*lose [lu:z] (lost [lɔst]) *vt.* 失去; 丢失 (17)
past *adv.* 过 (17)
give back 归还；送回 (17)
*corner ['kɔ:nə] *n.* 街道拐角; 角落 (18)
*suddenly ['sʌdnli] *adv.* 突然地 (18)
*land *vt.* (使)降落; (使)落到 (18)
or *conj.* 否则 (18)
travel ['trævl] *vi.* 旅行 (18)
lie [lai] (lay [lei]) *vi.* 平躺; (物件)平放在某处 (18)
*gate keeper ['geit ˌki:pə] = gateman ['geitmən] *n.* 看门人; 门警; 门卫 (18)
*crowd [kraud] *vt.* 拥挤; 群聚 (18)
move away 搬开; 搬走 (18)
library ['laibrəri] *n.* 图书馆(室) (18)
medicine ['medsin] *n.* 内服药 (18)
hurry ['hʌri] *vi.* 赶紧; 急忙 (18)
hurry up 赶快 (18)
hurry off 匆匆离去; 赶快去 (18)
Δblank [blæŋk] *n.* (表格等)空白处 (19)
*while [wail] *conj.* 当……的时候; 和……同时 (19)

Unit 6

*dictionary ['dikʃənəri] *n.* 词典; 字典 (21)
*several ['sevrəl] *pron.* 几个; 数个 (至少三个) *adj.* 若干 (21)
*shelf [ʃelf] *n.* (*pl.* shelves [ʃelvz]) 架子 (21)
*anywhere ['eniwεə] *adv.* 任何地方 (21)
yet [jet] *adv.* 尚; 还; 仍然 (21)
on *prep.* 关于 (22)
*helpful ['helpful] *adj.* 有帮助的; 有益的 (22)
reading room ['ri:diŋrum] *n.* 阅览室 (22)
Δstrict [strikt] *adj.* 严格的 (22)
*return [ri'tə:n] *vt.* & *vi.* 归还; 回; 归 (22)
on time 按时; 准时 (22)
*polite [pə'lait] *adj.* 有礼貌的; 有教养的 (22)
*politely [pə'laitli] *adv.* 有礼貌地 (22)
star [stɑ:] *n.* 星; 恒星 (22)
everywhere ['evriwεə] *adv.* 到处; 无论哪里 (22)
*pity ['piti] *n.* 怜悯; 同情 (22)
pay [pei] (paid [peid], paid) *vt.* & *vi.* 付款给…… 报酬 (22)
pay for 付款 (22)
from now on 从今以后 (23)
before *adv.* 以前 (23)
kindly ['kaindli] *adv.* 亲切地; 诚恳地 (23)
ever ['evə] *adv.* 曾经 (23)
Δknow-all ['nəu 'ɔ:l] *n.* 自称无所不知的人 (23)
*history ['histəri] *n.* 历史; 历史学 (24)

Unit 7

*person ['pə:sn] *n.* 人 (25)
film [film] *n.* 影片；电影 (25)
*forgetful [fə'getful] *adj.* 健忘的; 不留心的 (26)
*list [list] *n.* 一览表;清单 (26)
Mom [mɔm] *n.* = Mum (26)
*shopkeeper ['ʃɔpˌki:pə] *n.* 零售商人; 店主 (26)
arrive [ə'raiv] *vi.* (at) 到达; 抵达 (26)
already [ɔ:l'redi] *adv.* 已经 (26)
sweet [swi:t] *n.* 糖果; 甜食 (26)
break [breik] (broke[brəuk], broken['brəukən]) *vt.* & *vi.* 摔破; 撕开; 损坏 (26)
spend [spend] (spent [spent], spent) *vt.* 花费(金钱、时间等); 度过 (26)
Help yourself. 请自便；请随便吃。 (27)
*bicycle ['baisikl] *n.* 自行车 (bike 的全写形式) (28)

*noisy ['nɔizi] *adj.* 喧闹的; (人、地方等)嘈杂的 (28)
*noisily ['nɔizili] *adv.* 喧闹地 (28)
Δfill [fil] *vt.* 填空; 装满 (28)
Δform [fɔ:m] *n.* 表格 (28)

Unit 8

*cow [kau] *n.* 母牛; 奶牛 (29)
sheep [ʃi:p] *n.* 绵羊 (29)
field [fi:ld] *n.* 地; 田地 (29)
*tractor ['træktə] *n.* 拖拉机 (29)
*pig [pig] *n.* 猪 (29)
Δpan [pæn] *n.* 平底锅 (30)
play *n.* 戏剧; 话剧 (30)
with pleasure 高兴 (30)
as soon as ... 一 …… 就 …… (30)
hurry *n.* 着急 (30)
No hurry. 不忙。不必着急。(30)
lend [lend] (lent [lent], lent) *vt.* 把 …… 借给 (30)
hear of 听说 (30)
dead [ded] *adj.* 死的; 无生命的 (30)
die [dai] *vi.* 死 (30)
*joke [dʒəuk] *n.* 笑话 (30)
*wool [wul] *n.* 羊毛; 绒线 (31)
*mutton ['mʌtn] *n.* 羊肉 (31)
milk *vt.* 挤奶; 出奶 (31)
twice [twais] *adv.* 两次; 两倍 (31)
* pigsty ['pigstai] *n.* 猪圈 (31)
Δorder ['ɔ:də] *n.* 顺序 (32)

Unit 9

for *prep.* (表示时间、距离、数量等)达; 计 (33)
over *prep.* 超过; 多于 (33)
together [tə'geðə] *adv.* 一起; 一同; 合起来 (33)
since [sins] *prep.* & *conj.* 自从; 从 …… 以来; 由于 (33)
own [əun] *adj.* 自己的 (33)
*rush [rʌʃ] *vi.* 冲; 奔跑 (34)
through [θru:] *prep.* 通过; 穿过 (34)
part(s) [pɑ:t(s)] *n.* 零件; 部件 (34)
shop *n.* 车间 (34)
*step [step] *n.* 脚步;台阶; 梯级 (34)
*narrow ['nærəu] *adj.* 狭窄的 (34)
*touch *vt.* 触摸; 接触 (34)
cut [kʌt] (cut, cut) *vt.* & *vi.* 切;割; 砍 (34)
Δmetal ['metl] *n.* 金属 (34)
join [dʒɔin] *vt.* & *vi.* 连接; 接合;参加 (34)
take a look 看一看 (34)
*straight [streit] *adv.* & *adj.* 一直地(的); 直(的) (35)
*follow ['fɔləu] *vt.* 跟随 (35)
glasses *n.* *(pl.)* 眼镜 (35)
over *prep.* 蒙在 ……上，悬挂 ……上 (35)
*guess *vt.* 猜 (35)
life [laif] *n.* 生活; 生命 (35)
all one's life 一生; 终生 (35)
Δspy [spai] *vi.* & *vt.* 侦察; 刺探 (36)
*centre ['sentə] *n.* 中心 (36)

Unit 10

*headmaster ['hed'mɑ:stə] *n.* (英)中小学校长 (37)
hold on (打电话时)不挂断; (口语)等一等; 停住 (37)
*possible ['pɔsəbl] *adj.* 可能的 (37)
* as soon as possible 尽快 (37)
*able ['eibl] *adj.* 有能力的; 能干的 (37)
*be able to 能; 会 (37)
between [bi'twi:n] *prep.* 在(两者)之间 (37)
leave a message 留话 (37)
in trouble 处于困难中 (38)
*lazy ['leizi] *adj.* 懒惰的 (38)
*exam [ig'zæm] *n.* (口语)考试 (examination [ig ,zæmi'neiʃən] 的缩写形式) (38)
do one's best 尽力 (38)
*weak [wi:k] *adj.* 差的; 弱的; 淡的 (38)
*capital ['kæpitl] *n.* 首都; 省会 (38)
*miss [mis] *vt.* 失去; 缺; 错过 (38)

*even ['i:vn] *adv.* 甚至; 更 (39)
*fail [feil] *vi.* & *vt.* 不及格; 失败 (39)
true [tru:] *adj.* 真的; 真实的 (39)
learn by oneself 自学 (39)
during ['djuəriŋ] *prep.* 在…… 期间 (39)
mind [maind] *vi.* & *vt.* 介意; 反对 (39)
call *n.* 电话; 通话; 叫喊 (39)
give ... a call 给 …… 打个电话 (39)
go back 回去 (39)

Unit 11

*invent [in'vent] *vt.* 发明; 创造 (41)
*inventor [in'ventə] *n.* 发明者; 创造者 (41)
*invention [in'venʃən] *n.* 发明; 创造 (41)
change [tʃeindʒ] *vt.* & *vi.* 改变; 更换 (41)
world [wə:ld] *n.* 世界 (41)
call *vt.* 把 ……叫做; 称呼 (41)
*computer [kəm'pju:tə] *n.* 计算机 (41)
*fridge *n.* 电冰箱 (41)
*motor car 汽车 (41)
own *vt.* 所有; 拥有 (41)
send [send] (sent, sent) *vt.* 派; 派遣 (42)
send away 撵走; 开除; 解雇 (42)
try out 试验; 尝试 (42)
*hen [hen] *n.* 母鸡 (42)
*pupil ['pju:pl] *n.* 小学生; 学生 (42)
*strange [streindʒ] *adj.* 奇怪的; 古怪的; 陌生的 (42)
become [bi'kʌm] (became [bi'keim], become) *vi.* 变得; 成为 (42)
*interested ['intristid] *adj.* 感兴趣的; 关心的 (42)
*become (be) interested in 对 …… 感兴趣 (42)
*lab [læb] *n.* 实验室 (laboratory [lə'bɔrətəri] 的缩写词) (42)
*mirror ['mirə] *n.* 镜子 (43)
send for 派人去叫(请) (43)
light *n.* 光 (43)
*operate ['ɔpəreit] *vi.* & *vt.* 手术; 运转 (43)
clear [kliə] *adj.* 清楚地; 清晰的 (43)
clearly ['kliəli] *adv.* 清楚地; 无疑地 (43)
*save [seiv] *vt.* 救; 挽救 (43)
turn down (收音机,灯等) 关小; 调低 (43)
*line *n.* (电话的)线路 (44)

Unit 12

while *conj.* 当 …… 的时候 (45)
write down 写下; 记下来 (45)
*take (good) care of 照料; 照顾 (45)
*instruction [in'strʌkʃən] *n.* 说明; 须知 (45)
make sure 务必; 务请; 确信 (45)
*fill [fil] *vt.* 填空; 装满 (45)
*leaf [li:f] *n.* (*pl.* leaves) (树、菜)叶 (45)
cover ['kʌvə] *vt.* 盖; 遮盖
n. 盖子; 封面 (45)
Δcage [keidʒ] *n.* 笼; 鸟笼 (45)
*hate [heit] *vt.* 不喜欢;讨厌 (46)
each [i:tʃ] *pron.* & *adj.* 各个; 每件;每个 (46)
beside [bi'said] *prep.* 在 …… 旁边 (46)
*journey ['dʒə:ni] *n.* 旅行; 路程 (46)
*safely ['seifli] *adv.* 安全地; 平安地 (46)
by air 乘飞机 (46)
seat [si:t] *n.* 座位 (46)
*jacket ['dʒækit] *n.* 短上衣; 外套 (46)
*nearly ['niəli] *adv.* 将近; 几乎 (46)
come round 来; 再来 (46)
in a minute 一会儿; 立刻 (46)
just then 正在那时 (46)
mind *n.* 思想; 主意 (47)
change one's mind 改变想法(主意) (47)
Δflight [flait] *n.* 航班; 飞行 (47)
arrive in 到达; 抵达 (47)
furthest ['fə:ðist] *adj.* & *adv.* = farthest 最远 (48)

Unit 13

*merry ['meri] *adj.* 愉快的; 欢乐的 (49)
*Christmas ['krisməs] *n.* 圣诞节 (49)
*receive [ri'si:v] *vt.* 收到; 接收 (49)
news [nju:z] *n.* 新闻; 消息 (49)
whom [hu:m, hum] *pron.* 谁;哪个人 (49)
unhappy [ʌn'hæpi] *adj.* 不高兴的; 伤心的 (50)
without [wi'ðaut] *prep.* 无; 没有 (50)
*almost ['ɔ:lməust] *adv.* 几乎; 差不多(50)
member ['membə] *n.* 成员; 会员 (50)
*get-together ['get təˌgeðə] *n.* 聚集; 集会 (50)
*eve [i:v] *n.* (节日或大事件发生的)前夕 (50)
*Christmas Eve 圣诞节前夕(十二月二十四日) (50)
sitting room 起居室 (50)
fire ['faiə] *n.* 火; 火炉 (50)
fireplace ['faiəpleis] *n.* 壁炉 (50)
*burn [bə:n] (burnt [bə:nt], burnt or burned [bə:nd], burned) *vt. & vi.* 烧; 燃烧; 点(烛等) (50)
brightly ['braitli] *adv.* 闪烁地; 灿烂地; 明亮地 (50)
hear from 收到…… 的来信 (51)

Unit 14

foreigner ['fɔrinə] *n.* 外国人 (53)
Δfestival ['festəvəl] *n. & adj.* 节日(的); 喜庆(的) (54)
*Britain ['britn] *n.* 英国; 不列颠(英格兰、威尔士和苏格兰的总称) (54)
*stocking ['stɔkiŋ] *n.* 长统袜 (54)
heart [hɑ:t] *n.* 心(脏) (54)
kind-hearted ['kaind 'hɑ:tid] *adj.* 好心的 (54)
*top [tɔp] *n.* 顶部; (物的)上面 (54)
*on top of 在…… 上面 (54)
Δchimney ['tʃimni] *n.* 烟囱; 烟筒 (54)
dress up 穿上盛装; 乔装打扮 (54)
look up (在词典、参考书中)查寻 (54)
each other 彼此; 互相 (55)
ΔJesus Christ ['dʒi:zəs 'kraist] *n.* 耶稣基督 (55)
*follow ['fɔləu] *vt.* 照; 仿效; 跟随 (56)
Δdictation [dik'teiʃən] *n.* 听写 (56)

Unit 15

right away 立刻; 马上 (57)
whether ['weðə] *conj.* 是否 (57)
*lonely ['ləunli] *adj.* 孤独的; 寂寞的 (58)
*fight [fait] (fought [fɔ:t], fought) *vi. & vt.* 打架(仗); 与 …… 打架(仗) (58)
for long 长久 (58)
make friends 交朋友 (58)
get on ... with ... 与 …… 相处 …… (58)
mistake *vt.* 弄错
n. 错误 (58)
make a mistake 犯错误 (58)
dance [dɑ:ns] *vi.* 跳舞
n. 舞蹈; 舞会 (58)
either ['aiðə, 'i:ðə] *adv.* 也(不) (58)
light *adj.* 淡色的 (58)
dark [dɑ:k] *adj.* 深(浓)色的 (58)
*decide [di'said] *vi. & vt.* 决定; 下决心 (58)
*wool(l)en ['wulən] *adj.* 羊毛的; 羊毛制的 (59)
*hang [hæŋ] (hung [hʌŋ], hung) *vi. & vt.* 挂; 吊着 (59)
*cotton ['kɔtn] *n. & adj.* 棉花(的) (59)
take one's time 不急; 慢慢干 (59)
*expensive [iks'pensiv] *adj.* 昂贵的 (59)
*soft [sɔft] *adj.* 软的; 柔和的 (59)
cost [kɔst] (cost, cost) *vi.* 值(多少)钱 (59)
try ... on 试穿(衣、鞋、帽等) (60)

Unit 16

be made of …… 制的; 用 …… 制成的 (61)

key [ki:] *n.* 钥匙 (61)
stamp [stæmp] *n.* 邮票 (61)
*wood [wud] *n.* 木头; 木材 (61)
glass *n.* 玻璃 (61)
*lock [lɔk] *vt.* 锁; 锁上 *n.* 锁 (61)
by *prep.* 被; 由 (62)
*wide [waid] *adj.* 宽阔的; 广泛的 (62)
*widely ['waidli] *adv.*广阔地; 广泛地(62)
ΔNew Zealand [ˌnju:'zi:lənd] *n.* 新西兰 (大洋洲) (62)
*else [els] *adv.* 别的; 其他的 (62)
*Japan [dʒə'pæn] *n.* 日本 (62)
*German ['dʒə:mən] *adj.* 德国的; 德国人的; *n.* 德国人; 德语
*Germany ['dʒə:məni] *n.* 德国 (62)
*none [nʌn] *pron.* 没有任何东西或人; 一个人也没有(= no one) (62)
modern ['mɔdən] *adj.* 现代的 (62)
*business ['biznis] *n.* 事务; 商业; 生意 (62)
*Frenchman (*pl.*) Frenchmen *n.* 法国人 (62)
traveller ['trævlə] *n.* 旅行者 (62)
all over the world 全世界 (62)
*silk [silk] *n.* (蚕)丝; 丝织品 (63)
*produce [prə'dju:s] *vt.* 生产; 制造 (63)

Unit 17

*market ['mɑ:kit] *n.* 市场; 集市 (65)
bridge [bridʒ] *n.* 桥 (65)
*museum [mju(:)'ziəm] *n.* 博物馆 (65)
*crossing ['krɔsiŋ] *n.* 十字路口; 人行横道; 交叉点 (65)
*across [ə'krɔs] *prep.* 横过; 穿过 (65)
group [gru:p] *n.* 组; 一组 (66)
on show 展览; 陈列 (66)
*glass-topped *adj.*玻璃罩的;玻璃面的(66)
hundreds of ... 数百 …… (66)
*point [pɔint] (at)*vt.* & *vi.* 指; 指向 (66)
*king [kiŋ] *n.* 国王 (66)
*surprise [sə'praiz] *vt.* 使惊奇; 使感到意外 (66)
Δpot [pɔt] *n.* 壶; 罐; 锅 (66)
Δteapot ['ti:pɔt] *n.* 茶壶 (66)
Δthermos ['θə:mɔs] *n.* 热水瓶 (66)
*thirsty ['θə:sti] *adj.* 口渴的 (66)
ΔPLA 中国人民解放军 (67)
ΔPRC 中华人民共和国 (67)
Party *n.* 共产党 (小写指党; 政党) (67)
League *n.* 共青团 (67)
*found [faund] *vt.* 成立; 建立 (67)
Δsign [sain] *n.* 标志; 符号 (67)
*entrance ['entrəns] *n.* 入口; 入场; 进入 (67)
*exit ['eksit] *n.* 出口; 太平门 (67)
*smoke [sməuk] *vi.* & *vt.* 吸烟 *n.* 烟 (67)
*smoking ['sməukiŋ] *n.* 吸烟;冒烟(67)

Unit 18

plant [plɑ:nt] *vt.* 种植 *n.* 植物 (69)
*wonderful ['wʌndəful] *adj.* 极好的; 精彩的 (69)
neither ['naiðə,'ni:ðə] *adj.* , *adv.* & *conj.* (两者)都不 (69)
nor [nɔ:] *conj.* 也不 (69)
neither ... nor ... 既不 …… 也不 …… (69)
dig [dig] (dug [dʌg], dug) *vi.* & *vt.* 挖; 掘 (69)
*hole [həul] *n.* 洞; 坑 (69)
*deep [di:p] *adj.* 深的; 深厚的 (69)
*knock ... into ... 把 …… 插进; 把 …… 敲进 (69)
earth [ə:θ] *n.* 土; 泥; 地球; 大地 (69)
*tie [tai] *vt.* (用绳、线等) 系; 拴; 扎 (69)
water *vt.* 浇水; 灌溉 (69)
Δuntrue ['ʌn'tru:] *adj.* 不真实的; 假的 (69)
*forest ['fɔrist] *n.* 森林 (70)
*sand [sænd] *n.*沙; 沙子 (70)
*copy ['kɔpi] *vt.* 照搬; 誊写 (70)
*northern ['nɔ:ðən] *adj.* 北方的; 北部的 (70)

*million ['miljən] *num. & n.* 百万; 百万个(人或物) (70)
stop ... from 阻止; 阻拦 (70)
*toward(s) [tə'wɔ:d(z)] *prep.* 向; 朝; 对于 (70)
*save *vt.* 节省 (70)
workplace ['wə:kpleis] *n.* 工作场所; 车间 (70)
*among [ə'mʌŋ] *prep.* 在 …… 之中 (70)
mountain ['mauntin] *n.* 山; 山脉 (70)
*point to 指向 (70)
grow [grəu] (grew [gru:], grown [grəun]) *vt.* 种植; 生长 (70)
more or less 或多或少; 差不多 (72)

Unit 19

thousand ['θauzənd] *num. & n.* 千 (73)
*satellite ['sætəlait] *n.* 卫星 (73)
*universe ['ju:nivə:s] *n.* 宇宙 (73)
*man-made ['mæn meid] *adj.* 人造的; 人工的 (74)
*space [speis] *n.* 空间; 太空 (74)
 *spaceship ['speisʃip] *n.* 宇宙飞船 (74)
so far 到现在为止 (74)
send up 发射 (74)
with one's help 在(某人/物)的帮助下 (74)
*programme ['prəugræm] *n.* 节目 (74)
*knowledge ['nɔlidʒ] *n.* 知识; 学问 (74)
*develop [di'veləp] *vt. & vi.* 发展; 开发 (74)
*enjoyable [in'dʒɔiəbl] *adj.* 愉快的; 有趣的 (75)
Δchannel ['tʃænl] *n.* 频道 (75)

Unit 20

*population [ˌpɔpju'leiʃən] *n.* 人口; 人数 (77)
*billion ['biljən] *num.* 十亿 (77)
*India ['indjə] *n.* 印度 (77)
*following ['fɔləuiŋ] *adj.* 接着的; 以下的 (78)
on the earth 在地球上 (78)
hour after hour 一小时又一小时地; 连续地 (78)
mouth [mauθ] *n.* 嘴 (78)
grow (grew [gru:], grown [grəun]) *vi.* 增长 (78)
beginning [bi'giniŋ] *n.* 开始; 开端 (78)
 at the beginning of 起初; 开始 (78)
*century ['sentʃuri] *n.* 世纪; 百年 (78)
ΔUN = the United Nations [ju:'naitid 'neiʃənz] 联合国 (78)
by *prep.* 到 …… 为止 (78)

Unit 21

wear out 穿坏; 穿旧; 用尽 (81)
pair *n.* 一对; 一双 (81)
 a pair of 一对; 一双 (81)
*size [saiz] *n.* 尺寸; 大小 (81)
*bit [bit] *n.* 一点儿; 小片 (81)
 *a bit 有一点儿 (81)
*suit [sju:t] *n.* 一套(衣服) (81)
think about 考虑; 思考 (81)
name *vt.* 命名; 名叫 (82)
for *conj.* 因为 (82)
either ... or ... 或者 …… 或者 …… (82)
sell out 售完 (82)
never mind 不要紧; 没关系 (82)
*dollar ['dɔlə] *n.* 美元 (82)
*perhaps [pə'hæps] *adv.* 可能; 也许 (82)
*retell ['ri:'tel] *vt.* 重述; 重讲 (82)
so ... that ... 如此 …… 以致 (83)
be busy doing ... 忙着做某事 (83)
on and on 继续; 不断 (83)
dinner ['dinə] *n.* 正餐; 宴会 (83)
just a moment 等一会儿 (83)
in surprise 惊奇地 (83)
*pardon ['pɑ:dn] *n.* 原谅; 宽恕; 对不起 (83)
dirty ['də:ti] *adj.* 脏的 (83)
brush [brʌʃ] *vt.* 刷; 擦 *n.* 刷子 (83)
Δverb [və:b] *n.* 动词 (84)
Δsimple ['simpl] *adj.* 简单的; 简易的 (84)
*fall over 向前摔倒 (84)

*finger ['fiŋgə] *n.* 手指 (84)

Unit 22

*headache ['hedeik] *n.* 头痛 (85)
*cough [kɔf] *n.* & *vi.* 咳嗽 (85)
*have (have got) a cough (患)咳嗽(85)
till [til] *prep.* & *conj.* 直到; 直到…… 之时 (85)
by then 到那时 (85)
trouble *n.* 疾病 (85)
*serious ['siəriəs] *adj.* 严重的 (85)
catch a cold 伤风; 感冒 (85)
*terrible ['terəbl] *adj.* 可怕的; 极坏的(86)
*terribly 可怕地; 极坏地 (86)
*seem [si:m] *vi.* 好像 (86)
ever since 从…… 起一直到现在 (86)
nurse [nə:s] *n.* 护士 (86)
*pill [pil] *n.* 药丸; 药片 (86)
*common ['kɔmən] *adj.* 普通的; 一般的 (87)
match [mætʃ] *n.* 比赛; 竞赛 (87)
come along 走吧 (87)
*pain [pein] *n.* 疼痛; 疼 (87)

Unit 23

*in time 及时 (89)
league *n.* 联 盟; 社团 (89)
league match 联赛 (89)
such [sʌtʃ] *adj.* 这样(种)的 (89)
*against [ə'geinst] *prep.* 对着; 反对 (90)
*draw *n.* 平局 (90)
*be (feel) afraid of 害怕 (90)
*though [ðəu] *conj.* 虽然; 可是 (90)
beat [bi:t] (beat, beaten ['bi:tn]) *vt.* 打败; 敲打 (90)
*teamwork ['ti:mwə:k] *n.* 合作; 协同工作 (90)
*kick [kik] *vt.* & *vi.* 踢 (91)
*goal [gəul] *n.* (足球)球门;目标 (91)
song [sɔŋ] *n.* 歌曲 (91)
as *conj.* 照着 (91)

Unit 24

take *vt.* 耗费（时间）; 需要（多少时间） (93)
*rock [rɔk] *n.* 岩石; 大石头 (94)
ΔAyers [εəz] Rock 艾尔斯山（澳大利亚） (94)
*hardly ['hɑ:dli] *adv.* 几乎不 (94)
sky [skai] *n.* 天空 (94)
*low [ləu] *adj.* 低的; 浅的; 矮的 (94)
*rise [raiz] (rose [rəuz], risen ['rizn]) *vi.* 上升; 上涨 (94)
at the foot of 在 …… 的脚下 (94)
*grass [grɑ:s] *n.* 草 (94)
at all 全然 (94)
as *conj.* 因为 (94)
*famous ['feiməs] *adj.* 著名的 (95)
*photograph ['fəutəugrɑ:f] *n.* 相片 (96)

Vocabulary 词汇表

注: 带 • 的单词为第一、二册的三会要求转为四会要求，或转词类、转词义的单词。

A

*a bit 有一点儿 (81)
a moment later 片刻之后 (6)
a pair of 一对，一双 (81)
*able ['eibl] *adj.* 有能力的; 能干的 (37)
• about [ə'baut] *prep.* 关于 (2)
*accident ['æksidənt] *n.* 事故; 意外的事 (17)
*across [ə'krɔs] *prep.* 横过; 穿过 (65)
*against [ə'geinst] *prep.* 对着; 反对 (90)
agree [ə'gri:] *vt. & vi.* 同意; 赞成 (11)
  agree with 同意某人（或某人的意见）(11)
all one's life 一生; 终生 (35)
all over the world 全世界 (62)
*almost ['ɔ:lməust] *adv.* 几乎; 差不多 (50)
already [ɔ:l'redi] *adv.* 已经 (26)
*among [ə'mʌŋ] *prep.* 在 …… 之中 (70)
angry ['æŋgri] *adj.* 生气的; 发怒的 (14)
*anywhere ['eniwεə] *adv.* 任何地方 (21)
arrive [ə'raiv] *vi.* (at) 到达; 抵达 (26)
  arrive in 到达; 抵达 (47)
*art [ɑ:t] *n.* 艺术; 美术; 艺术品 (1)
as [æz, əz] *adv., conj. & prep.* 像 …… 一样; 同样地; 作为 (10)
  conj. 照着 (91)
  conj. 因为 (94)
  as soon as ... 一 …… 就 …… (30)
  as soon as possible 尽快 (37)
  *as usual 像平常一样 (10)
at all 全然 (94)
at noon 在中午 (15)
at the beginning of 起初; 开始 (78)
at the foot of 在 …… 的脚下 (94)
at the same time 同时 (6)
ΔAyers [εəz] Rock 艾尔斯山（澳大利亚）(94)

B

*Bad luck! 倒霉！(5)
badly ['bædli] *adv.* 坏; 恶劣地 (7)
Δbang [bæŋ] *interj.* 砰 (14)
*be able to 能; 会 (37)
*be(feel) afraid of 害怕 (90)
be angry with 生（某人）的气 (14)
be busy doing ... 忙着做某事 (83)
be made of …… 制的; 用 …… 制成的 (61)
beat [bi:t] (beat, beaten ['bi:tn]) *vt.* 打败; 敲打 (90)
become [bi'kʌm] (became [bi'keim], become) *vi.* 变得; 成为 (42)
  *become (be) interested in 对 …… 感兴趣 (42)
• before [bi'fɔ:] *adv.* 以前 (23)
beginning [bi'giniŋ] *n.* 开始; 开端 (78)
• behind [bi'haind] *adv.* 在后; 在后面 (6)
beside [bi'said] *prep.* 在 …… 旁边 (46)
between [bi'twi:n] *prep.* 在（两者）之间 (37)
*bicycle ['baisikl] *n.* 自行车（bike 的全写形式）(28)
*billion ['biljən] *num.* 十亿 (77)
*bit [bit] *n.* 一点儿; 小片 (81)
Δblank [blæŋk] *n.* （表格等）空白处 (19)
both [bəuθ] *adj. & pron.* 两个（人, …… ）都 (1)
break [breik] (broke [brəuk], broken['brəukən]) *vt. & vi.* 摔破; 撕开; 损坏 (26)
bridge [bridʒ] *n.* 桥 (65)
brightly ['braitli] *adv.* 闪烁地; 灿烂地; 明亮地 (50)
*Britain ['britn] *n.* 英国; 不列颠（英格兰、威尔士和苏格兰的总称）(54)
brush [brʌʃ] *vt.* 刷; 擦
  n. 刷子 (83)
*burn [bə:n] (burnt [bə:nt], burnt or burned [bə:nd], burned) *vt. & vi.* 烧; 燃烧; 点（烛等）(50)

*business ['biznis] *n.* 事务; 商业;
生意 (62)
• by [bai] *prep.* 被; 由 (62)
prep. 到 …… 为止 (78)
by air 乘飞机 (46)
by then 到那时 (85)

C

Δcage [keidʒ] *n.* 笼; 鸟笼 (45)
• call [kɔ:l] *n.* 电话; 通话; 叫喊 (39)
vt. 把 ……叫做; 称呼 (41)
*capital ['kæpitl] *n.* 首都; 省会 (38)
*card [kɑ:d] *n.* 卡片; 贺卡 (1)
catch a cold 伤风; 感冒 (85)
catch up (with) 赶上 (6)
*centre ['sentə] *n.* 中心 (36)
*century ['sentʃuri] *n.* 世纪; 百年 (78)
*chalk [tʃɔ:k] *n.* 粉笔 (13)
change [tʃeindʒ] *vt. & vi.* 改变; 更换 (41)
change one's mind 改变想法(主意) (47)
Δ channel ['tʃænl] *n.* 频道 (75)
*chick [tʃik] *n.* 小鸡 (9)
Δchimney ['tʃimni] *n.* 烟囱; 烟筒 (54)
*choose [tʃu:z] (chose [tʃəuz], chosen
['tʃəuzn]) *vt.* 选择 (2)
*Christmas ['krisməs] *n.* 圣诞节 (49)
*Christmas Eve 圣诞节前夕
(十二月二十四日) (50)
clear [kliə] *adj.* 清楚的; 清晰的 (43)
clearly ['kliəli] *adv.* 清楚地; 无疑地 (43)
come along 走吧 (87)
come back 回来 (14)
come on 赶快 (6)
come round 来; 再来 (46)
*common ['kɔmən] *adj.* 普通的;
一般的 (87)
*computer [kəm'pju:tə] *n.* 计算机 (41)
*comrade ['kɔmrid] *n.* 同志 (14)
*congratulation [kən ˌgrætju:'leiʃən]
n. (常用复数) 祝贺,庆贺 (7)
*copy ['kɔpi] *vt.* 照搬; 誊写 (70)
*corner ['kɔ:nə] *n.* 街道拐角; 角落 (18)
cost [kɔst] (cost, cost) *vi.* 值 (多少)
钱 (59)
*cotton ['kɔtn] *n. & adj.* 棉花 (的) (59)
*cough [kɔf] *n. & vi.* 咳嗽 (85)
*course [kɔ:s] *n.* 过程; 经过 (3)
cover ['kʌvə] *vt.* 盖; 遮盖
n. 盖子; 封面 (45)
*cow [kau] *n.* 母牛; 奶牛 (29)
*crossing ['krɔsiŋ] *n.* 十字路口;人行
横道;交叉处 (65)
*crowd [kraud] *vt.* 拥挤; 群聚 (18)
cut [kʌt] (cut, cut) *vt. & vi.* 切;割; 砍 (34)

D

dance [dɑ:ns] *vi.* 跳舞
n. 舞蹈; 舞会 (58)
dark [dɑ:k] *adj.* 深 (浓) 色的 (58)
dead [ded] *adj.* 死的; 无生命的 (30)
*decide [di'said] *vt. & vi.* 决定;下决心 (58)
*deep [di:p] *adj.* 深的; 深厚的 (69)
*develop [di'veləp] *vt. & vi.*
发展; 开发 (74)
Δdictation [dik'teiʃən] *n.* 听写 (56)
*dictionary ['dikʃənəri] *n.* 词典; 字典 (21)
die [dai] *vi.* 死 (30)
difficult ['difikəlt] *adj.* 难的; 困难的 (2)
dig [dig] (dug [dʌg], dug) *vi. & vt.*
挖; 掘 (69)
dinner ['dinə] *n.* 正餐; 宴会 (83)
dirty ['də:ti] *adj.* 脏的 (83)
do one's best 尽力 (38)
*dollar ['dɔlə] *n.* 美元 (82)
*downstairs ['daun'stɛəz] *adv.* 在楼
下; 到楼下 (14)
draw [drɔ:] (drew [dru:], drawn
[drɔ:n]) *vt. & vi.* 画; 绘制 (13)
* *n.* 平局 (90)
dress up 穿上盛装; 乔装打扮 (54)
*drop [drɔp] *vt. & vi.* (使) 落下 (6)
*drop (maths) 放弃 (数学) (12)
during ['djuəriŋ] *prep.* 在 …… 期间 (39)

E

each [i:tʃ] *pron. & adj.* 各个; 每个 (46)

each other 彼此; 互相 (55)
earth [ə:θ] *n.* 土; 泥;地球; 大地 (69)(78)
either ['aiðə, 'i:ðə] *adv.* 也（不） (58)
either ... or ... 或者 …… 或者…… (82)
*else [els] *adv.* 别的; 其他的 (62)
*enjoyable [in'dʒɔiəbl] *adj.* 愉快的; 有趣的 (75)
*entrance ['entrəns] *n.* 入口; 入场;进入(67)
*eve [i:v] *n.* （节日或大事件发生的）前夕 (50)
*even ['i:vn] *adv.* 甚至; 更 (39)
ever ['evə] *adv.* 曾经 (23)
ever since 从 …… 起一直到现在 (86)
everywhere ['evriwɛə] *adv.* 到处; 无论哪里 (22)
*exam [ig'zæm] *n.*（口语）考试 (examination [igˌzæmi'neiʃən] 的缩写形式) (38)
*except [ik'sept] *prep.* 除 …… 之外 (10)
• excuse [iks'kju:s] *n.* 借口; 托辞 (10)
*exit ['eksit] *n.* 出口; 太平门 (67)
*expensive [iks'pensiv] *adj.* 昂贵的 (59)

F

*fail [feil] *vi.* & *vt.* 不及格; 失败 (39)
fall asleep 睡着; 入睡 (14)
fall behind 落后; 跟不上 (7)
*fall over 向前摔倒 (84)
*famous ['feiməs] *adj.* 著名的 (95)
fast [fɑ:st] *adj.* & *adv.* 快的（地） (5)
Δfestival ['festəvəl] *n.*& *adj.* 节日(的); 喜庆(的) (54)
field ['fi:ld] *n.* 地; 田地 (29)
*fight [fait] (fought [fɔ:t], fought) *vi.* & *vt.* 打架（仗）; 与……打架（仗）(58)
Δfill [fil] *vt.* 填空; 装满 (28)(45)
film [film] *n.* 影片; 电影 (25)
*finger [fiŋgə] *n.* 手指 (84)
fire ['faiə] *n.* 火; 火炉 (50)
fireplace ['faiəpleis] *n.* 壁炉 (50)
Δflight [flait] *n.* 航班; 飞行 (47)
*follow ['fɔləu] *vt.* 跟随 (35)
vt. 照; 仿效; 跟随 (56)
*following ['fɔləuiŋ] *adj.* 接着的; 以下的 (78)
• for [fɔ:, fə] *prep.* （表示时间、距离、数量等）达; 计 (33)
conj. 因为 (82)
*for example 例如 (2)
for long 长久 (58)
foreign ['fɔrin] *adj.* 外国的 (9)
foreigner ['fɔrinə] *n.* 外国人 (53)
*forest ['fɔrist] *n.* 森林 (70)
*forgetful [fə'getful] *adj.* 健忘的; 不留心的 (26)
Δform [fɔ:m] *n.* 表格 (28)
*found [faund] *vt.* 成立; 建立 (67)
*Frenchman (*pl.*) Frenchmen ['frentʃmən] *n.* 法国人 (62)
*fridge [fridʒ] *n.*电冰箱 (41)
from now on 从今以后 (23)
• full [ful] *adj.* 全部的 (2)
full name 全名 (2)
furthest ['fə:ðist] *adj.* & *adv.* = farthest 最远 (48)

G

*gate keeper ['geit ˌki:pə] = gateman ['geitmən] *n.* 看门人; 门警; 门卫 (18)
*German ['dʒə:mən] *adj.* 德国的, 德国人的; *n.* 德国人; 德语
*Germany ['dʒə:məni] *n.* 德国 (62)
get back 回来 (14)
get on ... with ... 与 …… 相处 …… (58)
*get-together ['get tə ˌgeðə] *n.* 聚集; 聚会 (50)
give ... a call 给 …… 打个电话 (39)
give a talk 做一次演讲 (2)
give back 归还; 送回 (17)
given ['givn] (give的过去分词)
given name = first / middle name 名字 (2)
glad [glæd] *adj.*高兴的; 乐意的 (1)
• glass *n.* [glɑ:s] 玻璃 (61)
glasses *n.* (*pl.*) 眼镜 (35)
*glass-topped ['glɑ:stɔpt] *adj.* 玻璃罩的; 玻璃面的 (66)
go back 回去 (39)

*goal [gəul] *n.*（足球）球门; 目标 (91)
*Good luck! 好运气！ (1)
*grass [grɑ:s] *n.* 草 (94)
ground [graund] *n.* 地面 (5)
group [gru:p] *n.* 组; 一组 (66)
• grow [grəu] (grew [gru:], grown [grəun]) *vt.* 种植; 生长 (70)
vi. 增长 (78)
*guess [ges] *vt.* 猜 (35)

H

Hands up. 请举手。 (9)
*hang [hæŋ] (hung [hʌŋ], hung) *vi.* & *vt.* 挂; 吊着 (59)
*happen ['hæpən] *vi.*（偶然）发生 (14)
*hardly ['hɑ:dli] *adv.* 几乎不 (94)
*hate [heit] *vt.* 不喜欢; 讨厌 (46)
*have / have got a cough （患）咳嗽(85)
*headache ['hedeik] *n.* 头痛 (85)
*headmaster ['hed'mɑ:stə] *n.*（英）中小学校长 (37)
*headteacher ['hed'ti:tʃə] *n.* 中小学班主任 (8)
hear from 收到……的来信 (51)
hear of 听说 (30)
heart [hɑ:t] *n.* 心（脏） (54)
help ... with 帮助(某人做某事) (16)
Help yourself. 请自便；请随便吃。 (27)
*helpful ['helpful] *adj.* 有帮助的; 有益的 (22)
*hen [hen] *n.* 母鸡 (42)
*history ['histəri] *n.* 历史; 历史学 (24)
hold [həuld] *vt.* 举行; 进行 (5)
• hold a (sports) meeting 举行（运动）会 (5)
hold on （打电话时）不挂断; （口语）等一等; 停住 (37)
*hole [həul] *n.* 洞; 坑 (69)
Δhooray [hu'rei] *interj.* 好哇！（欢呼声） (7)
horse [hɔ:s] *n.* 马 (13)
hour after hour 一小时又一小时地; 连续地 (78)
How about ...? ……怎么样？ (4)
hundreds of ... 数百…… (66)
hurry ['hʌri] *vi.* 赶紧; 急忙 (18)
hurry off 匆匆离去; 赶快去 (18)
hurry up 赶快 (18)
n. 着急 (30)
*hurt [hə:t] (hurt, hurt) *vt.* 受伤; 伤害 (5)

I

important [im'pɔ:tənt] *adj.* 重要的 (3)
in a minute 一会儿; 立刻 (46)
in front 在前方（面）; 在正对面 (6)
in surprise 惊奇地 (83)
*in time 及时 (89)
in trouble 处于困难中 (38)
*India ['indjə] *n.* 印度 (77)
*instruction [in'strʌkʃən] *n.* 说明; 须知 (45)
*interested ['intristid] *adj.* 感兴趣的; 关心的 (42)
*invent [in'vent] *vt.* 发明; 创造 (41)
*invention [in'venʃən] *n.* 发明; 创造 (41)
*inventor [in'ventə] *n.* 发明者; 创造者 (41)

J

*jacket ['dʒækit] *n.* 短上衣; 外套 (46)
*Japan [dʒə'pæn] *n.* 日本 (62)
ΔJesus Christ ['dʒi:zəs 'kraist] *n.* 耶稣基督 (55)
join [dʒɔin] *vt.* & *vi.* 连接; 接合; 参加 (34)
*joke [dʒəuk] *n.* 笑话 (30)
*journey ['dʒə:ni] *n.* 旅行;路程 (46)
• jump [dʒʌmp] *n.* 跳 (5)
just [dʒʌst] *adv.* 正好; 恰好; 刚才 (14)
just a moment 等一会儿 (83)
just then 正在那时 (46)

K

key [ki:] *n.* 钥匙 (61)

*kick [kik] *vt. & vi.* 踢 (91)
kind-hearted ['kaind 'hɑ:tid] *adj.* 好心的 (54)
kindly ['kaindli] *adv.* 亲切地；诚恳地 (23)
*king [kiŋ] *n.* 国王 (66)
*knock [nɔk] *vi. & n.* 敲；击；打 (14)
*knock at 敲（门、窗等） (14)
*knock ... into ... 把 …… 插进；把 …… 敲 (69)
Δknow-all ['nəu 'ɔ:l] *n.* 自称无所不知的人 (23)
*knowledge ['nɔlidʒ] *n.* 知识；学问 (74)

L

*lab [læb] *n.* 实验室（laboratory [lə'bɔrətəri] 的缩写词） (42)
*land [lænd] *vt.* （使）降落；（使）落到 (18)
*language ['læŋgwidʒ] *n.* 语言 (9)
Δlap [læp] *n.* （跑道的）一圈 (6)
*lazy ['leizi] *adj.* 懒惰的 (38)
*leaf [li:f] *n.* (*pl.* leaves [li:vz]) （树、菜）叶 (45)
league [li:g] *n.* 联盟；社团 (16)(89)
league match 联赛 (89)
League [li:g] *n.* 共青团 (67)
League member 团员 (16)
learn by oneself 自学 (39)
leave a message 留话 (37)
lend [lend] (lent [lent], lent) *vt.* 把 …… 借给 (30)
• letter ['letə] *n.* 字母 (9)
library ['laibrəri] *n.* 图书馆（室） (18)
lie [lai] (lay [lei], lain [lein]) *vi.* 平躺；（物件）平放在某处 (18)
life [laif] *n.* 生活；生命 (35)
• light [lait] *n.* 光 (43)
adj. 淡色的 (58)
*line [lain] *n.* （电话的）线路 (44)
*list [list] *n.* 一览表；清单 (26)
*lock [lɔk] *vt.* 锁；锁上 *n.* 锁 (61)(68)
*lonely ['ləunli] *adj.* 孤独的:寂寞的 (58)
look up （在词典、参考书中）查寻 (54)
*lose [lu:z] (lost [lɔst], lost) *vt.* 失去；丢失 (17)
*loud [laud] *adj.* 大声的 (6)
*loudly ['laudli] *adv.* 大声地 (6)
*loudspeaker ['laud'spi:kə] *n.* 扬声器，喇叭 (7)
*low [ləu] *adj.* 低的；浅的；矮的 (94)
*luck [lʌk] *n.* 运气；好运 (1)
*lucky ['lʌki] *adj.* 运气好的；侥幸(10)(17)
*luckily ['lʌkili] *adv.* 运气好地 (10)

M

make a mistake 犯错误 (58)
make friends 交朋友 (58)
make sure 务必；务请;确信 (45)
*man-made ['mæn meid] *adj.* 人造的；人工的 (74)
*market ['mɑ:kit] *n.* 市场；集市 (65)
match [mætʃ] *n.* 比赛；竞赛 (87)
*maths [mæθs] *n.* （缩写词）数学 (11)
medicine ['medsin] *n.* 内服药 (18)
member ['membə] *n.* 成员；会员(16) (50)
*merry ['meri] *adj.* 愉快的；欢乐的 (49)
Δmetal ['metl] *n.* 金属 (34)
• milk [milk] *vt.* 挤奶；出奶 (31)
*million ['miljən] *num. & n.* 百万；百万个（人或物） (70)
mind [maind] *vi. & vt.* 介意；反对 (39)
n. 思想；主意 (47)
*mirror ['mirə] *n.* 镜子 (43)
*miss [mis] *vt.* 失去；缺；错过 (38)
• mistake [mis'teik] *vt.* 弄错 *n.* 错误 (58)
modern ['mɔdən] *adj.* 现代的 (62)
Mom [mɔm] *n.* = Mum (26)
more or less 或多或少；差不多 (72)
ΔMoscow ['mɔskəu] *n.* 莫斯科 (14)
*motor ['məutə] *n.* 发动机；马达
*motorbike 摩托车 (17)
*motor car 汽车 (41)
*mountain ['mauntin] *n.* 山；山脉 (70)
mouth [mauθ] *n.* 嘴 (78)

move away 搬开; 搬走 (18)
*museum [mju(:)'ziəm] *n.* 博物馆 (65)
*mutton ['mʌtn] *n.* 羊肉 (31)

N

• name [neim] *vt.* 命名; 名叫 (82)
*narrow ['nærəu] *adj.* 狭窄的 (34)
*nearly ['niəli] *adv.* 将近; 几乎 (46)
*neck [nek] *n.* 颈; 脖子 (5)
*neck and neck （赛跑时）齐头并进; 不分上下 (6)
neither ['naiðə, 'ni:ðə] *adj.*, *adv.* & *conj.*（两者）都不 (69)
neither ... nor ... 既不……也不…… (69)
never mind 不要紧; 没关系 (82)
ΔNew Zealand [ˌnju:'zi:lənd] *n.* 新西兰（大洋洲）(62)
news [nju:z] *n.* 新闻; 消息 (49)
*newspaper ['nju:sˌpeipə] *n.* 报纸 (9)
No hurry. 不忙。不必着急。 (30)
*noise [nɔiz] *n.* 嘈杂声; 响声 (14)
*noisily ['nɔizili] *adv.* 喧闹地 (28)
*noisy ['nɔizi] *adj.* 喧闹的;（人、地方等）嘈杂的 (28) (34)
*none [nʌn] *pron.* 没有任何东西或人; 一个人也没有 (62)
noon [nu:n] *n.* 中午 (15)
nor [nɔ:] *conj.* 也不 (69)
*northern ['nɔ:ðən] *adj.* 北方的; 北部的 (70)
nurse [nə:s] *n.* 护士 (86)

O

*of course [əfkɔ:z] 当然 (3)
• on [ɔn] *prep.* 关于 (22)
on and on 继续; 不断 (83)
on show 展览; 陈列 (66)
on the earth 在地球上 (78)
on time 按时; 准时 (22)
*on top of 在……上面 (54)
*operate ['ɔpəreit] *vi.* & *vt.* 手术; 运转 (43)
• or [ɔ:] *conj.* 否则 (18)
Δorder ['ɔ:də] *n.* 顺序 (32)
• over ['əuvə] *prep.* 超过; 多于 (33)
prep. 蒙在……上; 悬挂……上 (35)
own [əun] *adj.* 自己的 (33)
vt. 所有; 拥有 (41)

P

*pain [pein] *n.* 疼痛; 疼 (87)
pair [pεə] *n.* 一对; 一双 (81)
Δpan [pæn] *n.* 平底锅 (30)
*pardon ['pɑ:dn] *n.* 原谅; 宽恕; 对不起 (83)
• part(s) [pɑ:t(s)] *n.* 零件; 部件 (34)
• Party ['pɑ:ti] *n.* 共产党(小写指党; 政党) (67)
pass on 传递 (6)
• past [pɑ:st] *adv.* 过 (17)
pay [pei] (paid [peid], paid) *vt.* & *vi.* 付款; 给……报酬 (22)
pay for 付款 (22)
*P.E. ['pi:'i:] *n.* 体育(= physical education ['fizikəl ˌedju:'keiʃən]) (11)
*perhaps [pə'hæps] *adv.* 可能; 也许 (82)
*person ['pə:sn] *n.* 人 (25)
*photograph ['fəutəugrɑ:f] *n.* 相片 (96)
*pig [pig] *n.* 猪 (29)
*pigsty ['pigstai] *n.* 猪圈 (31)
*pill [pil] *n.* 药丸; 药片 (86)
*pity ['piti] *n.* 怜悯; 同情 (22)
Δ PLA ['pi:'el'ei] 中国人民解放军 (67)
plant [plɑ:nt] *vt.* 种植 *n.* 植物 (69)
• play [plei] *n.* 戏剧; 话剧 (30)
playground ['pleigraund] *n.*（学校的）操场 (5)
play with 玩耍 (13)
*point [pɔint] (at) *vt.* & *vi.* 指; 指向 (66)
*point to 指向 (70)

*polite [pə'lait] *adj.* 有礼貌的; 有教养的 (22)
*politely [pə'laitli] *adv.* 有礼貌地 (22)
*population [ˌpɔpju'leiʃən] *n.* 人口; 人数 (77)
*possible ['pɔsibl] *adj.* 可能的 (37)
Δpot [pɔt] *n.* 壶; 罐; 锅 (66)
ΔPRC ['pi:'ɑ:'si:] 中华人民共和国 (67)
*prefer [pri'fə:] *vt.* 宁愿（选择）; 更喜欢 (11)
*prefer ... to ... 比起 …… 来还是 …… 好; 喜欢 ……（而不喜欢 ……） (11)
*produce [prə'dju:s] *vt.* 生产; 制造 (63)
*programme ['prəugræm] *n.* 节目 (74)
*pupil ['pju:pl] *n.* 小学生; 学生 (42)

Q

quiet ['kwaiət] *adj.* 安静的; 平静的 (14)
quietly ['kwaiətli] *adv.* 安静地; 平静地 (14)

R

*race [reis] *n.* 赛跑;竞赛 (5)
*100-metre race 100米（赛跑） (5)
*rather ['rɑ:ðə] *adv.* 相当; 宁可 (7)
reading room ['ri:diŋrum] *n.* 阅览室 (22)
*receive [ri'si:v] *vt.* 收到; 接收 (49)
Δrelay ['ri:lei] *n.* 接力 (6)
relay race 接力赛 (6)
*result [ri'zʌlt] *n.* 结果; 效果 (7)
*retell ['ri:'tel] *vt.* 重讲; 重复; 复述 (82)
*return [ri'tə:n] *vt.* & *vi.* 归还; 回; 归 (22)
right away 立刻; 马上 (57)
right now 现在; 刚刚 (7)
*rise [raiz] (rose [rəuz], risen ['rizn]) *vi.* 上升; 上涨 (94)
*rock [rɔk] *n.* 岩石; 大石头 (94)
runner ['rʌnə] *n.* 赛跑的人 (6)
*rush [rʌʃ] *vi.* 冲; 奔跑 (34)
*Russian ['rʌʃən] *adj.* & *n.* 俄国的; 俄国人（的）; 俄语（的） (14)

S

*safely ['seifli] *adv.* 安全地; 平安地 (46)
*sand [sænd] *n.* 沙; 沙子 (70)
*satellite ['sætəlait] *n.* 卫星 (73)
*save [seiv] *vt.* 救; 挽救 (43)
vt. 节省 (70)
*science ['saiəns] *n.* 科学; 自然科学 (11)
seat [si:t] *n.* 座位 (46)
*seem [si:m] *vi.* 好像 (86)
sell out 售完 (82)
send [send] (sent [sent], sent) *vt.* 派; 派遣 (42)
send away 撵走; 开除; 解雇 (42)
send for 派人去叫（请） (43)
send up 发射 (74)
*serious ['siəriəs] *adj.* 严重的 (85)
*several ['sevrəl] *pron.* 几个;数个（至少三个） *adj.* 若干 (21)
sheep [ʃi:p] *n.* 绵羊 (29)
*shelf [ʃelf] *n.* (*pl.* shelves [ʃelvz]) 架子 (21)
• shop [ʃɔp] *n.* 车间 (34)
*shopkeeper ['ʃɔpˌki:pə] *n.* 零售商人; 店主 (26)
should [ʃud, ʃəd] *v. aux.* (shall的过去时态)会; 应该 (2)
• shout [ʃaut] *vt.* & *vi.* 喊; 呼喊 (6)
Δsign [sain] *n.* 标志; 符号 (67)
*silk [silk] *n.* （蚕）丝; 丝织品 (63)
Δsimple ['simpl] *adj.* 简单的; 简易的 (84)
since [sins] *prep.* & *conj.* 自从; 从…… 以来; 由于 (33)(34)
sitting room 起居室 (50)
*size [saiz] *n.* 尺寸; 大小 (81)
sky [skai] *n.* 天空 (94)
sleep [sli:p] (slept [slept], slept) *vi.* 睡;睡觉 (14)
smile [smail] *n.*, *vt.* & *vi.* 微笑 (10)
*smoke [sməuk] *vi.* & *vt.* 吸烟 *n.* 烟 (67)

*smoking ['sməukiŋ] *n.* 吸烟; 冒烟(67)
so ... that ... 如此…… 以致 (83)
so far 到现在为止 (74)
*soft [sɔft] *adj.* 软的; 柔和的 (59)
song [sɔŋ] *n.* 歌曲 (91)
sound [saund] *n.* 声音 (9)
*space [speis] *n.* 空间;太空 (74)
* spaceship ['speisʃip] *n.* 宇宙飞船 (74)
spend [spend] (spent [spent], spent) *vt.* 花费（金钱、时间等）; 度过 (26)
Δspy [spai] *vi.* & *vt.* 侦探; 刺探 (36)
stamp [stæmp] *n.* 邮票 (61)
star [stɑ:] *n.* 星; 恒星 (22)
*step [step] *n.* 脚步; 台阶; 梯级 (34)
*stick [stik] *n.* 木棒; 木棍; 枝条 (6)
still [stil] *adv.* 还; 仍旧 (6)
*stocking ['stɔkiŋ] *n.* 长统袜 (54)
stop ... from 阻止; 阻拦 (70)
*straight [streit] *adv.* & *adj.* 一直的(地); 直(的) (35)
*strange [streindʒ] *adj.* 奇怪的; 古怪的; 陌生的 (42)
Δstrict [strikt] *adj.* 严格的 (22)
subject ['sʌbdʒikt] *n.* 题目; 科目 (2)(11)
such [sʌtʃ] *adj.* 这样（种）的 (89)
*suddenly ['sʌdnli] *adv.* 突然地 (18)
*suit [sju:t] *n.* 一套（衣服） (81)
*surprise [sə'praiz] *vt.* 使惊奇; 使感到意外 (66)
*sweep [swi:p] (swept [swept], swept) *vt.* & *vi.* 扫; 扫除 (10)
sweet [swi:t] *n.* 糖果; 甜食 (26)

T

take [teik] *vt.* 耗费（时间）; 需要（多少时间） (93)
take a look 看一看 (34)
*take (good) care of 照料; 照顾 (45)
take one's time 不急; 慢慢干 (59)
Δtake turns 替换; 轮流 (7)
• talk [tɔ:k] *n.* 演讲; 谈话 (2)
*teamwork ['ti:mwə:k] *n.* 合作; 协同工作 (90)
Δteapot ['ti:pɔt] *n.* 茶壶 (66)
*terrible ['terəbl] *adj.* 可怕的; 极坏的 (86)
*terribly ['terəbli] *adj.* 可怕地; 极坏地 (86)
the high jump 跳高 (5)
the long jump 跳远 (5)
*the starting line 起跑线 (6)
Δthermos ['θə:mɔs] *n.* 热水瓶 (66)
think about 思虑; 思考 (81)
*thirsty ['θə:sti] *adj.* 口渴的 (66)
*though [ðəu] *conj.* 虽然; 可是 (90)
thousand ['θauzənd] *num.* 千 (73)
through [θru:] *prep.* 通过; 穿过 (34)
*tie [tai] *vt.* （用绳、线等）系; 拴; 扎 (69)
till [til] *prep.* & *conj.* 直到; 直到……之时 (85)
together [tə'geðə] *adv.* 一起; 一同; 合起来 (33)
*top [tɔp] *n.* 顶部; （物的）上面 (54)
• touch [tʌtʃ] *vt.* 触摸; 接触 (34)
*toward(s) [tə'wɔ:d(z)] *prep.* 向; 朝; 对于 (70)
*tractor ['træktə] *n.* 拖拉机 (29)
travel ['trævl] *vi.* 旅行 (18)
traveller ['trævlə] *n.* 旅行者 (62)
trouble ['trʌbl] *vt.* 麻烦; 使麻烦 (14)
n. 疾病 (85)
true [tru:] *adj.* 真的; 真实的 (39)
try [trai] *vt.* & *vi.* 试（做）; 试图; 努力 (13)
try ... on 试穿（衣、鞋、帽等） (60)
try out 试验; 尝试 (42)
turn down （收音机、灯等）关小; 调低 (43)
twice [twais] *adv.* 两次; 两倍 (31)

U

ΔUN=the United Nations [ju:'naitid 'neiʃənz] 联合国 (78)

unhappy [ʌn'hæpi] *adj.* 不高兴的；伤心的 (50)
Δuntrue ['ʌn'tru:] *adj.* 不真实的；假的 (69)
*universe ['ju:nivə:s] *n.* 宇宙 (73)
*upstairs ['ʌp'stɛəz] *adv.* 在楼上；到楼上 (14)
*useful ['ju:sful] *adj.* 有用的；有益的 (11)
*usual ['ju:ʒuəl] *adj.* 通常的；平常的 (10)

V

Δverb [və:b] *n.* 动词 (84)

W

• water ['wɔ:tə] *vt.* 浇水；灌溉 (69)
*weak [wi:k] *adj.* 差的；弱的；淡的 (38)
wear out 穿坏；穿旧；用尽 (81)
whether ['weðə] *conj.* 是否 (57)
while [wail] *conj.* 当……的时候；和……同时 (19)(45)
whom [hu:m, hum] *pron.* 谁；哪个人 (49)
*wide [waid] *adj.* 宽阔的；广泛 (62)(70)
  *widely ['waidli] *adv.* 广阔地；广泛地 (62)
*win [win] (won [wʌn], won) *vt.* 获胜；赢得 (5)
  *winner ['winə] *n.* 获胜者 (7)
*wish [wiʃ] *n.* & *vt.* 祝愿；希望；想要 (1)(3)
with one's help 在（某人）帮助下 (74)
with pleasure 高兴 (30)
without [wi'ðaut] *prep.* 无；没有 (50)
*wonderful ['wʌndəful] *adj.* 极好的；精彩的 (69)
*wood [wud] *n.* 木头；木材 (61)
*wool [wul] *n.* 羊毛；绒线 (31)
  *woollen ['wulən] *adj.* 羊毛的；羊毛制的 (59)
workplace ['wə:kpleis] *n.* 工作场所；车间 (70)
world [wə:ld] *n.* 世界 (41)
write down 写下；记下来 (45)

Y

yet [jet] *adv.* 尚；还；仍然 (21)

人名表：

Allan ['ælən] 艾伦 （男名） (2)
Catherine ['kæθərin] 凯瑟琳（女名） (3)
David ['deivid] 戴维 （男名） (3)
  Dave [deiv] （David的昵称） (3)
Henry ['henri] 亨利 （男名） (2)
Jill [dʒil] 吉尔 （女名） (3)
Linda ['lində] 琳达 （女名） (3)
  Lin [lin] （Linda 的昵称） (3)
Thomas Edison ['tɔməs 'edisn] 托马斯·爱迪生 （1847 - 1931, 美国发明家） (42)
Robert Thomas Brown ['rɔbət 'tɔməs 'braun] 罗伯特·托马斯·布朗 (3)
Ron [rɔn] 罗恩 （男名） (83)

Irregular verbs 不规则动词

Infinitive	Past tense	Past participle
be		
am, is	was [wɔz; wəz]	been
are	were [wə:; wə]	been
beat	beat	beaten ['bi:tn]
become	became	become
begin	began	begun
blow	blew [blu:]	blown [bləun]
break	broke	broken ['brəukən]
bring	brought [brɔ:t]	brought
build	built [bilt]	built
burn	burnt, burned	burnt, burned
buy	bought [bɔ:t]	bought
can	could [kud]	——
catch	caught [kɔ:t]	caught
choose	chose	chosen ['tʃəuzn]
come	came	come
cost	cost	cost
cut	cut	cut
dig	dug	dug
do	did	done [dʌn]
draw	drew [dru:]	drawn [drɔ:n]
drink	drank	drunk
drive	drove	driven ['drivn]
eat	ate	eaten ['i:tn]
fall	fell	fallen ['fɔ:lən]
feel	felt	felt
fight [fait]	fought [fɔ:t]	fought
find	found [faund]	found
fly	flew [flu:]	flown [fləun]
forget	forgot [fə'gɔt]	forgotten [fə'gɔtn]
get	got	got

Infintive	Past tense	Past participle
give	gave	given ['givn]
go	went	gone [gɔn]
grow	grew [gru:]	grown [grəun]
hang	hung; hanged	hung; hanged
have, has	had	had
hear	heard [hə:d]	heard
hit	hit	hit
hold	held	held
*hurt	hurt	hurt
keep	kept	kept
know	knew [nju:]	known [nəun]
learn	learnt, learned	learnt, learned
leave	left	left
lend	lent	lent
let	let	let
lie [lai]	lay [lei]	lain [lein]
lose [lu:z]	lost	lost
make	made	made
may	might [mait]	——
mean	meant [ment]	meant
meet	met	met
mistake	mistook	mistaken [mis'teikən]
must	must	——
put	put	put
read	read [red]	read
ride	rode	ridden ['ridn]
ring	rang	rung
rise	rose	risen ['rizn]
run	ran	run
say	said [sed]	said
see	saw [sɔ:]	seen
sell	sold [səuld]	sold
send	sent	sent
shall	should [ʃud]	——

Infinitive	Past tense	Past participle
shine	shone [ʃɔn], shined [ʃaind]	shone, shined
show	showed [ʃəud]	shown [ʃəun]
sing	sang	sung
sit	sat	sat
sleep	slept	slept
smell	smelt, smelled	smelt, smelled
speak	spoke	spoken ['spəukən]
spend	spent	spent
stand	stood [stud]	stood
sweep	swept	swept
swim	swam	swum
take	took	taken ['teikən]
teach	taught [tɔ:t]	taught
tell	told [təuld]	told
think	thought [θɔ:t]	thought
throw	threw [θru:]	thrown [θrəun]
understand	understood	understood
wake	waked, woke	waked, woken ['wəukən], woke
wear	wore [wɔ:]	worn [wɔ:n]
will	*would [wud]	——
win	won [wʌn]	won
write	wrote	written ['ritn]

九年义务教育三年制初级中学英语

练习册

第三册

JUNIOR ENGLISH FOR CHINA

WORKBOOK 3

(中国) 人民教育出版社
(英国) 朗文出版集团有限公司 合编

人民教育出版社

说　明

根据我国政府与联合国开发计划署达成的协议，由联合国开发计划署提供资助，联合国教科文组织任执行机构，人民教育出版社与英国朗文出版集团有限公司合作编写九年义务教育初中英语教材。本书由人民教育出版社教科书编辑人员、设计人员与英方作者、编辑和设计人员合作编制而成，由人民教育出版社出版。遵照协议规定，本书版权归人民教育出版社所有。

本练习册配合义务教育三年制、四年制初级中学教科书英语第三册教学使用。

参加本书编写工作的还有董蔚君。

CONTENTS

Unit 1 Lesson 1

1 Fill in the blanks and compare the dialogues.

1 **A**: How do you do?
B: ____ ____ ____ ____?
A: My name is Tom Green. Nice to meet you.
B: My name is Wang Haiming. ____ ____ ____ ____, too.

2 **A**: Good morning, Miss Zhao!
B: ____ ____, Mrs King!
A: Happy Teachers' Day! Here are some flowers for you, with our best wishes.
B: What ____ ____! ____ ____ very much.

3 **A**: Hi, Li Lei! ____ ____ ____?
B: Hi, Jim! I'm very well, and you?
A: ____, too. Glad to see you again.

4 **A**: Hello, Lucy! Glad to see you again.
B: Hello, Han Meimei! I'm ____ to see ____, too. How are you?
A: I'm fine. What about you?
B: ____ ____, too.

2 Make a Teachers' Day card like this. Write some words on it.

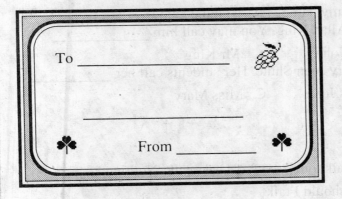

To ____

____

From ____

3 Write down the -s / -es, -ing and past forms of these verbs.

begin	blow
bring	catch
come	do
eat	fall
feel	see
have	hope
teach	wish

4 Fill in each blank with the right verb form.

MEIMEI: Hi, Ann! Where ____ you ____ (go)?
ANN: Hi, Meimei! I ____ (go) shopping. I want to ____ (buy) Mr Wu a present. The day after tomorrow ____ (be) Teachers' Day.
MEIMEI: Hmm, I don't think it ____ (be) a good idea. I think you'd better ____ (make) a Teachers' Day card instead.
ANN: How about you? ____ you ____ (go) to make a Teachers' Day card?
MEIMEI: No, I'm not. I ____ (make) one yesterday evening and I ____ (give) it to Mr Wu the day after tomorrow.

Lesson 2

1 Read Lesson 2 again and answer the questions. Write the answers in your exercise books.

1 What does the teacher ask Jim to do?
2 What subject did Jim choose?
3 How many names do most English people have? What are they?
4 What's Jim's full name?
5 Which is Jim's given name? Which is his family name?
6 What's your full name? Which is your family name?
7 What did Jim's parents call him when he was born?
8 Why do people usually call him Jim instead of James?

2 Choose the right answers.

1 In China, the first name is the ____________.
A. given name B. family name C. middle name
2 In England, the first name is the ____________.
A. given name B. family name C. middle name
3 In England, the last name is the ____________.
A. given name B. family name C. middle name
4 The man's name is John Allan King. You may call him ____________.
A. Mr Allan B. Mr John C. Mr King
5 The teacher's name is Mary Joan Shute. Her students call her ____________.
A. Miss Shute B. Miss Joan C. Miss Mary

3 Complete the dialogue.

A: Tom, can you give us a talk tomorrow? An easy talk. Nothing ________.

B: A talk? What ________ should I talk ________?

A: ________ any subject. Something ________ England, for ________.

B: That's difficult! Maybe I could talk ________ English names.

A: Yes, ________ please! That's a good ________.

4 Fill in each blank with the right verb form.

Jim's parents ________ (call) Jim "James" when he ______ (be) born because James ________ (be) the name of his grandfather. In England, people usually ________ (call) him Jim for short because Jim ______ (be) shorter and easier to say than James.

Lesson 3

1 Ask and answer these questions in pairs.

1 What's your full name?
2 Which is your family name? Which is your given name?
3 Which comes first, your family name or your given name?
4 What did your parents call you when you were born? What does it mean?

2 Fill in the blanks and practise the dialogue.

TOM: Hi, Linda! Glad to ______ you again.
LINDA: Hi, Tom! ______ to see you, too. ______ ______ my friend. Her ______ is Catherine Green.
TOM: ______, Catherine! My ______ is Thomas. You can call me ______.
KATE: Nice ______ meet you.
TOM: Hmm, shall I call you Catherine or ______?
KATE: It doesn't ______. It's not ______. You may call me ______ for short.

LINDA: Who's the little boy there?
TOM: Oh, he's my brother ______.
KATE: David? May I ______ him Dave?
TOM: Of ______, if you ______! Dave, come here please!
LINDA: ______ to meet you, Dave!
DAVE: Me too. I'm playing football with those boys. I must go there now.
KATE: That's all right. ______ luck, Dave!
DAVE: Thank you. Bye!

3 Make dialogues like this and write one in your exercise books.

A: Shall I call you *James* or *Jim*?
B: It doesn't matter. It's not important. But my friends call me *Jim* for short.

Thomas	Tom
Linda	Lin
David	Dave
Catherine	Kate

Lesson 4

1 Listen to the tape and write the names in the form below.

	Family names	Given names
1		
2		
3		

2 Read and learn the word stress.

□□□ 'difficult 'January 'family 'cinema 'beautiful
'February 'elephant 'diary 'bookseller
'Saturday 'radio 'telephone 'factory 'carefully
'yesterday 'animal 'hospital 'somebody

□□□ ba'nana e'raser po'liceman Aus'tralian

□□□□ 'vegetable 'everybody 'dictionary 'temperature

3 Fill in the blanks with the right verb form.

Teachers' Day is coming soon. Miss Zhao is talking to her students and her students______ ______ (listen) to her.

"Good morning, girls and boys!" said Miss Zhao. "Teachers' Day ______ (be) on September 10th. I hear some students ______ ______ (go) to ______ (buy) presents for their teachers. They ______ (want) to show their love for their teachers. That ______ (be) very good, of course. But teachers ______ (not like) to get presents from students. So please______ ______ (not buy) any! I ______ (think) one Teachers' Day card from you all ______ (be) enough. And the best present for us teachers ______ (be) your good work!"

4 Make new dialogues, using the words in the box and write one in your exercise books.

A: Shall we make a card for Teachers' Day?
B: Yes, of course. What should we write on it?
A: I think we can write: "*Happy Teachers' Day !*"
B: That'll be fine.

Thank you for teaching us so well! Thank you for your help! Thank you for your hard work! Best wishes for Teachers' Day! We hope you enjoy teaching us. We wish you a happy Teachers' Day!

Unit 2 Lesson 5

1 Add -er and -est to these words. Change the letters where necessary.

Model: fast → faster → fastest

big	slow	early	late
fat	far	empty	long
thin	high	hungry	thick
wet	few	easy	rich

2 Look at these pictures and complete these sentences.

Lin Tao ran ______. Jim ran ______ ______ Lin Tao.
Li Lei ran ________ of all.

Li Lei played football well.
Jim did ____________ Li Lei.
Bill did ______ of all.

Cheng Hui jumped quite ______.
Lily jumped ______ ______ her.
Han Meimei jumped ______ of all.

Zhang Jun jumped ______.
Bill jumped ______ ______ Zhang Jun.
Jim jumped ________ of all.

3 Complete this passage with the words in the box.

on	first
held	won
third	boys'
girls'	quite
best	farthest
in	because
after	happily

Last Saturday No.14 Middle School ______ a sports meeting ______ the playground. Class 3, Grade 3 did very well. Wu Dong was ______ in the Girl's 100-metre race. She ______ the race. Zhang Jun won the ______ high jump. Bill was second. Lin Tao also did ______ well. He was ______. In the ______ long jump, Liu Mei jumped ______ of all. She was the ______ of all. I was not ______ any of the sports ______ I wasn't very well. But I watched the sports meeting ______ and looked ______ my classmates' clothes.

Lesson 6

1 Read the passage in the Students' Book. Answer right or wrong.

		Right	Wrong
1	Mr Hu stood at the starting line. All the girls got ready to run.	/ /	/ /
2	The runners started to run. All the students began to shout very loudly.	/ /	/ /
3	At the end of the first lap, Li Lei quickly passed the stick on to Yu Yan.	/ /	/ /
4	Yu Yan caught up with Jim. They were neck and neck.	/ /	/ /
5	At the end of the second lap, Yu Yan and Jim passed on their sticks at the same time.	/ /	/ /
6	"Come on" means "Run, run quickly!"	/ /	/ /
7	The other runners were far behind.	/ /	/ /
8	The Class 2 runner dropped his stick on the ground when he was passing it on to the last runner.	/ /	/ /
9	The Class 4 runner fell and hurt his leg. He stopped running.	/ /	/ /
10	The Class 3 runner and the Class 4 runner were still neck and neck on the last lap.	/ /	/ /

2 Polly says: Can you read and write these words?

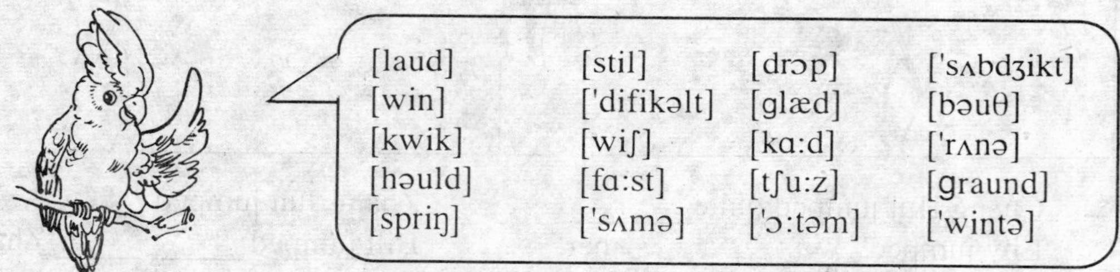

3 Fill in the blanks with *to, on, with, behind, neck ... neck, moment* or *same*.

No. 14 Middle School were having a relay race. At first Yu Yan was far ________ Jim, but Yu Yan ran much faster than Jim. "Come ________!" shouted everyone. A ________ later, Yu Yan caught up ______ Jim and they were ______ and ________. At the end of the second lap, they passed their sticks on ________ the next runners at the ________ time.

Lesson 7

1 Read the whole story in Lesson 6 and Lesson 7 again. Answer these questions. Write the answers in your exercise books.

1 Is a relay race a team race?
2 What does "Come on!" mean?
3 Who ran fastest on the first lap?
4 Who did Li Lei pass the stick on to?
5 Did Yu Yan catch up with Jim?
6 Who passed on their sticks at the same time?
7 When did the Class 2 runner drop his stick?
8 What was wrong with the Class 4 runner? Did he go on running?
9 Who had bad luck and fell behind?
10 Who was first past the finishing line? Which class won the race?

2 Complete the dialogue, and then practise it.

WEI HUA: Well _____ ! Congratulations, Lin Tao!

LIN TAO: Thank you. I felt sorry for Wu Peng. He and the Class 2 runner had _____ luck. Both of them _____ their sticks.

WEI HUA: Who _____ the boys' high jump? Do you know the _____ ?

LIN TAO: I don't know. Oh! Listen to the _________ . It's telling the result of the high jump.

LOUDSPEAKER : Boys and girls, here is the result of the high jump. Zhang Jun is the winner. He jumped over one metre and sixty-seven!

LIN TAO: Hooray! It's a new record (记录) in our school.

WEI HUA: ______ done! But I must go. The next is the girls' 400-metre race.

LIN TAO: _____ luck! I hope you will win!

WEI HUA: Thank you. See you later!

3 Make new sentences, using the words in the box.

Mr Read	*swims*	drives a car	very well.
But he	*skates*	rides a bike	rather badly.
Tom	*plays basketball*	dances	better than Ann.
But he	*plays pingpong*	sings	worse than Ann.
Li Lei	*jumps*	climbs	higher than Jim.
But he	*runs*	comes down	slower than Jim.
Mrs Read	*writes English*	speaks Japanese	best in the family.
But she	*writes Chinese*	speaks French	worst in the family.

4 Look at the colour page i, say which sport you like best. Why?

Lesson 8

1 Listen to the results of the relay races on the loudspeaker, and write down the results in the form below.

Results	1st	2nd	3rd
Boys' relay race			
Girls' relay race			

2 Read and learn the word stress.

□□ 'classmate 'playground 'homework 'postcard
'penfriend 'doorbell 'housework 'Sunday

□□□ 'difficult 'favourite 'opposite 'interesting
'beautiful 'dangerous 'popular 'similar

3 Ask and answer questions about the sports meeting at No. 14 Middle School.

1 Who jumped higher / farther, ... or ...?
2 Who jumped highest of all?
3 Did ... run faster / slower than ...?
4 Did ... do better in the relay race than ...?
5 Who won the boys' / girls' 100-metre race?

4 Fill in the blanks with *in, on, from, of, at, to* or *behind*.

1 No. 5 Middle School are now holding a sports meeting ____ the playground.
2 Mr Hu stood ____ the starting line and the runners got ready to run.
3 Fang Fang was ____ front, but soon Wu Dong caught up ____ her. ____ the end of the race, Wu Dong was first past the finishing line.
4 ____ the 1000-metre race, Li Lei was far ____ the other runners at first. "Come ____!" his friends shouted. A moment later, Li Lei caught up ____ the others and won the race.
5 "Did Wu Dong win the Girls' 100-metre race?" a student asked. "____ course, she did," Lucy answered. "She ran much faster than the other girls."
6 A runner ____ Class 3 and a Class 2 runner were neck and neck.
7 They passed ____ the sticks ____ the next runners ____ the same time.
8 The headteacher said: "Well done! Congratulations ____ the winners!"

Unit 3 Lesson 9

1 Make dialogues like this and write one in your exercise books.

A: Excuse me, what does this word mean?
B: Which one? Show me the word please!
A: Here's this word [nju:s'peipə].
B: Oh, *newspaper*. You say it like this: ['nju:s,peipə]. Here *ew* makes a [ju:] sound. It means *baozhi*.

2 Fill in the blanks with *more carefully* / *heavily* / *quickly* / *slowly* or *happily*. Then turn these sentences into Chinese.

1 I'm afraid I can't understand you. Can you speak ________ ________, please?
2 I'm sorry I can't understand your writing. Could you write ________ ________ next time?
3 I'm afraid it's rather late. Will you please walk ________ ________?
4 It's raining much ________ ________ now. I'm afraid we'll have to stay here for the night.
5 The old man was pleased to be back home. When he saw his grandson, he laughed ____________.

*** 3 Read the short story and then answer the questions**

An English woman came to China. She didn't know any foreign languages. She only knew a few Chinese words and she liked to use them here and there. One day she went into a shop and wanted to buy a cup. She said:

"*bèizi, bèizi.*" She didn't make the right sound. So the girl in the shop gave her a quilt (被子). The woman was unhappy. She said again:

" I want *bèizi, bèizi*! Not a quilt."

"Yes, that's right. It's a *bèizi*," the girl answered.

1 Did the woman know any foreign languages?
2 What does *bèizi* mean in Chinese?
3 What did the woman want?
4 Why didn't the girl give her a cup?
5 How do you say "cup" in Chinese?

Lesson 10

1 Read the passage on page 10 of the Students' Book. Ask and answer these questions.

1 Do Miss Zhao's students like her? How do you know that?
2 Was she very glad when she came into class yesterday morning? Why?
3 What was wrong with the classroom last Saturday?
4 What did some students forget to do?
5 What should the students do every day?
6 Who was on duty that day?
7 What was the date that day?
8 When and how did they go to the Great Wall?
9 What was the weather like last Sunday?
10 Where did they have their picnic? What did they do later?

2 Complete the short passage and retell it.

Miss Zhao is one of the _______ _______ teachers in the school. Yesterday she came into class with a big _______ _______ her face. She said congratulations _____ her students on their good results in the sports meeting. But she was not pleased to see the classroom last Saturday not as clean _____ usual. She told them to _______ the floor and _______ the classroom every day. Wei Hua was _____ duty yesterday. She said everyone was at school _______ Lin Tao. Then she told Miss Zhao and the class about their picnic last Sunday. They _______ the Great Wall. Luckily the weather was _____ fine _____ usual. They had a very _______ time. After Wei Hua finished her talk, it was time _____ them to _____ their lesson.

3 Practise the dialogues. Make a similar dialogue and write it down in your exercise books.

A: Is Bill as [tall / careful / strong / healthy] as Li Lei?

B: No, he is not so / as [tall / careful / strong / healthy] as Li Lei. He is as [tall / careful / strong / healthy] as Jim.

Lesson 11

1 Choose the right answers.

1 Do you think maths is _______ than foreign languages?
A. as difficult as B. more difficult C. most difficult
2 The elephant is much _______ than the panda.
A. as strong as B. strongest C. stronger
3 Are the flowers on the right _______ than the ones on the left?
A. as beautiful as B. more beautiful C. most beautiful
4 I think maths is not _______ P.E.
A. so easy as B. less easy C. easier
5 Is Lucy _______ than Lily in her work?
A. as careful as B. more careful C. not as careful as
6 "She'll be _______ usual after the small operation," said the doctor.
A. healthier B. healthiest C. as healthy as

2 Practise the dialogue and then make new ones, using the words in the box. Write one of the new dialogues in your exercise books.

A: Which do you prefer, *chicken* or *fish*?
B: I prefer *fish* to *chicken*. I think *fish* is more delicious than *chicken*.
A: I don't agree with you. I prefer *chicken* to *fish*. *Chicken* is more delicious.

beef	pork
tomatoes	potatoes
meat	vegetables
apples	oranges

***3 Fill in the blanks and practise the dialogue.**

A: Do you think a foreign language is _______ interesting as art?
B: Yes, but it is _______ important and _______ useful than art.
C: No. I really can't _______ with you. I prefer _______. A foreign language is not so interesting _______ art. And it's _______ difficult than art.
D: I agree _______ you. For example, English is much _______ difficult than art. Art is _______ popular than a foreign language, I think.
B: Yes, art is very popular. But I don't think art is _______ useful than a foreign language. More and more foreign visitors come to China and more and more Chinese go to _______ countries. People have to talk to each other in _______ languages. So foreign languages are _______ important.
A: I think a foreign _______ is _______ useful as art. Both are important and interesting and both are difficult. We must work hard and learn them well.

Lesson 12

1 Listen to the tape and complete the form below.

Name	Likes best	Likes	Doesn't like at all
Lucy			
Wei Hua			
Han Meimei			

2 Read these long sentences.

He 'stopped to 'get the 'stick | and of 'course 'fell be`hind.
'Well 'done, | ´everyone, | and con,gratu'lations to the `winners.
I was 'very 'glad | when the 'boys 'won the 'relay race.
'Which is 'more `difficult, | ´science or `English?

3 Make up dialogues using the words in the box.

tiger
elephant
monkey
dog
cat
panda

1 **A**: Which animal is quicker, the *monkey* or the *elephant*?
B: I think the ....
2 **A**: Which animal is the most dangerous?
B: I think the ....
3 **A**: Is the *dog* as clever as the *cat* ?
B: I think ....

4 Complete and practise the dialogue.

PETER : Which do you prefer, art _____ music?
MARY : I _____ music to art. I think music is more interesting _______ art.
PETER : No, I really can't agree _______ you. Art is_____ interesting and important than music. You can see nice art everywhere. I prefer art _______ music.
MARY : No. Music is _______ more popular. We can hear it every day.
PETER : But I'm sorry to say you sing badly. Nobody likes to listen _____ you when you sing.
MARY : But you draw badly. Nobody enjoys your pictures.
MUM : Oh, my dear children, stop talking like that, please. Art is as popular _____ music. They are both important. They make our life _____ interesting.

Unit 4 Lesson 13

1 Look at the pictures. Ask and answer the questions in pairs.

What was *Kate* / were *Meimei and Lily* doing yesterday afternoon?

She was flying a kite. Meimei and Lily .... Uncle Wang ....

2 Fill in the blanks and practise the dialogue.

MR WU: What are you doing, Xiao Mao?
XIAO MAO: I'm drawing a panda ______ the wall ______ some chalk.
MR WU: Mmm, it's quite a nice ______. But please don't play ______ the ______, and don't ______ on the wall.

3 Ask and answer questions about your classmates.

Model: What was he / she doing when the teacher came in?
What were they doing when Mr / Miss ... came in?

4 Write down the -s / -es, -ing and past forms of these verbs.

fly	find	forget	get	draw	give
hold	hit	keep	hurt	know	use
cry	put	wear	bring	ring	move

***5 Ask three of your friends the question and write down long answers in the form.**

Name	What were you doing when your father came back yesterday evening?
Li Lei	I was tidying my room when my father came back yesterday evening.

Lesson 14

1 Read the story on page 14 of the Students' Book. Answer these questions.

1 Where did the man live? Why did he like to live there?
2 What did the man upstairs always do when he came home every night?
3 What was the man downstairs trying to do at this time?
4 Was he happy when he heard the noise? Why?
5 What did he ask the man upstairs not to do?
6 Why did he ask the man upstairs not to drop his shoes again?
7 What did the man upstairs say to him?
8 Did the man upstairs remember his comrade downstairs at first the next evening? What did he do with his first shoe?
9 What did he do with his second shoe? Why didn't he throw his second shoe?
10 What did he do after that?
11 Was the man downstairs happy because the man upstairs didn't throw his second shoe? Why not?

2 Complete the short passage and retell it.

The story happened in a ______ building in Moscow. A man lived downstairs. He found it ________ to ________, because the man upstairs _______ ______ his shoes and threw them ______ the floor every night when the man ________ was ______ to sleep. The _______ woke him up and ______ him rather angry. One night, the man went upstairs and told the man above him ________ the problem. The man upstairs said: "I'm sorry, _________. I won't do it again." The next evening the man upstairs ______ one shoe on the floor before he ______ the man downstairs. Then he put his other shoe _______ under his bed. The poor man downstairs could not get to ______ . He kept _______ for the sound of the second ______ .

3 Fill in each blank with the right verb form.

Liu Ying and her friends _______ ______ (play) games upstairs last Sunday morning. A man downstairs came up and _______ (knock) at the door. He said: "I'm sorry to ______ (trouble) you, but I _______ (work) at night, so I must get to ______ (sleep) in the daytime. If you _____ (make) a lot of noise, I can't ______ (sleep) at all. Would you please _______ (keep) quiet?" Liu Ying _____ (say) sorry to the man. After that they _____ (go) out of the building.

Lesson 15

1 Look at the picture on page 15. Ask and answer these questions. Write down the answers.

1 What was the man (in the building) doing?
....

2 What was the man (by the lake) doing?
....

3 What was the man (in the park) doing?
....

4 What were the girls doing? What were the boys doing?
....

5 What were the children doing?
....

6 What were the women doing?
....

2 Complete and practise the dialogue.

MOTHER: What ______ you doing ______ noon today?

JIM: I ____ mending my bike in the garden.

MOTHER: What ______ Kate doing _____ that time?

JIM: She ______ drawing some animals for the art lesson. It was a nice picture.

MOTHER: Can you show me the picture?

JIM: Of _______. Kate, bring your picture here please! Mum wants to have a look.

KATE: OK! But it's upstairs. Let me go and get it. Wait a moment, please.

3 Fill in the blanks with *a, an* or *the* where necessary.

1 Do you remember _______ name of _______ cinema?

2 They waited for the bus for ______ quarter of _______ hour. Then _______ queue jumper came and stood in ______ front of them.

3 ______ elephant is much heavier than ______ tiger.

4 Yesterday evening Mingming was reading ______ story. ______ story was very interesting. He laughed from ______ beginning to ______ end.

5 **A**: Where shall I put _______ box?

B: You'd better put it under _______ bed.

6 "What ______ fine weather!" ______ tallest boy said.

7 **A**: Which would you like, ______ orange or ______ apple or ______ banana?

B: Thank you. But I never eat before I go to ______ bed.

Lesson 16

1 A policeman is asking three people some questions. Listen carefully, and write down their answers in the form below.

Question	What was he / she doing at eight o'clock last night?
Mr Green	He was ....
Mrs Black	
Mr Brown	

2 **Read these long sentences.** (| means a little pause.)

Do you 'think | that 'art is as 'interesting as ´music?

I 'think | Chi´nese is 'more ´popular | than 'any 'other `subject.

A 'man 'lived in a 'tall ´building | in the 'city of `Moscow.

The 'next ´evening | the 'man 'upstairs 'came 'home from `work | 'late as `usual.

3 Fill in the blanks with the right verb forms.

1 Father ______ still ______ (sleep) when I ______ (get) up yesterday morning.
2 Grandma ______ ______ (cook) breakfast when I ______ ______ (wash) my face this morning.
3 I ______ ______ (eat) bread and porridge when mother ______ (leave) home.
4 Many of my classmates ______ ______ (read) English when I ______ (go) into the classroom.
5 We ______ ______ (do) our homework when the headmaster ______ (come) in.
6 Some students from Class 4 ______ ______ (do) sports when I ______ (see) them on the playground.
7 The students on duty ______ ______ (sweep) the floor when I ______ (walk) out of the classroom.
8 Grandpa ______ ______ (mend) his clock when I ______ (reach) home.
9 The young man ______ ______ (fish) when the boy ______ ______ (read) a book under the tree.

***4 Retell the story in Lesson 14 of the Students' Book.**

Begin: The story happened in a tall building in Moscow. The man downstairs found it difficult to get to sleep ....

Unit 5 Lesson 17

1 Look at the picture on page 15 of the Students' Book and answer the questions after the model. Write down your answers in your exercise books.

Model: Were the children playing football in the park?
Yes, they were. / No, they weren't. They were flying kites in the park.

1 Was the man selling pears in the park?
2 Were the boys playing basketball?
3 Was the man watching TV in the building?
4 Was the man fishing by the lake?
5 Were the girls swimming in the lake?
6 Were the girls boating in the lake?
7 Were the women sweeping the ground in the park?
8 Were the women reading newspapers under a tall tree?

2 Ask two of your classmates the following questions, and then write down their answers.

1

Name	What were you doing last Sunday afternoon?

2

Name	What was your mother doing at that time?

3 Make sentences using the Past Continuous Tense.

1 We *were having* a P.E. lesson at a quarter to three yesterday afternoon.
2 Uncle Li ________ at ten o'clock yesterday morning. (have a meeting)
3 Miss White ______ ______ at noon last Sunday. (wash clothes)
4 Mrs King ______ ______ at this time yesterday. (go shopping)
5 The twin brothers ______ ______ on Monday evening. (study Chinese)
6 The Reads ______ ______ last night. (watch TV)

Lesson 18

1 Read the passage on page 18 of the Students' Book and answer the questions.

1 What were the children doing at the time of the accident?
2 What happened suddenly?
3 What did they hear when they were running to move the bag of rice?
4 Was the man on the motorbike travelling fast?
5 What happened then?
6 Was he badly hurt?
7 Whose room did the two boys carry the man to?
8 What did the gate keeper ask the children not to do?
9 Where did Li Lei find Miss Zhao?
10 What was she doing when Li Lei told her about the accident?
11 What did she get as quickly as she could?
12 What did Miss Zhao want to do?

2 Complete the story and then retell it.

The children ______ ______ school when they saw a truck. Suddenly ______ _____ _____ rice fell off the _____ . It landed ______ ______ ______ the road. A man on ______ ______ ______ ______ too fast. His motorbike ______ the bag, and the man ______ ______ . Two boys ______ the man to ______ ______ ______ ______ room and the girls went ______ ______ corner to stop _____ ______. The gate keeper and Lin Tao ______ ______ the bag. Then Li Lei ______ into the school and told Miss Zhao about ______ ______. With a ______ ______ under her arm Miss Zhao ______ off to look ______ the man. At the same time Li Lei ______ the police.

3 Rewrite these sentences after the model in your exercise books.

Model: Kate *went* to bed *at* nine o'clock *after* her mother came back.
Kate *didn't go* to bed *until* nine o'clock.
Kate *didn't go* to bed *until* her mother came back.

1 The children *left* school at five *after* they finished their homework.
2 The man on the motorbike *went* home *when* he felt better.
3 The girls *let* the traffic go again *at* twelve o'clock *after* the boys moved away the bag.
4 The policemen *knew* about the accident half an hour later *when* Li Lei telephoned them.

***4 Make four sentences using *not ... until*.**

Lesson 19

1 Listen to the tape and write down what they were doing last Sunday evening in the form below.

Kate	She
Jim	
Jim's parents	

2 Answer the policemen's questions. Write them in your exercise books.

1 Did you see the accident?
2 What happened to the man?
3 When did you see the accident?
4 Was the man travelling fast?
5 Where did the accident happen?
6 Where did the bag come from?
7 Did anyone else see the accident?

3 Practise the dialogues.

A: What were you doing while
- the farmers were picking apples?
- your mother was cooking?
- he was mending the TV set?

B: I was
- lifting the baskets on to the truck.
- washing my clothes.
- drawing horses.

4 Complete and practise the dialogue.

A: Did you see the ________ at noon yesterday?
B: Yes. I was travelling past the corner near the school when the accident ________.
A: It was really dangerous. The motorbike ________ came and hit the bag in the middle of the road.
B: ________, the man wasn't hurt badly. Some children carried him into a room ________ quickly ________ possible.
A: Miss Zhao brought some ________ and looked ________ the man. The policemen hurried there a moment later. By the ________, do you know the man on the motorbike?
B: Yes, I know him very well.
A: Who was the man?
B: It's me.

Lesson 20

1 Ask two of your classmates these questions and then fill in the forms.

Name	1 What were you doing while the TV was giving the weather report at half past seven yesterday?

Name	2 What were you doing when the bell rang at the beginning of this class?

Name	3 Were you doing your homework while your mother / father was cooking supper yesterday?	4 Were you watching TV when your father came home yesterday?

2 Read and learn the word stress.

□□ 'sunshine 'playground 'bedroom 'weekday
'bookshop 'football 'classroom 'birthday

□□□ 'basketball 'volleyball 'waiting-room 'holiday
'motorbike 'Englishman

3 Fill in the blanks with *corner, standing, accident, careful, happening, travelling, while, hurt, dangerous*, *badly* or *sorry*.

A: Look! A lot of people are ______ round the truck. What is ______ ?
B: Maybe it's an ________. Is anybody ______ ?
C: Yes. A man on the bike was ________ too fast ______ the truck was stopping round the _____. The bike hit the truck and the man got ____ hurt.
A: Oh, poor man! I'm very ________ to hear that.
B: It's ________ to travel too fast in the street. We must be _______.

Unit 6 Lesson 21

1 Look at the pictures and ask your friends the following question. Then write down their answers in your exercise books.

Have you or your family got any of these?
Yes, I / we have got a radio. No, I / we haven't got a TV set.

2 Say and write the following sentences in another way.

Model: I have a ruler. → I have got a ruler.
Do you have any colour pens? → Have you got any colour pens?
I don't have an eraser. → I haven't got an eraser.

1 Do you have any pork here?
2 We have beef and potatoes.
3 They don't have any fish.
4 I have only a little meat.
5 The farmers have several trucks.
6 I don't have enough fruit for so many people.

3 Read and learn these verb forms.

get → got → got　see → saw → seen　give → gave → given
lose → lost → lost　find → found → found　have → had → had

***4 Fill in the blanks with the right verb forms.**

1 **A**: Hello! Have you _____ (see) my pen? I can't _____ (find) it.
B: I'm afraid I haven't.
2 **A**: Excuse me. Have you ______ (see) my dictionary? I _____ (put) it on the shelf a moment ago.
B: Oh, yes, I have. I'm sorry I forgot to ______ (give) it back to you.
3 **A**: Bruce, I've ______(lose) my cup. Have you ______ (see) it anywhere?
B: Look! It's over there. I ______ (see) you put it there.
4 **A**: Have you ______ (find) your knife yet?
B: Not yet.

Lesson 22

1 Read the story on page 22 of the Students' Book and answer the questions.

1 Who works in the school library?
2 How does Miss Yang work? Why?
3 She's very strict, isn't she? Why do you think so?
4 What did Han Meimei say to Miss Yang one day?
5 What was the name of Meimei's library book?
6 Did Meimei have to pay for it if she couldn't find it?

2 Read and learn these verb forms.

look → looked → looked
finish → finished → finished
borrow → borrowed → borrowed
return → returned → returned
turn → turned → turned
stay → stayed → stayed
cry → cried → cried
study → studied → studied
pay → paid → paid
buy → bought → bought
bring → brought → brought
come → came → come
go → went → gone [gɔn]
do → did → done[dʌn]
forget → forgot → forgotten [fə'gɔtn]
write → wrote → written ['ritn]

3 Fill in the blanks with the right verb forms. Then practise these dialogues.

1 **A**: Are you sure you _____ _____ (lose) your dictionary?
B: Yes. I _____ _____ (look) for it everywhere, but I still can't find it.
2 **A**: John, _____ you _____ (return) my ladder yet?
B: Not yet. Don't worry! I _____ _____ (return) it soon.
3 **A**: Jim, _____ you _____ (write) a letter to your aunt?
B: Yes, I _____. I _____ (write) one last week.
4 **A**: _____ you _____ (finish) your homework, Lucy?
B: Not yet, Mum. I _____ _____ (do) my homework right now.
5 **A**: I'm sorry I _____ _____ (forget) to bring you the photos.
B: What a pity! I wanted to show them to the comrades here.

4 Fill in the blanks with *at, like, for, after, over, with* or *around*.

1 The doctor looked _____ the baby, and then said to the woman: "Don't worry. There is nothing much wrong _____ your baby."
2 Jo's younger brother was ill. Jo was looking _____ him yesterday morning.
3 "You must look _____ before you cross the street," mother told her.
4 "What are you doing?" the policeman asked.
"I'm looking _____ my cat," the old woman answered and showed him a photo. He looked _____ the photo. It was a beautiful cat. It looked _____ a tiger.

Lesson 23

1 Complete the questions on "The Lost Book" in pairs. Then ask and answer them.

1 Who _____ (come) into the library while Miss Yang and Meimei were talking?
2 What _____ Lucy _____ (give) Miss Yang?
3 Whose library book _____ it?
4 What _____ Miss Yang _____ (say) to Meimei?

2 Fill in the blanks with verbs in their proper forms.

Miss Yang works in the library of No. 14 Middle School. She _____ very helpful and _____ after the books very carefully. She _____ very strict. Everybody must _____ the books on time.

One day Meimei _____ to the library. She said she _____ not find her library book "Red Star Over China". Miss Yang _____ her to pay for it. At that moment, Lucy _____ and showed a book to Miss Yang. It _____ Meimei's library book! Meimei _____ very pleased. She _____ Lucy. Miss Yang _____ Meimei to be more careful from then on.

3 Ask and answer the questions in pairs. Write down any four of them.

Have you ever Have they ever	studied Russian? spoken to an Englishman? visited a hospital? travelled by air? mended a bike? worn a raincoat? written a book? read an English book?	Yes, I have. Yes, we have. Several times. Yes, they have. Quite often. No, never.

4 Complete and practise the dialogues.

A: Have you	returned the book yet? borrowed an English dictionary? read today's newspaper?

B: Yes, I have. I've just	____________ it. ____________ it. ____________ it.

Lesson 24

1 Listen to the tape and write down the students' favourite kinds of books in the form below.

Name	Kinds of books
Jim	
Li Lei	
Wei Hua	
Han Meimei	

2 Read and learn the word stress.

'news,paper
'book,seller
'grand,parents

,loud'speaker
,head'teacher
,kind'hearted

'kilo,metre
'tele,vision

,pio'neer
,under'stand
,Japa'nese

,ope'ration

con,gratu'lation

3 Ask questions about Bruce. Write down the questions in your exercise books.

Model: I've never visited the Great Wall. →
Has Bruce ever visited the Great Wall? No, he hasn't.

I've seen the Yellow River.
I've never tried to skate.
I've read a few picture-books in Chinese.
I've studied French for three years.
I've never travelled on a train.

4 Ask and answer questions in pairs after the model.

Model: **A:** Have you returned the book?
B: Yes, I have.
A: When did you return it?
B: I returned it last Monday.

Unit 7 Lesson 25

1 Make as many dialogues as possible.

A: Was it [raining / blowing / snowing] when you [got home? / woke up? / left school?]

B: Yes, it was still [raining heavily. / blowing hard. / snowing, but not heavily.]

2 Write down the different forms of adverbs.

Models: well → better → best　　badly → worse → worst
politely → more politely → most politely

late　　early　　hard　　far　　fast

slowly　　quickly　　happily　　carefully　　suddenly

3 Fill in each blank with the right form of the adjective in the brackets.

1 **A**: Maths is as ________ as English, I think.
B: I don't think so. English is ________ ________ than maths. (interesting)

2 **A**: Which is the ________ ________ subject in the school?
B: I think English is. (difficult)

3 **A**: I think science is ________ ________ than foreign languages.
B: I think they are both ________. (important)

4 **A**: Which is ________ ________, music or art?
B: I think both of them are ________. (useful)

5 **A**: Do you think Chinese is ________ than English?
B: I think so, but Jim doesn't. (easy)

6 **A**: Is Russian as ________ as Japanese?
B: I've no idea. Maybe Russian is not so ________ as Japanese. (popular)

7 **A**: Is P.E. the ________ ________ subject at school?
B: Most of us think it is. A few of us don't. (popular)

8 **A**: Which subject is the ________ ________ of all?
B: I think Chinese is. (important)

***4 Which school subject do you think is the most important. Write down your reasons in your exercise books.**

Lesson 26

1 Read the story "Miss Forgetful" quickly and choose the right answers.

1 Mrs King asked __________ to do shopping for her.
A. Lily B. Lucy C. Mr King
2 The girl bought ____________ on the shopping list.
A. most of the things B. some of the things C. all of the things
3 The shopkeeper kept the things __________.
A. on a table B. in a bag C. on a shelf
4 Miss Forgetful dropped a bag of _______ on the floor.
A. sweets B. salt C. sugar
5 Lucy spent __________ the money.
A. some of B. all C. most of

2 Read the story again more carefully and answer these questions. Write down the answers in your exercise books.

1 What did Mrs King give Lucy before she went shopping?
2 Why did the girl have to run home?
3 What did her mother tell her to take?
4 Did Lucy get everything at last?
5 What happened when she was taking the things out of the basket?
6 Do you sometimes help your parents do shopping? Are you more careful than Lucy?

3 Make dialogues.

A: Please	turn on the TV. tell Mary to come. close the windows. turn off the lights. go and help your mother.

B: I think	Bill /he /she has already	turned it on. told her. closed them. turned them off. finished cooking.

***4 Fill in the blanks with *something, everything, anything, anywhere* or *everywhere*.**

1 Has Lucy forgotten _________? No, she hasn't forgotten _________.

2 I have looked for my handbag ___________, but I can't find it.

3 Have you seen my handbag ___________? I've put ___________ in it.

4 Have you got ___________ to eat? Yes, I've got ___________ nice for you.

Lesson 27

1 Fill in each blank with *yet, just, ever, never* or *already*.

1 Have you finished your work ____________?
2 I've had my breakfast ________________.
3 Has Miss Yang ______________ worked in the Beijing Library?
4 The bus has ____________ left. You have to wait for the next.
5 I know nothing about the film because I have ___________ seen it.

2 Look at the pictures and retell the story about Miss Forgetful.

3 Write down the different verb forms.

Model: break → broke → broken

build spend pay lie take try feel grow

smell win choose give think find buy

***4 Complete and practise the dialogue, then copy it.**

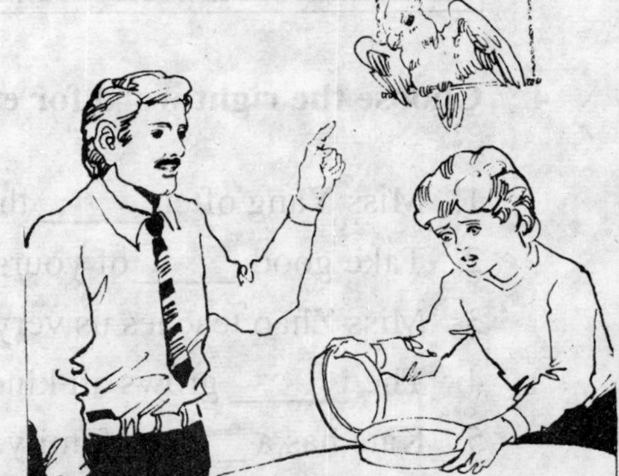

A: Dad, I've just __________ a volleyball game. I'm so tired and hungry. Have you __________ anything to eat?
B: Supper's not ready. But you may have some chocolate.
A: Oh, dear. The box is empty. Who has __________ all the chocolate?
B: Go and ask Polly!

Lesson 28

1 Listen to the tape carefully, and complete the form below.

Place	Weather	Temperature
Beijing	It was	
Shanghai		
Harbin		
Nanning		
Fuzhou		

2 Read and learn the word stress.

□□□ con'ductor Sep'tember Oc'tober No'vember
De'cember Au'stralia Ca'nadian po'tato
for'getful de'licious im'portant un'happy
al'ready re'member a'nother e'xample

3 Make up compound words and put them into Chinese.

1	2
pencil-	shine
day-	day
north	ball
sun	friend
basket	work
week	time
pen	box
house	west

1	2
post	man
police	board
birth	seller
class	bag
grand	parent
black	day
book	mate
hand	card

4 Choose the right word for each blank.

1 Miss Yang often ______ the students. She is very ______. (helps, helpful)

2 Take good ______ of yourself. Be ______. Don't catch cold. (care, careful)

3 Miss Zhao teaches us very ______. She is a ______ teacher. (good, well)

4 The ______ grows all kinds of vegetables on his ______. (farm, farmer)

5 Kate has a ______ family. She lives ______ with her parents. (happily, happy)

Unit 8 Lesson 29

1 Practise the dialogue. The answers should be true.

A newsman (记者) has come to visit your school. He's now talking with your headteacher.

N: When did you build this school?
H: We built it ______________.
N: How many buildings did you have at that time?
H: Let me see. We had ______________.
N: How many have you got now?
H: ______________.
N: How many students and teachers have you got?
H: ______________.
N: Have you got a school farm or a factory?
H: ______________.
N: You have got a school library, haven't you?
H: ______________.
N: How many books have you got in the library?
H: ______________.

2 Ask and answer in pairs. Write two dialogues in your exercise books.

Have you ever been to	Xinjiang? Hainan? Taiwan? Xi'an? Beijing? Tianjin?	Has Jim / Ann ever been to	England? the USA? France? Canada? Australia? Japan?

***3 Make up dialogues using the words in the box.**

A: Have you ever been to the zoo?
B: No. I've never been there before.
Have they got many animals there?
A: Yes. It's quite a big zoo.
B: How many kinds of animals have they got?
A: More than 70. They've got *large elephants and a baby elephant.*
B: Really? I've never seen a young elephant before.
I'd like to go and have a look.

tigers
sheep
pandas
monkeys
horses
cows
birds
lions (狮子)

Lesson 30

1 Read the short play on page 30 of the Students' Book. Answer right or wrong.

	Right	Wrong
1 The farmer had to borrow a pan because he couldn't find his.	/ /	/ /
2 He returned the pan very soon.	/ /	/ /
3 The woman only took the big pan.	/ /	/ /
4 The farmer came to borrow the woman's pan again.	/ /	/ /
5 The farmer used the pan for one week.	/ /	/ /
6 The farmer was joking when he said the pan was dead.	/ /	/ /

2 Read the play more carefully and answer these questions. Write down the answers in your exercise books.

1 What did the farmer borrow from the woman?
2 Did he return the pan to the woman?
3 How many pans did he give the woman?
4 What did he say about the small pan?
5 Did the woman take the small pan?
6 Why did the farmer come to borrow the woman's pan again?
7 How long did the farmer use the pan?
8 Did the woman go to get the pan herself?
9 Did the man let the woman have her pan back?
10 Why did he say "The pan is dead"?

3 Fill in the blanks with *borrow* or *lend* in their right forms.

LUCY: Hi! I'm sorry to trouble you. Could you ______ me your bike?

MEIMEI: Certainly I can ______ it to you. But Li Lin ______ just ______ it from me. He'll come back in five minutes. You can ______ it when he comes back.

4 Choose the right answer.

1 **A**: Is the old woman still alive?
B: I'm sorry she's ______ (died, dying, dead). She ______ (died, has died, dead) one week ago.

2 **A**: Comrade Lei Feng is ______ (die, dead), but he always lives in our hearts (心脏).
B: When did he ___ (die, dead)?
A: In 1963.

Lesson 31

1 Ask and answer in pairs. Write one of the dialogues in your exercise books.

1

A: Have you ever *travelled on a train*?
B: Yes, I have.
A: How many times have you *done that?*
B: Only once. / Twice. / Several times. / Many times. / Sorry, I don't know.

2

A: Has Wei Hua *come* yet?
B: Yes. She has *come* already.
A: When did she *come*?
B: She *came* here a moment ago.

cooked a meal	
cried	
made a dress	
made dumplings	
moved your house	
broken a cup	
arrived	gone
finished	left
started	sung
spoken	tried

2 Fill in the blanks with the proper words.

One day a farmer______ (arrive) at a woman's house. He ______ (borrow) a pan from her. Very soon he ______ (return) it to her. He ______ (give) her another small one and ______ (say) it was a baby. The woman was pleased and ______ (take) it.

A few days later the farmer ______ (have) visitors. He______ (ask) the woman to lend him the pan again. He __________ (not return) it until the woman ______ (come) to ask for it. He played a joke with her and _______ (say) the pan ______ (die). But of course, he______ (give) it back to her at last.

3 Look at the pictures and retell the story of "Borrowing a pan". Then write out this story in your exercise book.

Lesson 32

1 James Teller has got several kinds of animals on his farm. Listen to the tape and write the answers in the form.

Kinds of animals	Number

2 Listen and read these words.

[tw-] **tw**in **tw**elve **tw**enty **tw**ice

[kw-] **qu**estion **qu**ite **qu**een **qu**iet **qu**arter **qu**ick

[sw-] **sw**eet **sw**eater **sw**im **sw**eep

[gr-] **gr**ow **gr**een **gr**and **gr**eat

3 Complete the dialogue with the sentences in the box.

(*Lin Tao arrives at the school library.*)

LIN TAO: Excuse me. Have you got the book "Clouds of War (战争风云)"?

MISS YANG: ____________

LIN TAO: Oh sorry! It should be "Winds of War".

MISS YANG: ____________

LIN TAO: Thanks very much.

MISS YANG: ____________

LIN TAO: I'll try to finish it as soon as I can.

MISS YANG: ____________

1 I see. Yes, there's still one on the shelf. Here you are.

2 "Clouds of War"? I've never heard of it.

3 No hurry. You may keep it for two weeks.

4 You're welcome.

***4 Fill in the blanks with the right verb forms.**

A: I'm not feeling well. I ________ (get) a cold.
B: ______ you ______ (be) to the hospital yet?
A: Yes, I ______ (go) to see Doctor Li this morning and he ______ (give) me some medicine.
B: ______ you ______ (take) the medicine?
A: Yes, I ______ (take) it just a moment ago.
B: Mr Li is a good doctor. I think you'll ______ (be) all right soon.

Unit 9 Lesson 33

1 Ask and answer questions about these people.

Model: Bruno went to Paris two years ago. →
How long has Bruno been in Paris?
He's been there for two years.

1 James went to Toronto three years ago.
2 The Turners came to Zhengzhou four months ago.
3 Bruce came to No. 14 Middle School a year ago.
4 The Shute family moved to the southern part of the USA the year before last.

2 Talk about your friends or your family members.

How long	have you has your teacher have your parents has your uncle has your aunt	been	in this city? at this school? in this town? at that village? in that hospital?

I've He / She's They've	been	here / there	since 1990. since 1984. since 1949. for 6 years. for 5 months.

3 Make up similar dialogues with the words in the box. Write one in your exercise books.

A: Our *Maths* teacher has been here *for just over two years.*
B: That means he started to teach here in 19_ _.
A: Yes, I think so.

English	Chinese
art	P.E.
for only one year	
since three years ago	
for over ten years	

***4 Learn these words with the help of a dictionary.**

something
someone
somebody
somewhere
anything
anyone
anybody
anywhere
everything
everyone
everybody
everywhere

Lesson 34

1 Read the story on page 34 of the Students' Book. Answer these questions. Write the answers in your exercise books.

1 When did Uncle Wang's factory open?
2 How long has Uncle Wang worked in the factory?
3 Is the factory far from No. 14 Middle School?
4 What do the students often do there?
5 What did Uncle Wang say to the Class 3 students when they came to visit the factory one morning?
6 What does the factory make?
7 Which workshop (车间) did the students go to first?
8 Why didn't Uncle Wang let them touch the machines?
9 What do the machines do?

2 Fill in the blanks with *Don't rush / crowd / worry, Take care, Be quiet, Please hurry* or *Be careful.*

1 This is a difficult problem. Think carefully. ___________!
2 ___________! You shouldn't make any noise in the reading room.
3 Get on the bus one by one. ___________!
4 It's getting late. ___________ or we can't catch the train.
5 It's getting colder. Put on your coat. ___________ of yourself.
6 ___________! If you can't say it in English, speak Chinese.
7 The road is rather narrow. ___________ when you are driving.

3 Ask your teacher these questions and write down the answers in your exercise books.

1 How long has this school been open?
2 How long have you taught in this school?
3 Where do you live?
4 How long have you lived there?

4 Fill in the blanks with *back, in, off, on, with* or *up.*

1 The twins have been in China for three years. They get on quite well _______ their Chinese friends.
2 Li Lei helped the old woman get _______ the bus and said, "Don't get _______ until the bus stops at the end of the road."
3 Mary got _______ too late to have breakfast. She felt hungry at school.
4 Mr White stopped at a food shop, went _______ and bought two kilos of eggs.
5 Kate passed the message on to Jim as soon as he got _______.

Lesson 35

1 Read the second part of the story about Uncle Wang's factory and tick the right answers.

1 Uncle Wang asked the students to keep together. He didn't want them to ___________.
A. get wrong B. get lost C. get away

2 The students saw the workers wearing ___________.
A. warm clothes B. thin clothes C. thick clothes

3 The workers wore glasses over their eyes to ___________.
A. see better B. keep safe C. look nice

4 The workers were making ___________.
A. ladders B. lights C. loudspeakers

2 Put the following sentences in order and retell the story.

1 This factory makes all kinds of useful things.
2 Uncle Wang works in a machine factory near No. 14 Middle School.
3 The workers were wearing thick clothes and glasses to keep themselves safe.
4 They were making ladders.
5 Uncle Wang welcomed them and showed them round the factory.
6 One day last November Class 3, Grade 3 went there.
7 Every year several classes visit the factory.
8 There were lots of machines in the shop.
9 For example, they make bicycle and tractor parts.
10 The students visited No. 1 Machine Shop.
11 They cut metal into small pieces or join pieces of metal together.

3 Ask about your friend's family and write the answers in the form.

Your friend's father	How long has he worked in ...?
...	
...	
...	

A: Where does your ... work?
B: He / She works ....
A: How long has he / she worked there?
B: He's / She's worked there since ... / for only / about / just ... / for ... years already.

4 Write down the four different verb forms.

blow	hit	catch	sell	meet	lend	leave	buy
grow	put	teach	spell	make	lose	tell	bring
throw	hurt	feel	send	mean	pay	run	stand

Lesson 36

1 Listen to the tape and write down the answers to the questions.

Where does Mr Green work?	Where does Mrs Green work?
He ____________________.	She ____________________.
How long has he worked there?	How long has she worked there?
____________________.	____________________.
What work does he do?	What work does she do?
____________________.	____________________.

2 Listen and read these words.

[sp-]	**sp**eak	**sp**ell	**sp**end	**sp**ort	[spr-]	**spr**ing
[st-]	**st**and	**st**art	**st**ay	**st**ill		
[str-]	**str**eet	**str**ict	**str**ong			
[sk-]	**sk**ate	**sk**irt	**sc**ore	**sch**ool		
[sl-]	**sl**eep	**sl**ow	a**sl**eep			
[sm-]	**sm**all	**sm**ell	**sm**ile		[sn-]	**sn**ow
[sw-]	**sw**eep	**sw**eet	**sw**im	**sw**eater		

***3 Ask and answer questions about the person in each picture.**

Model: A: When did *Uncle Wang* come to this *factory*?

B: He came in ________.

A: How long has he been a *worker* here?

B: About *2 years.*

Unit 10 Lesson 37

1 Choose the right sentences from the box for each blank in the dialogue.

A: Hello! May I speak to Miss Zhao?
B: ____________. (*A moment later*) I am sorry, ____________. Could I take a message?
A: Certainly, ____________. I want to speak to her about my son Bill Smith. ____________. I'm afraid he isn't able to go to school today.
B: ____________. I hope he'll be all right very soon.
A: ____________. Could I leave my telephone number for you?
B: OK. ____________. I'll go and get a pen and a piece of paper. OK! Please give me your phone number.
A: **3579860**. That's my office telephone number. My name is Allan Smith.
B: All right. I'll leave the message on her desk. I'll tell her to call you back.
A: ____________. Thank you very much. Goodbye!
B: Goodbye!

1 that's very kind of you.	5 That'll be fine.
2 **she** isn't here right now.	6 He has a bad cold today.
3 I'm sorry to hear that.	7 Thank you!
4 Hold on for a moment, please!	8 Wait a moment, please!

2 Ask questions in pairs and write them down in your exercise books.

Model: A: What does Polly say?
B: Polly says that *she wants to have an apple.*

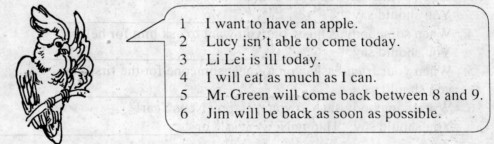

1 I want to have an apple.
2 Lucy isn't able to come today.
3 Li Lei is ill today.
4 I will eat as much as I can.
5 Mr Green will come back between 8 and 9.
6 Jim will be back as soon as possible.

***3 Tell one of your friends what the radio says.**

Now the weather report for the next 24 hours. Beijing will be fine with the temperature from 4 to 13. Tokyo will be fine too and cloudy later in the day. The lowest (最低的) temperature is 12 and the highest is 13. Paris will be wet and the temperature is 1 to 8. London will be rainy and windy later in the day. The highest temperature is 8 and the lowest is 4. New York will be sunny and cloudy later in the day. The temperature is 13 to 19.

Model: The radio says that Beijing will be fine with ....

Lesson 38

1 Read the dialogue on page 38 in your Students' Book and answer these questions. Write down your answers.

1. Is Jim doing well in all his lessons?
2. What does the headmaster think of Jim?
3. Jim doesn't work hard enough, does he?
4. Jim is good at Chinese, isn't he?
5. How long have the Greens lived in China?
6. What are they travelling back to England for?
7. How long are they going to stay in London?
8. What is the capital city of England?
9. Can Mr Green help Jim with his Chinese lessons?
10. What is Mr Green's problem? Why is he worried?

2 Choose the right sentences for the blanks.

a I'm sorry to trouble you.	d Not at all.
b No, thanks.	e Glad to meet you!
c I'm sorry to hear that.	f The same to you!

1 When somebody says: "Thank you very much!"
You should say: "__________"
2 When somebody asks you: "Would you like a cup of tea?"
If you don't want it, you should say: "__________"
3 When somebody tells you some sad news.
You should say: "__________"
4 When somebody is busy, but you want to ask him for help,
You should say: "__________"
5 When your friend asks you to meet someone for the first time,
you should say: "__________"
6 When somebody says to you: "Happy New Year!"
You should say: "Happy New Year!" or "__________"

3 Fill in the blanks with the words in the box.

weak
lazy
except
exam
missed
fell behind

Tom is a clever boy, but he is ______. He doesn't work very hard. His teacher says that he is very ______ in Chinese. Last week he ______ a lot of lessons, so he ______ other students in all the lessons ______ English. He also did very badly in the Chinese ______. Everyone knows that if he works harder, he'll do much better.

Lesson 39

1 Which is the closest in meaning to the underlined part?

1 Mr Green is afraid that Jim'll forget his Chinese if he <u>misses</u> so many lessons.
A. forgets B. loses C. gets D. studies

2 Mr Green is afraid that Jim may even <u>fail his Chinese exam.</u>
A. do well in his Chinese exam B. do badly in his Chinese exam
C. take his Chinese exam D. not take his Chinese exam

3 Mr Green thinks that maybe Jim's Chinese teacher will give him some work to do <u>during the holiday.</u>
A. on Sunday B. on the weekend
C. in the holiday D. before holiday

4 The headmaster is sure that Mr Hu <u>won't mind.</u>
A. will agree B. won't ask Jim to do anything
C. won't agree D. won't give Jim any trouble

5 Mr Green will <u>give the headmaster a call.</u>
A. give ... a ring B. call ... out C. call ... on D. give ... a message

2 Dictate what your teacher says. Write them down on the notice board, and then check them with your teacher.

3 According to the dictation, ask and answer questions after the model.

Model: **A:** What does your teacher say to the students?
B: She / He says tomorrow is Sunday, December 22nd.

Lesson 40

1 Write in today's date and time in the right places. Listen to the tape and write down the message in the form.

TELEPHONE MESSAGE

From: .... To: ....

Date: .... Time: ....

Message: ....

....

....

....

2 Listen and read these words.

[-pl]	app**le**	peop**le**		[-bl]	ta**ble**	possi**ble**
[-tl]	lit**tle**	bot**tle**	capi**tal**	[-dl]	can**dle**	mid**dle**
[-sl]	pen**cil**			[-zl]	puz**zle**	

3 Make up similar dialogues with the sentences in the box.

A: He says that *he'll come home* early.
B: I think that *he'll come home* early.
C: I hope that *he'll come home* early.
D: I'm afraid that *he won't come home* early.

1 Lucy is right.
2 he can mend the radio.
3 he has seen the doctor.
4 he will pass the exam.
5 she will be well soon.

***4 Play the game "HOT SEAT".**

One student is in the "HOT SEAT". The rest of you must ask this student questions. He or she must answer them without saying *yes* or *no*. See how long you can last in the "HOT SEAT"!

Model:

A: Your name's Jim, isn't it?
JIM: You're right.
B: Do you come from England?
JIM: I'm afraid you've made a mistake.
C: Do you have a sister?
JIM: Yes.
C: Oh! You said "YES". Please get out of the "HOT SEAT". It's my turn. (*C sits in the "HOT SEAT" and the game goes on.*)

Unit 11 Lesson 41

1 Guess what it is and write its name on each box below.

1 Here is a box with a beautiful glass face. It looks like a TV, but it isn't a TV. It's very clever and can work very fast. It can help you study or work, but you can't watch TV plays on it.

2 This little thing has got numbers from 0 to 9. It has no legs but has an arm and its arm has got a long tail. It can't walk, but it can talk. It likes to sleep. You can lift up its arm and wake it up at anytime. It is pleased to help you talk to your friend far away.

3 There is a long and large house. It can run like a bus on the ground and it can also fly like a bird in the air. It is very strong. It can take several hundred people to any places in the world.

4 Here is an interesting box. It's not very big, but you can find everything in it, for example, people, birds, animals, flowers, tall buildings, even rivers and sea. From the face of the box you can see things and people moving, and you can hear all kinds of sound, too.

5 Here is another box. It's rather tall. It can help to keep your vegetables, fruit and meat for a long time even in hot summer. When you can't finish your food, you should put it into the box for the next meal. If you leave it outside for too long, it'll be bad for your health.

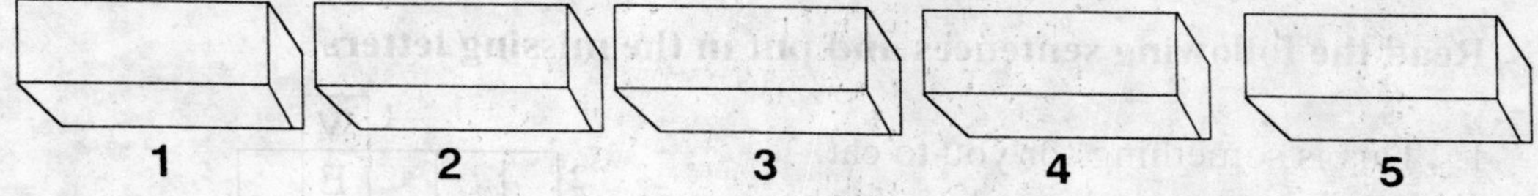

2 Write 5 or 6 sentences about each of the following pictures in your exercise books.

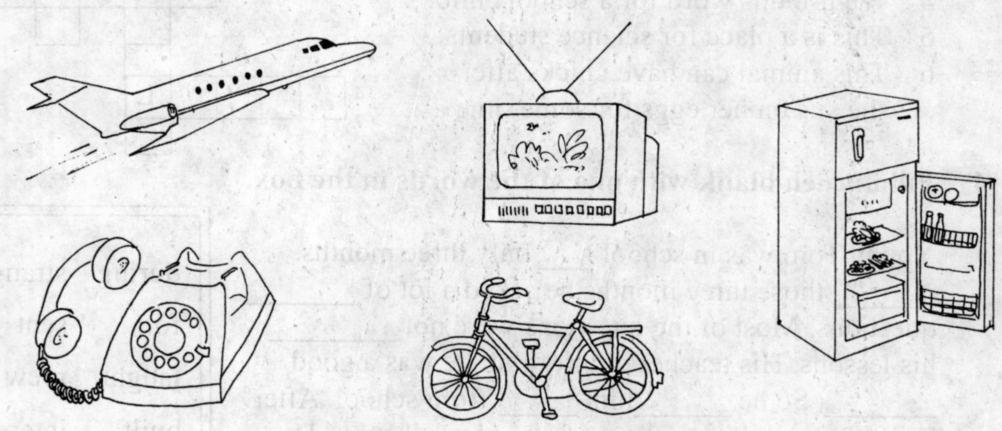

***3 Can you name other inventions? If you can, please make a riddle (谜语) about each of them and ask your classmates to guess what it is.**

Lesson 42

1 Read the story on page 42 of the Students' Book. Answer right or wrong.

		Right	Wrong
1	Thomas Edison was a great American inventor.	/ /	/ /
2	Thomas Edison died at the age of sixty-five.	/ /	/ /
3	When Thomas Edison was young, he always asked a lot of strange questions about his lessons.	/ /	/ /
4	Tom's teacher didn't like him because he didn't study hard.	/ /	/ /
5	Tom's mother took him out of school and she taught him at home.	/ /	/ /
6	Tom became interested in science even before he was ten.	/ /	/ /

2 Read the story again and answer the questions.

1 Why did Tom sit on some eggs one day?
2 How long did Tom stay in school?
3 Why did Tom's teacher ask his mother to take him out of school?
4 Do you think Tom was clever? Why?
5 Who taught him after he left school? Did he learn fast?
6 How did he build his science lab?

3 Read the following sentences and put in the missing letters.

1 This is something for you to eat.
2 You have to use this to buy things.
3 You'll use this word when you think something is unusual.
4 We use this word for a school child.
5 This is a place for science students.
6 This animal can have chicks after she sits on her eggs for some time.

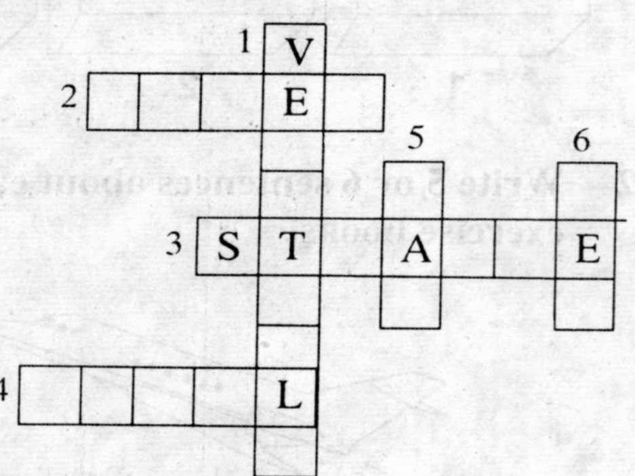

4 Fill in each blank with one of the words in the box.

Young Tom was in school ____ only three months. _______ those three months he asked a lot of ________ questions. Most of the questions were not _________ his lessons. His teacher didn't think he was a good _______. So he _______ him ______ from school. After he left school, his mother ______ him at home. He became very __________ in science. He __________ vegetables and __________ them. With the money he __________ a science lab.

during	strange
for	sent
taught	grew
built	interested
sold	about
pupil	away

Lesson 43

1 Fill in the blanks with proper words, and then retell the story.

Tom was a clever boy. He was always trying out new _______. One day his mother was very ill. She _______ _______ a doctor. When the doctor came, he looked over Tom's mother carefully and said that she needed an operation _______ _______. But it was night, and the _______ in the room was very _______. Tom thought for a moment. Then he had _______ _______. He took _______ _______ lights in the house and _______ _______ on a long table. Then he put a big mirror _______ them. Now the doctor was able to _______ _______. He _______ on her at once. Edison's mother was saved.

2 Make up dialogues in pairs and write them down in your exercise books.

A: Don't you think	B: Yes, I do.
1 he is running too fast?	Tell her to take off her coat.
2 she is making too much noise?	Tell her to keep quiet.
3 his TV is too noisy?	Tell him to eat less.
4 she is driving too slowly?	Tell him to run more slowly.
5 he is drinking too much?	Tell him to drink less.
6 he is eating too much?	Ask him to turn it down.
7 she is wearing too much?	Ask her to drive faster.

***3 Fill in this form about Thomas Edison.**

Family name: .... Given name: ....

Country of birth: .... Year of birth: ....

Year of death: .... Work: ....

Write something about Thomas Edison.

....

....

....

....

Lesson 44

1 Listen to the tape, write in today's date and time in the right places and write down the message in the form.

TELEPHONE MESSAGE

From: .... To: ....

Date: .... Time: ....

Message: ....

....

....

2 Listen and read these words.

[pr-]	present	practise	problem	April	surprise		
[br-]	bread	break	broom	brown	February	library	
[kr-]	cross	cry	secret	Christmas			
[gr-]	great	group	grow	ground	agree	hungry	
[fr-]	France	free	friend	front	fruit	afraid	Friday
[θr-]	three	through	throw				

3 Look at the pictures, and say what Dr. Clarke told you to do.

Model: Picture 1 Dr Clarke told me to have a good rest.

Have a good rest. 1

Drink more water every day. 2

Get up early and do morning exercises. 3

Have a walk after meals. 4

Wear more clothes. 5

Take the medicine three times a day. 6

Unit 12 Lesson 45

1 Read Part 1 on page 45 of the Students' Book and answer the questions.

1 Where's Jim going next week?
2 What's he worried about?
3 What will he do with Polly?
4 Who will help him look after the bird?
5 Does Ling Feng know how to take care of Polly?
6 What has Jim done for Ling Feng?

2 Read Part 2 on page 45 of the Students' Book. Write down what Jim asked Ling Feng to do for Polly.

1 Jim told Ling Feng to ....

2 Jim asked him to ....

3 ....

4 ....

5 ....

6 ....

3 Say what the signs mean.

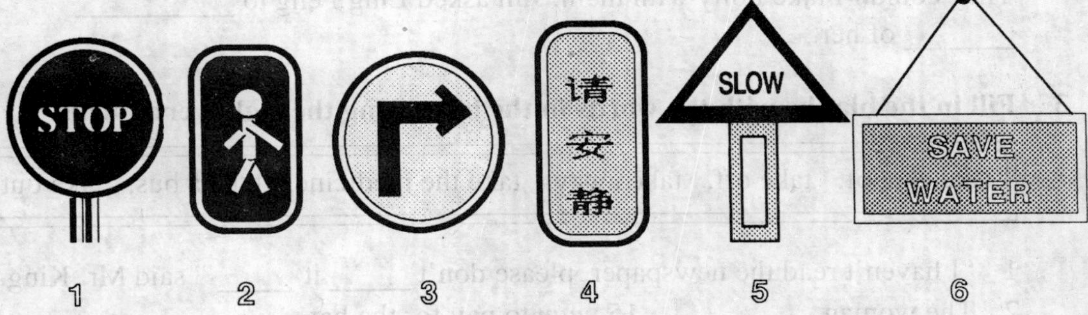

Model: Sign No. 2 tells people to cross the street.

Sign No. 1 tells ....

Sign No. 3 ....

Sign No. 4 ....

Sign No. 5 ....

Sign No. 6 ....

Lesson 46

1 Read the story on page 46 in your Students' Book and answer the questions.

1 Where were the Greens getting ready to fly for their holiday?
2 What were the children doing on Friday evening?
3 Did Mrs Green like or hate travelling? Why?
4 Was she able to sleep well on the plane?
5 Was Polly going to England with them?
6 Where were their air tickets?
7 Who got the money for their journey?
8 How did Jim ask Ling Feng to take care of his bird?
9 What did Mrs Green call Jim's father?

2 Fill in the blanks with proper words from the text.

It was Friday evening. Mr and Mrs Green _______ _______ to go to England _______ their holiday. The children _______ _______ their bags _______ clothes and other things. Mrs Green told her children to _______ their bags_______ hers when they were ready.

Mrs Green was _______ _______ their journey. She _______ travelling by air. She _______ to stay safely in the same place because the seats on the plane were too _______, and the _______ was always too long. She tried to sleep, but she was never _______ _______ sleep very well.

Mr Green told Mrs Green that he had the _______ and _______ in his jacket. They couldn't take Polly with them. Jim asked Ling Feng to _________ _______ of her.

3 Fill in the blanks with the words in the box, using the right verb forms.

take care of, take off, take away, take the medicine, take a bus, take out

1 "I haven't read the newspaper, please don't _____ it _____" said Mr. King.
2 The woman _____ _____ 15 *yuan* to pay for the hat.
3 "The village is quite far from here. I'm afraid you have to _____ _____," the policeman told the man.
4 "Can you _____ _____ _____ my Mimi when I go back to England?" Kate asked Da Mao.
5 "You should _____ _____ _____ three times a day and you'll get better soon," said the doctor.
6 Mrs Green _____ _____ her coat after she came into the room. It was quite warm inside.

Lesson 47

1 Talk about the Green family's flight to London in pairs.

Model: Do you know / Can you tell me	what their flight number is? what time their plane leaves? where they will have to stop? why they will stop in Moscow? when they will arrive in London?

2 Make similar dialogues in pairs.

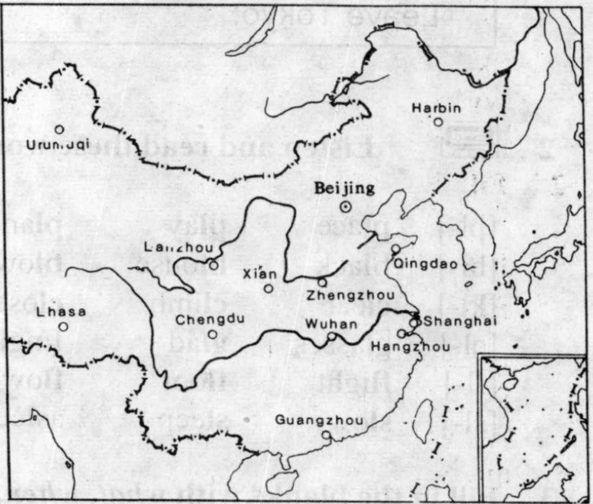

A: Do you know where I want to go for my holiday?
B: Sorry! I don't know.
A: Please guess!
B: I think you'll go to Guangzhou.
A: Why do you think so?
B: Because Guangzhou is in the south. The weather is warm there even in the winter. It's near the sea. And you can enjoy a lot of sea food, too.

***3 Look at the flight time table. Ask and answer questions.**

Flight No.	Departure (离站)	Arrival (到达)	From	To	Stop
CA 907	0745	1130	Beijing	Moscow	\
CA 981	0915	1835	Beijing	New York	Shanghai
CA 147	1555	1015	Beijing	Sydney	Guangzhou
CA 949	1725	0735	Beijing	Paris	Shanghai
CA 937	2125	0810	Beijing	London	Hongkong

		A:	B:
Models:	1	Could you tell me which plane I should take to go to *Paris*?	You should take ....
	2	Could you tell me what time the plane leaves?	It leaves at ....
	3	Do you know what time the plane arrives in *Paris*?	It arrives at ....
	4	Do you know where I'll have to stop on the way?	I think you'll have to stop in ....

Lesson 48

1 Listen to the tape and fill in the form.

Mrs King wants to buy some air tickets to New York. You must write down the date, the flight number, and the leaving and arriving time.

Flight No.:	Date:
Leave Beijing:	Stop in Tokyo:
Leave Tokyo:	Arrive in New York:

2 Listen and read these words.

[pl-]	**pl**ace	**pl**ay	**pl**ane	**pl**ate	**pl**ease	**pl**easure
[bl-]	**bl**ack	**bl**ouse	**bl**ow	**bl**ue	pro**bl**em	
[kl-]	**cl**ear	**cl**imb	**cl**ose	**cl**othes	**cl**oudy	
[gl-]	**gl**asses	**gl**ad	En**gl**ish	En**gl**and		
[fl-]	**fl**ight	**fl**oor	**fl**ower	**fl**y		
[sl-]	**sl**ow	**sl**eep	a**sl**eep	**sl**ept		

3 Fill in the blanks with *what, when, where, which, who, why* and *how*.

1 **A**: Excuse me! Could you tell me ________ the nearest post office is?
B: Certainly! Go down this road and turn right, then you'll find it.

2 **A**: Could you please tell me _____ time the plane to New York leaves?
B: It leaves at 9:15 in the morning.

3 **A**: Do you know _______ I have to give this letter to?
B: To Mr Jenkins.

4 **A**: Mum, do you know _____ gate we have to go through?
B: Gate 9.

5 **A**: Dad, do you know ________ we must leave?
B: Early tomorrow morning.

6 **A**: Could you tell me ______ I can get to the plane, madam?
B: Sorry! I don't know. Please ask the policeman over there.

7 **A**: Do you know ______ I have to take with me?
B: Money, of course!

8 **A**: Can you tell me _______ I will have to change planes?
B: Look at your air ticket and you'll find the answer.

9 **A**: I don't know ________ I shall buy for my daughter.
B: What about the yellow skirt?

10 **A**: Please tell me ______ you didn't come this morning.
B: I got up too late. I was afraid ....

Unit 13 Lesson 49

1 Find the right answer.

1 A: Where's Jim?
B: He ____________ England.
A. has gone to B. has been to C. went to

2 Mr Green ______________ China for three years.
A. has been to B. has come to C. has been in

3 Bruce is young, but he ______________ many foreign countries.
A. has been in B. has been to C. has gone to

4 Ann's grandpa was not in good health. Ann __________ see him last week.
A. has gone to B. has been to C. went to

5 How wonderful the Great Wall is! I __________ a place of interest like that.
A. have never been to B. didn't go to C. have never gone to

2 Choose the right preposition for each blank.

beside	in
except	at
with	on

1 Betty left her office ____ the end of April.
2 Does Mrs Green always travel _____ her husband?
3 Everybody went to visit the factory _____ Liu Ying.
4 The students _____ duty should sweep the floor today.
5 I sat _____ Mr Hu _____ the centre of the cinema.

3 Rearrange the dialogue between Mr Hu and Lily, and practise it in pairs.

1 He's gone to England.
2 How did he travel?
3 Are we all here today?
4 He went with his family.
5 No, Jim is not here.
6 Where's Jim?
7 Why did he go there?
8 He went last week.
9 When did he go?
10 Whom did he travel with?
11 He travelled by air.
12 For how long will he be away?
13 He'll be away for about 8 weeks.
14 He went for a holiday.

MR HU: Are we all here today?
LILY: ....
MR HU: ....
LILY: ....
MR HU: ....
LILY: ....
MR HU: ....
LILY: ....
MR HU: ....
LILY: ....
MR HU: ....
LILY: ....
MR HU: ....
LILY: ....

Lesson 50

1 Read Jim's letter and answer the questions.

1 How long has Jim been away from school?
2 What does Jim hope?
3 What did Jim tell Ling Feng not to forget to do in his letter?
4 Did they have a good journey home?
5 Why didn't Jim see much during his flight?
6 Where and how long did they stop on the way?
7 What was the weather like in Moscow when they got there?
8 Did they get to England before Christmas or after it?
9 Whom has Jim seen since he got home?
10 Can you say something about Jim's family's sitting room?
11 What's Jim's address in London?
12 When did Jim write this letter?

2 Fill in the blanks with the proper prepostions.

They had a very good journey home. Jim sat ______ the window, but he didn't see much ______ his flight because there were too many clouds. Mrs Green slept almost the whole way. They stopped ______ Moscow ______ the way, but only ______ an hour or two, so there was no time to go ______ the centre ______ the city. Jim didn't mind, because it was really cold ______ Moscow. There was thick snow everywhere. Nobody liked to go out ______ the bad weather.

3 Fill in the blanks with the right verb forms.

On Christmas Eve, Jim ______ (go) with his father to choose a Christmas tree. They ______ (choose) a big one. It ______ (be) almost as tall as the room! They ______ (put) it in the corner of their sitting room. Kate ______ (cover) it with Christmas lights. The sitting room ______ (look) really beautiful. There was a fire ______ (burn) in the fireplace, and the Christmas tree lights ______ ______ (shine) brightly. The whole family ______ (be) happy.

***4 Put these sentences into Chinese.**

1 How time flies!
2 Please give them all my best wishes.
3 Everybody here is busy getting ready for Christmas.
4 Merry Christmas, and best wishes for the New Year!
5 Mum slept almost the whole way.
6 We had a very good journey home.
7 No news is good news.
8 We won't have our big family get-together until Christmas.

Lesson 51

1 Make up dialogues as the models.

Models: 1 **A**: *Keep quiet, please*!
B: Sorry! What did he tell me to do?
C: He told you to keep quiet.
2 **A**: *Don't make any noise*!
B: Sorry! What did he ask me to do?
C: She asked you not to make any noise.

1 Give Polly some food every day.	6 Don't draw on the wall.
2 Cover her cage every night.	7 Don't run so fast!
3 Remember to clean her cage.	8 Don't forget to tell her the news.
4 Take good care of Polly!	9 Don't play with fire!
5 Give your family my best wishes.	10 Don't read in poor light.

2 Read the answers, and then write their questions.

1 **A**: Did Jim have a good journey home?
B: Yes, he said that he had a very good journey home.
2 **A**: ....?
B: Yes, he said that they stopped in Moscow on the way.
3 **A**: ....?
B: No, he said that it was very cold in Moscow.
4 **A**: ....?
B: No, he said that they didn't go to the centre of the city.
5 **A**: ....?
B: No, I haven't heard from her yet.

3 Make up dialogues using the words in the box. Then put one of the dialogues into Chinese.

A: Where's *Mike*?
B: He has gone to *Xi'an*.
A: When did *he* go there?
B: *He* went there last Thursday.
A: Has *he* been there before?
B: Yes, *he* has been there twice. / No, never. / No, *he* has never been there before.

Sam	Bill
Ann	Lucy
Luoyang	Nanjing
Kunming	Chengdu

Lesson 52

1 Listen to the tape and choose the right answers.

1 What is the first problem?
A. Making a Christmas cake. B. Getting enough food and drink.
C. Cooking a Christmas chicken.
2 Who makes the Christmas cake? A. Grandma. B. Mrs Green. C. Kate.
3 When does she make it? A. October. B. November. C. December.
4 What is a Christmas cake full of? A. Nuts. B. Sweets. C. Fruit.
5 Who usually buys the Christmas tree?
A. Mother. B. Father. C. The children.
6 Who puts lights on the tree? A. Kate. B. Jim. C. The children.
7 Who cuts up wood for the fire? A. Father. B. Mother. C. Jim.
8 Where do the presents go?
A. On the tree. B. Under the tree. C. On the floor near the fireplace.
9 When do the Greens open their presents?
A. On Christmas Day. B. On Christmas Eve.
C. The day before Christmas.
10 When is Christmas Day? ____________.

2 Listen, read and learn the syllabic (成音节的) [n].

[-tn]	**mutton**	**certainly**	[-dn]	**garden**	**suddenly**
[-sn]	**lesson**	**listen**	[-zn]	**present**	**season**
[-fn]	**often**		[-vn]	**seven**	**eleven**

3 What did Polly say ?

1 Ling Feng is very good to me.
2 Ling Feng gives me some clean water to drink.
3 Ling Feng speaks to me in English.
4 Ling Feng covers my cage every night.
5 I am very pleased to stay with Ling Feng.

Model: Polly said that Ling Feng was very good to her.

*4 Fill in the blanks with proper prepositions.

1 Everybody is here __________ Jim Green.
2 He's gone to England __________ his family.
3 Have you heard __________ Jim, Ling Feng?
4 Jim thought that Polly might be unhappy __________ him.
5 Merry Christmas, and best wishes __________ the New Year!

Unit 14 Lesson 53

1 Make up some similar dialogues and act them in pairs.

Model 1:

NICK: Mum, could I ask you a question?
MOTHER: Certainly. What is it?
NICK: Have you ever *read this book*?
MOTHER: Yes, I have.
NICK: When did you read it?
MOTHER: *Two weeks ago.*

1	ride a horse last summer
2	visit the Great Wall three weeks ago
3	use a computer just a few years ago
4	study French when I was at school

Model 2:

MOTHER: Where has *Linda* gone?
JILL: *She*'s gone to the *zoo*.
MOTHER: Has *she* been there before?
JILL: Sorry, I don't know / Yes, I think so.

1	Nick	Shanghai
2	Jim	Lanzhou
3	Lily and Lucy	Guilin
4	Dick	Beihai Park
5	Mr Green	the West Lake
6	Mary	America

2 Complete the dialogues and then put them into Chinese.

1 **A**: How long________ your aunt ________ (live) in that village?
B: Let me see. She ________ ________ (live) there for ten years.
A: So she _______ (go) there in 199_ , __________ she?
B: Right. She _________ _________ (be) there ever since then.

2 **A**: __________ Sam ___________ (return) the library book?
B: No, he ___________ not ___________ (finish) it yet.
A: When __________ he ___________ (return) it?
B: I don't know. You'd better ask him.

3 **A**: Hello! __________ you _________ (be) here long?
B: No, not very long.
A: When __________ you __________ (arrive)?
B: About ten minutes ago.

4 **A**: __________ you __________ (see) the TV play?
B: Yes, I __________.
A: When __________ you __________ (see) it?
B: I __________ it on New Year's Eve.

Lesson 54

1 Read the story on page 54 of the Students' Book and answer the questions.

1 When is Christmas Eve?
2 What do children in England do on Christmas Eve?
3 What kind of person is Father Christmas?
4 How does Father Christmas come into the house?
5 What does Father Christmas do when he gets into the house?
6 Do you think there is really a Father Christmas in the world?
7 Who is "Father Christmas" in Jim and Kate's house?
8 When does Mr Green put the presents into his children's stockings?
9 Do the children know who "Father Christmas" really is?
10 Which countries have Christmas Day? Say three or four of them.

2 Give the four forms of the following verbs.

Model: try → tries → trying → tried → tried

arrive	fail	win	die	happen	agree
pass	pay	begin	draw	catch	lend
hit	mean	bring	forget	prefer	travel
join	burn	cover	keep	remember	return
spend	sleep	shine	send	sell	break
come	go	have	do	take	run

3 Fill in the blanks with the words in the brackets, and then put them into Chinese.

1 Tomorrow is Children's Day. They won't have any ______. They'll have ______ ________ to the Great Wall. They're sure to have ________ ________ ________. (a visit, lessons, a good time)

2 **A**: I'm not feeling well, Doctor. Yesterday I had ________ in a river. I'm afraid I've got ________ ________.

B: Yes, you must have ________ ________ in bed. Have ________ before you have ________ at noon.

(lunch, a rest, a cold, a swim, the medicine)

3 **A**: Let's have ________ ________. We can have ________ ________ when we're walking.

B: Good idea. We can talk about the match. Do we ______ ______ have ______ ______ before the match? (a talk, have to, a meeting, a walk)

4 Mrs King is going to have ________ ________ in her house. She went shopping this morning. "May I have ________ ________ at the green skirt?" she asked the girl in the shop. The girl showed her the skirt. "Very nice, I will have it," she said. (a look, a party)

Lesson 55

1 Choose the right answer.

1 Christmas Eve is ____________________.
A. the night before December 24 B. the night after December 25
C. the night of December 25 D. the night of December 24

2 Father Christmas often puts the presents __________________.
A. into children's hats B. into children's stockings
C. under children's beds D. into children's shoes.

3 Father Christmas comes into the house through the __________________.
A. window B. front door C. chimney D. back door

4 On the morning of Christmas Day, children wake up their parents very early and say "______________________".
A. Good morning! B. Happy New Year!
C. Best wishes to you! D. Merry Christmas!

5 On Christmas Day, people often ____________________ to each other.
A. give money B. ask for money
C. ask for presents D. give presents

2 Fill in the blanks according to the text.

On Christmas Eve, children are very happy. They put their stockings ________ ________ ________ of their beds before they ________ to _________. They want Father Christmas to ________ them some presents.

Mr Green tells his children that Father Christmas is a very ________ man. He comes on Christmas Eve. He lands ________ ________ of each house and comes _________ the chimney into the fireplace and bring them a lot of _________.

Christmas Day always begins ________ _________. The children ________ ________ very early. They can't ________ to ________ the presents in their stockings. Then they ________ ________ their parents and call: "________ ________!"

Do you know what Christmas means? Christmas Day is the _________ Jesus Christ. When Christ _________ _________, many people _________ him _________. So today, people still do the same thing to _________ _________.

***3 Look at different cards on page ii of the Students' Book and make a Christmas card or a New Year card for your parents.**

***4 Say a few words about each card on page ii of the Students' Book.**

Lesson 56

1 Fill in the blanks with *that, who, where, whom, what , how or if / whether*.

1 I hear __________ he'll be back before noon.
2 Do you know __________ the man over there is?
3 He asked me __________ I was waiting for.
4 Can you tell me __________ the No. 5 bus stop is?
5 I don't know __________ he will be able to come back.
6 They want to know __________ time the meeting will start.
7 He told me __________ he could join the two pieces of metal together.
8 I'm sure __________ I can catch up with the others.
9 Lily wants to know ______ Lucy has spent too much money on her clothes.
10 Could you please show me __________ I can turn on the computer?

2 Listen and read these long sentences.

1 'Mr and 'Mrs 'Green | were 'getting 'ready | to 'fly to 'England | for their `holiday.
2 We've 'seen 'several 'members of the 'family | since we a'rrived | — my 'grandfather, my 'aunt and `uncle.
3 Their 'parents 'usually 'tell them | that 'Father 'Christmas will 'come | during the `night.

3 Make a plan to tell how you are going to spend your winter holiday.

*** 4 Sing this old Christmas song, and learn it by heart.**

1 = ♭B 3/4

A Merry Christmas

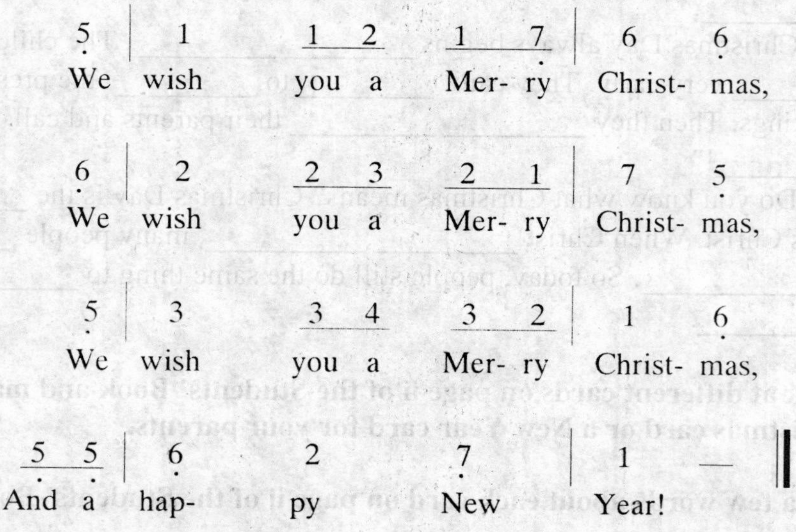

5 | 1 1 2 1 7 | 6 6
We wish you a Mer- ry Christ- mas,

6 | 2 2 3 2 1 | 7 5
We wish you a Mer- ry Christ- mas,

5 | 3 3 4 3 2 | 1 6
We wish you a Mer- ry Christ- mas,

5 5 | 6 2 7 | 1 — ‖
And a hap- py New Year!

Unit 15 Lesson 57

1 Complete the dialogue.

1 GIRL: ______ I have a toy (玩具) horse, Daddy?
FATHER: Sure, dear. I'm ________ to get one for you today.

2 MAN: ____ I ______ you, sir?
FATHER: ____ you ____ any toy horses, please?
MAN: Yes, here you ______ .
FATHER: Oh, no, that's a *house*. My daughter ______ a *horse*.
MAN: I'm sorry. Look at that shelf. There ____ lots of horses. Which kind ____ your daughter ____?
FATHER: The black one is beautiful. I'll ______ one.

2 Fill in the sentences with *whether / if, that* or *which*.

1 The girl asked ______ she could have a toy horse.
2 Her father said ______ he was going to get one for her.
3 The man asked ______ he could help him.
4 The father asked the man ______ they had any toy horses.
5 The man said ______ there were many on the shelf.
6 The man asked ______ kind his daughter would like.

3 Make similar dialogues with the words in the box and write one in your exercise books.

pork	noodles	tomatoes
potatoes	fish	salt

DAD: Do we need some more *dumplings*?
MUM: Jill, what did your Dad say?
JILL: Dad asked whether we needed some more *dumplings*.
MUM: Yes, I think we do. Dick, we need some more *dumplings*. Can you get some, please?
DICK: Jill, what did Mum say?
JILL: Mum asked if you could get some more *dumplings*, please.
DICK: Oh, the music is too loud. I can't hear what you say. Would you please turn off the radio?

Lesson 58

1 Answer these questions and write the answers in your exercise books.

1 What do people often ask Lucy?
2 Do the twins get on well with each other?
3 Why do people mistake them for each other?
4 Do the twins feel the same? Give two examples.
5 What are the differences between them?
6 What did their mother give them for their birthday one year?
7 What colour does Lucy prefer?
8 Who is a little younger, Lily or Lucy?
9 What do they fight about when the present is open?
10 Do they fight very often?

2 Complete the passage with the words in the box.

fight, decide, dance, lonely, dark, green, either, prefers, if, together, strange, whether, example, make friends, get on

"Do you want to know ________ I like being a twin?" Lucy asked. "Yes, it feels ________ to have a twin sister. We're ________, most of the time. So we never feel ________. Certainly, sometimes we fight. For ________, we ________ about who should open a present first and we fight when we can't ________ who should play with it first. But we never fight for long. We always ________ ________ with each other again! Usually we ________ ________ very well with each other."

"We look the same. We usually feel the same. We like the same music, the same food and the same books.

"You want to know ________ we have any differences, don't you?" Lucy went on talking. "Of course, we have a few differences. Lily likes to ________. I like to sing. We don't like the same colours, ________. Lily ________ ________ blue. I like light ________. It's great to have a twin sister."

3 Fill in the blanks with *too* or *either*.

1 Lily hasn't finished her homework. Lucy hasn't, ________.
2 Lily has bought a dark blue sweater. Lucy has bought one, ________.
3 Lily wanted to open the present first. Lucy wanted to open it first, ________.
4 Lily doesn't like pork for dinner. Lucy doesn't like it, ________.

***4 Read the passage on page 58 of the Students' Book and say something about the twin sisters.**

Lesson 59

1 Put the sentences in the right order with numbers and write down the dialogue in your exercise books.

( ) MRS KING: I'd like a sweater, please.
( ) SHOPKEEPER : All right. What about this one? It's a little larger.
( ) SHOPKEEPER: Would you like a woolen one or a cotton one?
( ) MRS KING: It's great. But it costs too much.
(1) SHOPKEEPER : Good morning. What can I do for you, Madam?
( ) MRS KING: I like the colour, but it's not large enough.
( ) SHOPKEEPER : Certainly! What about this green one?
( ) MRS KING: I haven't decided which one to buy. Mm, can I have a look at a woolen sweater, please?
( ) MRS KING: OK. I'll take it. Thank you.
( ) SHOPKEEPER : Good things always cost too much. You decide!

2 Complete the dialogue.

SHOPKEEPER : Good afternoon! What can I do ________ you?
HAN MEIMEI: ________ like a skirt, please.
SHOPKEEPER : ________ kind do you want? The cotton ones are hanging here and the woolen ones are ________ there.
HAN MEIMEI: Can I have a ________ the cotton ones, please?
SHOPKEEPER: Yes, of course. Here you are.
HAN MEIMEI: Can I have a look at the ________ ones, please?
SHOPKEEPER: Yes, please. No ________! Please ________ your time!

3 Write down what Lucy said to the shopkeeper.

1 Do you have red woolen skirts?	4 Can I try it on?
2 Do you have anything cheaper?	5 Is it a woolen skirt?
3 Can I have a look at the red one?	6 Is it made in Shanghai?

Model: 1 Lucy asked the shopkeeper *if he had red woolen skirts*.

2 Lucy asked the shopkeeper if ....

3 ....

4 ....

5 ....

6 ....

Lesson 60

1 Listen to the tape and choose the right answers.

1 Who is Lucy talking to?
A. Her mother. B. Her sister. C. Her teacher.
2 What does Lucy want to do?
A. She wants to mend her shoes. B. She wants to go shopping.
C. She wants to buy some new shoes.
3 What size shoes does she wear?
A. Six. B. Seven. C. She doesn't know.
4 What colour shoes does she want to get?
A. Blue. B. Green. C. Black.
5 When do they decide to go shopping?
A. On Saturday. B. Saturday afternoon. C. Sunday afternoon.

2 Fill in the blanks with *on, off, up* or *down*.

1 "The radio is too loud. Tell Jim to turn it ____, Kate!" said Mr. Green.
2 " I've finished my homework, Mum. May I turn ____ the TV now? I want to watch the film The Flying Doctor," said Tom.
3 He turn ____ the radio because he couldn't hear the weather report clearly.
4 The TV film was not interesting. She turned ____ TV and went to bed.

***3 Complete the passage with right prepositions.**

It was Christmas Eve. It was very cold. A poor girl was selling flowers ____ the street. Her parents were ill, so she had to get money ____ food. She felt cold and hungry. She stopped ____ front of a beautiful house. The girl knocked ____ the door and a man came out. She asked him if he needed some flowers. The man said he didn't want any. She left the house and felt tired. She sat down ____ the foot of a tall wall. She looked ____ the flowers. The flowers smelled very nice. She suddenly had a strange feeling. She felt she was becoming light, and slowly she began to fly ____ the sky (天空). She flew higher and higher and ____ last she found herself ____ the clouds. A group of people were coming to meet her. ____ the head of them was her granny. Granny welcomed her and asked her why she didn't stay ____ home. The girl told her that she had to sell flowers to get money because her parents were badly ill. Granny told her not to worry and gave her lots ____ beautiful clothes and delicious food. The girl laughed happily.

It snowed heavily that night. The girl died ____ a smile ____ her face. ____ the same time, the people in the beautiful house began to sing Christmas songs and enjoyed themselves.

Unit 16 Lesson 61

1 Make up dialogue.

A: What's this ... made of?	B: It's made of	It's used for
1 hat	1 metal.	A sleeping.
2 bed	2 wool.	B travelling.
3 bottle	3 glass.	C keeping water.
4 knife	4 paper.	D sending letters.
5 stamp	5 wood.	E keeping warm.
6 mirror		F looking at yourself.
7 clock		G cutting things.
8 bicycle		H telling the time.

2 Look at these pictures. Ask and answer in pairs and write down the answers in your exercise books.

What're these? What're they made of? What're they used for?

3 Fill in the blanks with *my, mine, your, yours, her* or *hers*.

A: I'm afraid I've lost my coat.

B: Is this ________ ? It's made of cotton.

A: No, it's not ________ . It's Miss Turner's. It's ________ coat. ________ is made of cotton.

B: Is that ________ coat? It's made of wool.

A: No, it's not ________ coat, either.

B: What's ________ coat made of?

A: ________ is made of paper, a kind of strong paper. It's a new invention.

B: A paper coat! What's it used for?

A: It's used for keeping off the rain.

Lesson 62

1 Read the passage on page 62 of the Students' Book again. Answer right or wrong.

		Right	Wrong
1	English is spoken by the largest number of people in the world.	/ /	/ /
2	English is more widely used than any other languages.	/ /	/ /
3	English is spoken as the second language in Australia.	/ /	/ /
4	English is not the first language in Germany.	/ /	/ /
5	When you look at the back of a watch, you may see the English words "Made in China".	/ /	/ /
6	English is very widely used for business between different countries.	/ /	/ /
7	When an Indian sells something to a Frenchman, they may speak English.	/ /	/ /
8	Most business letters around the world are written in French.	/ /	/ /
9	Three quarters of the world's telephone calls are made in English.	/ /	/ /
10	English is very popular with travellers and business people in foreign countries.	/ /	/ /

2 Read and learn. Pay attention to the silent letters.

Chris**t**mas	**k**nife	i**s**land	**w**rite	w**h**en
san**d**wich	**k**now	clim**b**	**w**rong	w**h**at
We**d**nesday	**k**nock	autum**n**	**w**ho	**h**our

3 Fill in the blanks with right prepositions.

Look ____ the back ____ your watch. You may see the English words "Made ____ China". Look _____ something else. You may find the words " Made _____ Japan" or "Made ____ Germany". But English is spoken ____ the first language _____ none _____ these countries. It's widely used _____ different countries. It's used _____ travellers and business people all _____ the world. It's one _____ the most important languages ______ the world. And it's getting more and more popular _____ the modern world.

***4 Give a short talk about the English language.**

Begin: English is the most widely spoken language in the world. It is spoken as the first language by ....

Lesson 63

1 Look at the map on page 63 of the Students' Book. Answer the questions and write them down in your exercise books.

1 Where are ships made in China? ....

2 Where are trucks made? ....

3 Where are radio sets produced? ....

4 Where are apples grown? ....

2 Ask a friend these questions and then write down the answers.

1 What's your desk made of?	
2 What's the door of the classroom made of?	
3 What're the windows made of?	
4 What's your sweater made of?	
5 What're your socks made of?	

3 Fill in the blanks and practise the dialogue in pairs.

A: Hello! I haven't seen you ____ a long time.

B: Hello! How are you?

A: Fine. Oh, your skirt looks beautiful. What's it made ______?

B: It's made ______ silk.

A: Where's it ________?

B: It's ______ in Suzhou.

A: Would you like to have a cup ______ tea?

B: Yes, please. Mm, the tea is very nice. Where's it grown?

A: It's _______ in Zhejiang.

B: What ______ the oranges? Are they ______ in South China?

A: I think so.

B: That's a new TV set, isn't it? Is it made in Japan?

A: I'm afraid you're wrong. It's made in China.

Lesson 64

1 Fill in the blanks with *in, on, by, over, with, for, of* or *as*.

1 English is spoken ____ the first language ____ New Zealand.
2 Bicycles are widely used ____ Chinese people.
3 Woolen clothes are used ____ keeping warm.
4 **A**: How are you getting ____ with each other?
B: Very well. We have made good friends ____ each other.
5 These modern cars are used all ____ the world.
6 Planes, cars and trains are used ____ business people ____ travelling.
7 **A**: Where are potatoes grown?
B: Good potatoes are grown ____ north China.
8 The Smiths travelled ____ China last year.
9 **A**: What's the cup made ____?
B: It's made ____ china (瓷料). China is made in China. Do you know?
10 She asked the shopkeeper whether she could try ____ the shoes.

2 Turn these sentences into the passive voice after the models.

Model 1: No.14 Middle School teaches **English**. →
English is taught in No.14 Middle School.

1 Some people speak French in Canada.
2 They make TV sets in that factory.
3 Northwest China grows the best cotton.
4 This farm grows beautiful flowers.

Model 2: Students learn English as the second language in China. →
English is learned as the second language in China.

1 Some Canadians use French as their first language.
2 People speak English as the first language in New Zealand.
3 The girl studies German as her second foreign language.

Model 3: People use knives for cutting things. →
Knives are used for cutting things.

1 People use tractors for farming.
2 They use this room for playing pingpong.
3 Uncle Wang uses this machine for making things.
4 We use brooms for sweeping the floor.

3 Look at the pictures on page iii and ask each other questions in pairs.

Where're [ships / trucks / ...] made / produced? Where's [tea / salt / ...] grown / produced?

Unit 17 Lesson 65

1 Look at the map and mark the way to the market according to the dialogue.

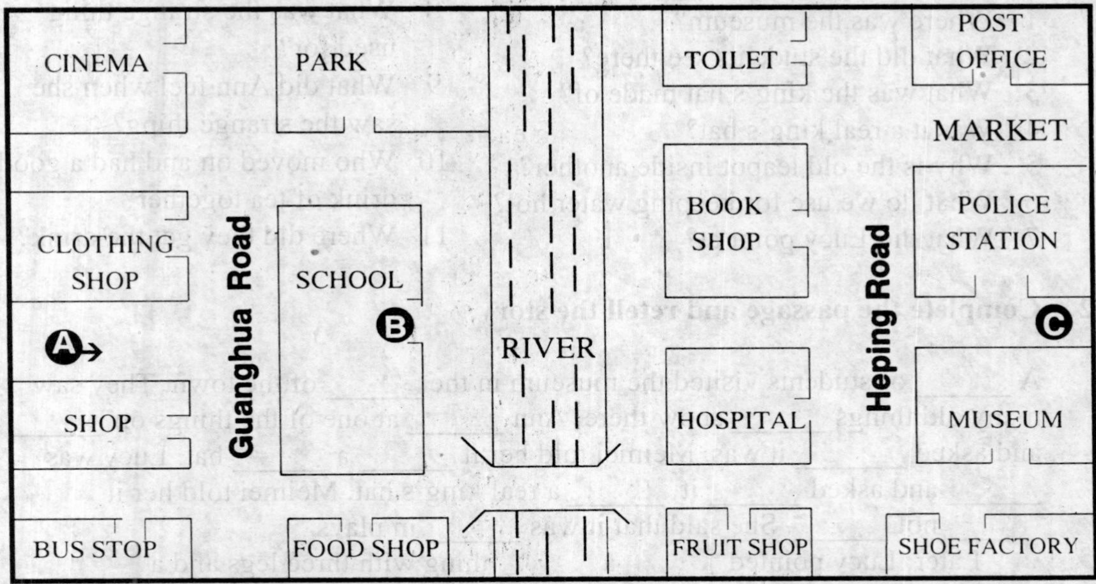

Example: Someone is standing at A. He's asking you the way to the market.

A: Excuse me! Can you tell me the way to the market, please?

B: Yes. Go along the street, and take the first turning on the right. Go along Guanghua Road, and take the first turning on the left. Go straight along the street and cross the bridge. Then turn left and walk along the river. Take the second turning on the right. Walk on till you get to Heping Road. Cross the road. You'll see the market between the post office and the police station. You can't miss it.

A: Thank you very much.

2 Look at the map in Part 1. Do the following exercises.

1 Start from **A**. Go along the street, turn left. Walk along **Guanghua** Road. Turn right at the first crossing. The ______ is on your left hand side.

2 Start from **B**. Go along the river. Then turn left and cross the bridge. Go straight and take the second turning on the left. Go along **Heping** Road and turn right at the second crossing. Then you'll find the ____ ______ on your left hand.

3 If you are standing at **C**, how can you get to the cinema? Write down the instructions in your exercise books.

4 If you are in the cinema enjoying a film, suddenly someone is very ill. Please show him how to get to the hospital quickly. Write down your instructions in your exercise books.

Lesson 66

1 Answer these questions.

1 Where was the museum?
2 What did the students see there?
3 What was the king's hat made of?
4 Was it a real king's hat?
5 Why is the old teapot inside another?
6 What do we use for keeping water hot?
7 What did Lucy point at?
8 What was the strange thing used for?
9 What did Ann feel when she saw the strange thing?
10 Who moved on and had a good drink of tea together?
11 Where did they get the drink?

2 Complete the passage and retell the story.

A ______ of students visited the museum in the ______ of the town. They saw many old things ______ show there. Ann ______ at one of the things on ______ and asked ______ it was. Meimei told her it ______ a ______ hat. Lucy was ______ and asked ______ it ______ a real king's hat. Meimei told her it ______ not ______. She said that it was ______ in plays.

Later, Lucy pointed ______ a ______ thing with three legs and a ______ top. It was made of ______. Wei Hua said it was used ______ drinking. The girls began to feel ______. They all moved ______ and had a good drink of tea ______ from a ______ thermos.

3 Write a few words about the teapot or the strange cup.

Model: In the museum we saw something very interesting. It was a hat. It was made of red silk. It was worn by a king in plays. It was very beautiful.

4 Do you know what they are?

1 Its outside is made of metal. Its inside is made of glass. It has a cork (软木塞) made of soft wood. It is used for keeping hot water.

2 What word begins with **T**, ends with **T**, and is full of **T**?

*** 5 Fill in the blanks with the right verb forms.**

MUM: What an interesting picture! Peter, ______ it ______ (draw) by you?

PETER: Yes. The picture tells you bread ______ ______ (harvest) from trees.

MUM: Where ______ this tree ______ (grow)?

PETER: It ______ ______ (grow) in the clouds.

MUM: Who ______ ______ (stand) on the ladder?

PETER: You and me, Mum. We ______ ______ (pick) bread from the tree!

Lesson 67

1 Make up dialogues.

A: When was	your school Uncle Wang's factory the hospital the train station the museum the cinema	built?	B: It was built in	....

2 Look at the picture on page 67 of the Students' Book. Find the right sign for the following sentences.

1 Excuse me. I'm afraid you can't take photos here.
2 Look at that sign. You may get out of the cinema from that door.
3 Where's the door? Oh, there it is. Let's go in.
4 Excuse me. I'm afraid you can't smoke here.
5 It's 4:45. It's still open. We're lucky.
6 If you push, you can't open the door.
7 If you pull, you can't open the door.
8 It's too late. The shop is closed. Bad luck!

3 Fill in each of the blanks with the right verb form.

A: When _____ the museum ________(found)?
B: It ________ (found) in 1952. There _______ (be) many interesting things on show in it. Would you like to _______ (visit) the museum?
A: Yes, I'd love to. Where is the entrance?
B: Here, this side door is _______ (use) as an entrance. There's something wrong with the front door. It's _______ (lock).
A: What's that? It ______ (look) strange. It ______ (have) three legs and a strange top.
B: It's an old cup. It ______ ______ (use) for ________ (drink) a thousand years ago.
A: It's very beautiful. What _____ it ______ (make) of?
B: It ______ ______ (make) of metal.
A: What's that?
B: It's a king's hat.
A: Is it a real king's hat?
B: No, it's not real. It ______ ______ (use) in plays. It ______ _______ (make) of silk.

Lesson 68

1 Listen to the tape and choose the right answers.

1 Who did Mrs Clarke want to buy a watch for?
A. Her daughter. B. Her son. C. Her husband.
2 Where were the watches made?
A. In China. B. In Japan. C. In England.
3 Why didn't Mrs Clarke buy a watch in the shop?
A. Because they were too cheap. B. Because they were too expensive.
C. Because they were not made in China.
4 Where were the watches in the market made?
A. They were made in Japan. B. They were made in China.
C. We don't know.
5 Why did Mrs Clarke buy one?
A. She wanted a watch for her daughter. B. They were cheap.
C. They were made in China.
6 What happened?
A. The watch stopped. B. She lost the watch.
C. Dr Clarke mended it after it was broken.
7 What did Mrs Clarke decide?
A. She decided to get a clock instead.
B. She decided never to buy a watch in the market again.
C. She decided never to buy a cheap watch again.

2 Fill in the blanks.

A: Excuse me. Can you tell me the way ________ the museum, please?
B: Certainly. Go ________ the street, and go ________ the bridge, and then turn right. You'll see a white building ________ the police station and the post office. You can't miss it. The white building is the __________.
A: Thank you very much. By the way, do you know what are ____ show in it?
B: I'm sorry I ________ know. But I'm afraid it's ________ now. You'll have to go tomorrow if you want to visit it.

3 Complete the dialogue.

A: Look! I've got a new machine.
B: How long ....?
A: Only a week.
B: It looks strange. What ....?
A: It's used for making noodles.
B: Where ....?
A: It was made in Guangzhou.
B: Have ....?
A: Yes. I've used it seven times already.

Unit 18 Lesson 69

1 Complete the dialogues.

1 FRED: My father has bought two young trees. Will you please help me ________ them in the garden, Jack?
JACK: Certainly! What ________ we do first?
FRED: I'll ________ two holes. You go and ________ some water for me.
JACK: That's easy. Then I can ________ you with digging.

2 FRED: Dad, do you think the holes are big and deep ________?
DAD: I think they are just ________. You've done very well.

3 FRED: Jack, please ________ the tree in the hole and make ________ it's straight. I'll put the ________ back in the hole.
JACK: OK.

2 Make new sentences with *neither ... nor.*

Model: The ground must not be too cold or too hot. →
The ground must be neither too cold nor too hot.

1 The ground must not be too wet or too dry.
2 The stick should **not** be too long or too short.
3 The holes must **not be** too big or too small.
4 The temperature must not be too high or too low.

3 Do you know how to plant a tree? Complete the instructions.

1 Dig a ______ for the tree. The hole should be ________ enough, but not too _______.
2 Knock a ________ into the earth to help the tree ________.
3 Put the ________ in the ________. Make ________ that it is ________.
4 ________ the ________ back into the ________. ________ it hard with your ________ several times.
5 Tie the ________ ________ the top of the stick to ________ it straight.
6 ________ the tree well, as ________ as possible.

Lesson 70

1 Answer these questions. Write down the answers in your exercise books.

1 What has happened to the forests of the USA in the last 350 years?
2 What has gone and what was left?
3 What's still happening in the USA?
4 Why has China built the Great Green Wall?
5 How long and how wide is the Great Green Wall?
6 What will the Great Green Wall do?
7 Where did the writer find Wang Feng?
8 What will happen to the high mountains in a few years' time?

2 Match the phrases with the words.

1 forest	a in the middle of
2 copy	b (moving) near to a place
3 towards	c a very high hill
4 farmland	d a large place where many trees grow
5 among	e land used by farmers to grow things
6 mountain	f try to do the same as others

3 Fill in the blanks. Then try to retell the text "the Great Green Wall".

In 1620, about half the USA was covered by ________. Today the forests have almost gone. A lot of good ________ has gone with them, leaving only ________. China doesn't want to ________ the USA's example. We're planting ________ and _____ trees. We've built the "Great Green Wall" of trees _____ northern part of our country. The Great Green Wall is 7,000 kilometres ________, and between 400 and 1,700 kilometres ________. It will stop the wind ________ blowing the earth away. It will ________ the sand from moving ________ the rich ________ in the south. More "Great Green Walls" are needed. Trees must ________ grown all over the world. Great Green Walls will make the world better.

4 Choose the right answers.

1 There are about two _____ workers in the factory.
A. thousand B. thousand of C. thousands of D. thousands

2 Many _____ trees should be planted on the mountains.
A. thousand B. thousand of C. thousands D. thousands of

3 We have planted _____ trees in San Bei. It's a "Great Green Wall" of trees.
A. million B. millions C. millions of D. million of

4 _____ people were hurt in the train accident. So we must be more careful.
A. Hundred B. Hundred of C. Hundreds D. Hundreds of

Lesson 71

1 Put these sentences into the passive voice.

Model: We should look after old people very well.→
Old people should be looked after very well (by us).

1 You should answer these questions as soon as possible.
2 We must clean our classroom this afternoon.
3 You must finish your homework before nine o'clock.
4 You can bring your friends to my birthday party tomorrow evening.
5 You should not touch the things on show in the museum.
6 They may grow fruit trees next spring.
7 They may grow cabbages after they harvest the carrots.

2 Fill in the blanks with *high, tall, deep, thick, long* or *wide*.

1 **A**: Can I skate on the river?
B: Of course. The ice of the river is over one metre ________.
It's strong enough.
2 The Great Wall is more than 6,000 kilometres ________, and between 4 - 5 metres ______. In most places it is ______ enough for five horses or ten men to walk side by side (并排) along the top.
3 **A**: How ________ is the river, do you know?
B: It's more than 20 metres ________, I think. I'm afraid it's dangerous to swim in it.
4 **A**: What a ________ building!
B: It's about 200 metres ________, the highest one in the city.
5 **A**: The young man plays basketball very well.
B: Yes. You know, he's over 2 metres ________.

3 Fill in the blanks.

Can vegetables be planted in winter? Yes, but a greenhouse (暖房) must ______ built first. The greenhouse should be ______ of glass. A large greenhouse may be 10 metres ______, 3 metres ______, and 2.5 metres high. The sunshine can reach the vegetables ______ the glass. The wind and the cold air can be ______ from getting in. The air inside the greenhouse is always ______. More and ______ greenhouses are being built ______ over the world. All kinds of vegetables can be brought on to our dinner tables ______ winter.

Lesson 72

1 Listen to the tape and choose the right answers.

1 When was Tree Planting Day started?
A. In 1987. B. In 1971. C. In 1980.

2 What day is Tree Planting Day?
A. March 7th. B. March 12th. C. March 11th.

3 Where did Class Three meet?
A. At the school. B. About six kilometres from the school.
C. In a park.

4 How did they get to the park?
A. By bus. B. On foot. C. By truck.

5 Who went with them?
A. Miss Zhang. B. Uncle Wang and several teachers.
C. Miss Zhang and several other teachers.

6 How many trees did they plant?
A. 250. B. 350. C. 550.

2 Complete these dialogues with the right verb forms.

1 **A**: Do you know how to grow rice?
B: Yes, more or less.
A: Can rice ________ ________ (grow) in water?
B: Sure. It's usually ________ (grow) in water.
A: Can rice ________ ________ (harvest) twice a year?
B: Yes. In South China, it may ________ ________ (harvest) three times a year.

2 **A**: How many holes must ________ (dig) today?
B: Miss Zhang told us 20 holes must ________ ________ (dig) today.
A: Oh, we ________ ________ (finish) 19 holes. I think we'll have time to________ (dig) five more holes.
B: Good. The more, the better. Maybe six or even more holes can ________ ________ (finish).

3 Fill in the blanks with the right verb forms.

A: Why should trees ________ ________ (plant) on the mountains?
B: Forests are very important to the world. The wind can ________ ________(stop) from ________ (blow) the earth away. The sand can ________ ________ (stop) from ________ (move) towards the rich farmland.
A: We ________ already ________ (plant) about eight thousand trees. Millions of trees may ________ ________ (need) for all the mountains here. You'll ________ (see) a "Great Green Wall " in a few years' time.
B: That'll be really wonderful!

Unit 19 Lesson 73

1 Look at the diagram (图表). Ask and answer like this:

A: How many kilos of *milk* was produced on Green Lake Farm last year?

B: *48,400* kilos.

A: What about 1996?

B: *53,500* kilos. *5,100* kilos more was produced than last year.

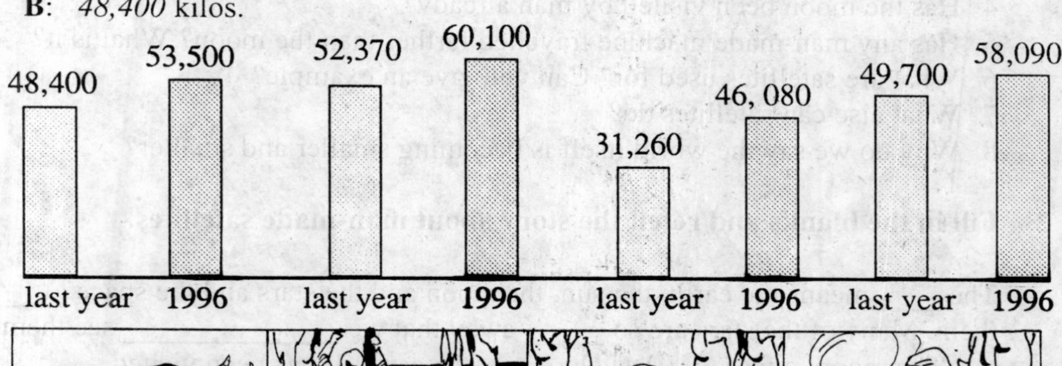

2 Ask and answer these questions. Write down the answers in your exercise books.

1 What're watches used for?
2 What're TV sets used for?
3 What're computers used for?
4 What're keys used for?
5 What're fridges used for?
6 What're stamps used for?
7 What're pigs kept for?
8 What's this machine used for?

*** 3 Fill in the blanks with the right words.**

What machine is this?

A: What's that? It looks strange.
B: It's ______ old machine.
A: What's it used ______?
B: It's used by people for getting water ______ a river or a lake.
A: How ______ it work?
B: Usually two people stand ______ it. They push the pedals (踏板) down hard with their ______. Then ______ can be brought up.
A: What is it made ______?
B: It's made of ______. It can be seen ______ south China.

Lesson 74

1 Answer these questions. Write down the answers in your exercise books.

1 What do we mean when we talk about the universe?
2 Why can't many stars be seen?
3 How far is the moon away from the earth?
4 Has the moon been visited by man already?
5 Has any man-made machine travelled farther than the moon? What is it?
6 What are satellites used for? Can you give an example?
7 What else can satellites do?
8 Why do we say the world itself is becoming smaller and smaller?

2 Fill in the blanks and retell the story about man-made satellites.

The ____ means the earth, the sun, the moon and the stars and the space ______ them. Many of the stars are so _____ away that we ______ ______ see them.

The moon, our ______, travels _____ the earth. It has been visited ______ man from the earth.

Man-made ______ have been sent up _____ space by many countries. They go _____ the earth. They are used for helping us to learn more _____ the earth, the weather and other things. They are also used for sending and ______ messages. It makes people _____ different countries understand each other much better. So people say the world itself is becoming a much ______ place.

3 Fill in each blank with a word beginning with the given letter.

1 We call the moon our s______________.
2 Man-made satellites can be used for sending and receiving m__________.
3 We can never say we have learned enough k________________.
4 Man-made satellites can be used for sending TV p___________ to other countries.
5 The earth, the sun, the moon and the stars are all in the u_____________.
6 Thanks to space satellites, people from different countries u_____ each other better

4 Fill in the blanks with *with* or *without*.

1 The poor car went past ______ heavy smoke behind it.
2 Vegetables and trees can't grow ______ water.
3 He can't pass the exam ______ her help.
4 "No hurry. Don't forget to take the coat ______ you!" said she.

Lesson 75

1 Complete the dialogue.

A: What are you doing?
B: I'm trying to _____ our favourite TV programme.
A: Have you found ________ yet?
B: Yes. I've found two programmes, but I can't decide which is ______ enjoyable.
A: Which channels are they ________?
B: One is on Channel 2 and the _____ is on Channel 8.
A: The one on Channel 8 is a TV play ______ a village in Northeast China. The story is _____ interesting. Why not sit down and _____ it?

2 Practise the dialogues, and then write one in your exercise books.

A: Which radio programme do you think is more [interesting / enjoyable] ?

B: Well, I don't think any of them is very interesting.

A: Why don't you go and [visit a museum / play football / take a walk in the park / have a swim] instead?

B: Good idea! [Visiting a museum / Playing football / Taking a walk / Having a swim] is better than listening to the radio.

3 Fill in the blanks with the phrases in the box.

put on	put up	put down	put away

1 "If you know the answer, _____ _____ your hand, please," the teacher said.
2 The students _____ their books _____ as soon as the class was over.
3 It was very cold. Mr Smith _____ _____ his coat and went out.
4 "The bag is too heavy. May I _____ it _____ on the ground and have a rest?" the boy asked.
5 Lucy, could you please help me _____ _____ the map on the blackboard?
6 "Can I _______ these books ________ your desk?" Lily asked the teacher.

Lesson 76

1 Listen to the tape and choose the right answers.

1 Yuri Gagarin was the first man ______________.
A. to fly in a plane B. to travel in space C. to land on the moon
2 Yuri Gagarin was ______________.
A. a Russian B. an American C. an Englishman
3 How long did he stay in space? ______________.
A. Twelve days B. 108 minutes C. Nineteen minutes
4 In what year did the first man fly in space? ______________.
A. 1957 B. 1959 C. 1961
5 Who was the first woman in space? ______________.
A. An American B. A Russian C. A Canadian
6 How far did she travel? ______________.
A. Nearly two thousand kilometres B. Nearly two billion kilometres
C. Nearly two million kilometres
7 Who was Neil Armstrong? ______________.
A. The first American in space B. The first man in space
C. The first man to land on the moon
8 In what year did the first man land on the moon? ______________.
A. 1969 B. 1959 C. 1979

2 How many compound words can you find when you join the words from Box A with the words from Box B? Write them down in your exercise books.

A

birth	bed	class
grand	foot	basket
home	house	north
south	week	reading
sitting	meeting	down
book	loud	head

B

room	parents	son
speaker	ball	town
work	east	west
day	seller	shop
mate	stairs	master

3 Put the following sentences into Chinese.

1 We never fight for long and we **make friends with** each other again.
2 I don't always tell them that they've **made a mistake**.
3 The sweaters **are made of** wool and cotton.
4 Our colour TV set **is made in** Japan.
5 Lily, would you please **make** some **tea**?
6 It **makes** me feel thirsty.

Unit 20 Lesson 77

1 Write out the following in numbers.

1 forty five million ( )
2 fifty-seven million two hundred and eighteen thousand ( )
3 one billion one hundred and thirty-two million ( )
4 one billion three hundred and thirty-six million eight hundred and twenty thousand ( )
5 three hundred and eight million ( )
6 four hundred and three million five hundred and ninety thousand and eighty-seven ( )

2 Write out the numbers in English and read them aloud.

987	654	711	201	1,300	5,110
4,944	64,000	150,000	8,670,000	1,200,000,000	

3 Find out and write down the answers in English.

1 What's the population of China?
2 What's the population of Beijing?
3 What's the population of Shanghai?
4 What's the population of Sichuan?
5 What's the population of your city / town / county (县城)?

***4 Talk about the rivers on the map of China.**

Model:

A: How long is the Yellow River?
B: I think it's over 5,000 kilometres long. Oh, look! It's 5,464 kilometres long.

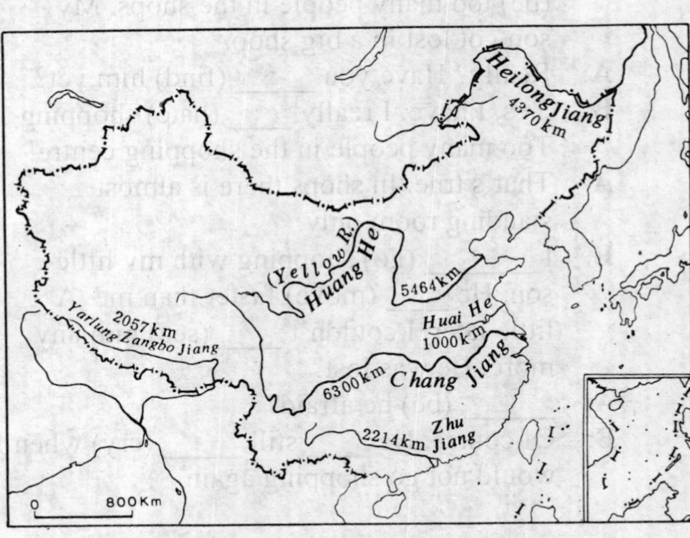

Lesson 78

1 Read this passage on page 78 of the Students' Book and then answer these questions.

1 About how many babies are born in one hour?
2 How many new babies do people have to find food for in one day?
3 What may be the greatest problem of the world today?
4 How is the population growing?
5 When was the population over 500 million?
6 What does a UN report say about the world's population?
7 What will happen in about 600 years?
8 Do you think that a family should have many children? Why?

2 Complete the passage and then talk about the population problem.

174 babies ______ born ______ the world in just one ______. That means people have to find food ______ over 250,000 ______ more in one day. The population ______ may be the greatest one of the world today. The world's ______ is growing faster and ______. In 1990, the ______ was over five billion. A UN ______ says that the ______ population will pass six ______ by the end of the twentieth ______. People say that ______ the year 2010, it may be seven ______. That means that ______ about 600 years, there will be standing ______ only on the earth. There won't be enough ______ for anybody ______.

3 Fill in the blanks with the right verb forms.

A: Where ___ you ______ (go) this morning?
B: I _____ (go) shopping.
A: _____ you ______(buy) anything?
B: No, I _____ (buy) nothing. There _____ (be) too many people in the shops. My son got lost in a big shop.
A: Really? Have you _____ (find) him yet?
B: Yes, I have. I really ____ (hate) shopping. Too many people in the shopping centre!
A: That's true. In shops there is almost standing room only.
B: I ______ (go) shopping with my little son. He ____ (move) faster than me. A little later, I couldn't ____ (see) him any more. He was lost.
A: ______ (be) he afraid?
B: Of course. He ____ still _____ (cry) when I ______ (find) him. He said he would not go shopping again.

Lesson 79

1 Fill in the blanks and practise the dialogue.

A: _________ you read today's newspaper?
B: No, I _________. _________ there any important news?
A: There's a report about the population of our country. It says China had got another 16,000,000 people in 1990.
B: Oh, the population is growing _________ and _________.
A: If the population goes on growing like this, it will be the biggest _________ in our country.
B: _________ course it will. China has the _________ population in the world. The babies born in one year are almost as many _________ the population of Australia.
A: I'm afraid there will be standing _________ only in our country some day.
B: But if every family has only one _________, things will turn for the better.

2 Rewrite these sentences after the model.

Model: I don't know if they will visit our school. →
I *didn't* know if they *would* visit our school.

1 We do not know whether we will have an English test this week.
2 They can't decide when they will visit the farm.
3 I can't find out if the doctor will operate on him.
4 Tom asks Ann when she will return the book.
5 She asks me where I will wait for her.
6 Mrs Jenkins says that she will look after Mary.
7 Robert hopes that you will help him with his Chinese.

***3 Look at the table and talk in pairs.**

A: How many .... were made / produced in 1985 in China.
B: About ....
A: How about 1990?
B: About ... / Sorry, I don't know.

Items	1985	1992
Bicycles	32,277,000	40,836,000
Watches	54,311,000	86,104,600
Fridges	1,448,100	4,857,600
TV sets	16,676,600	28,678,200
Radio sets	16,003,000	16,489,000
Washing machines	8,872,000	7,079,300

Lesson 80

1 Listen to the tape, and choose the right answers.

1 How many different languages are spoken in the world today?
A. 5,000. B. 500. C. 50,000.
2 How many languages are spoken in India?
A. Nearly 9,000. B. Nearly 900. C. About 1,900.
3 Which language is spoken by the most number of people?
A. Chinese. B. Indian. C. English.
4 How many people speak English as their first language?
A. 650 million. B. 33 million. C. 330 million.
5 How many people speak English as a foreign language?
A. 330 million. B. 650 million. C. 65 million.
6 How many words are there in the English language?
A. 790,000. B. 490,000. C. 300,000.
7 How many words do 16-year-old school leavers know?
A. 60,000. B. 6,000. C. 15,000.
8 How many words do most people use?
A. 60,000. B. 6,000. C. 16,000.

2 Put in the missing letters.

1 100
2 1,000
3 1,000,000
4 1,000,000,000

3 1
4 L N
2 N

3 Fill in the blanks with the right form of the words in the brackets.

1 China is developing ________ (quick) than ever before.
2 I could understand what the foreigner said when he spoke ________ (slow) and clearly.
3 By the year 2010, the world's population will be much ________ (large) than today's.
4 The boy ran away as _____ (fast) as he could when he saw his father coming.
5 English is one of the ________ (hard) subjects at school.
6 Chinese is the language spoken by the ________ (large) number of people in the world, but it's not as ________ (wide) spoken as English.

*4 Guess what it is.

It has one or two doors. But it doesn't have any windows. It's usually white or light green. It's made of metal. It's used for keeping food cold.

Unit 21 Lesson 81

1 Practise the dialogues with the words in the box.

A: What can I do for you, Miss?
B: I'm looking for *a dark blue skirt.*
A: What size do you want, please?
B: *Size M.*
A: Yes, we've got Size M, but the blue ones are sold out.
B: Have you got any other colours?
A: Yes. What about those ones over there?
B: Well, this colour looks nice. How much do they cost?
A: *Thirty-eight dollars.*
B: Hmm! That's a bit expensive. Can I try it on, please?
A: Of course.
B: It's just right. I'll take it.

a white shirt a light yellow suit a green dress

Size L Size S

$ 39 $ 25

2 Complete the dialogue.

SON: Look at my trousers, Mum.
MUM: What's wrong, dear?
SON: My trousers are ______ ______.
MUM: Can't they be ________?
SON: No! Look at these holes.
MUM: You'd ______ buy a new ______.
SON: OK. Let's go shopping this Sunday.

3 Give the opposites of the following words.

far	easy	black	right	dark
early	young	large	expensive	short
wide	warm	cold	rich	quiet
borrow	buy	go	take	push
up	after	in	big	slow
inside	without	upstairs	long	behind

4 Fill in the blanks with *make a noise, make a mistake* or *make faces.*

1 "I'm afraid you've ______ ______ ______. I'm Lily. I'm not Lucy," said Lily.
2 Bill sat on the desk and ______ ______. The other students laughed.
3 Li Lei came into the classroom and said, "Stop ______ ______! I have something important to tell you all."

Lesson 82

1 Read this passage on page 82 of your Students' Book and answer the questions.

1 What did John decide to buy?
2 Why did he want to buy some new **clothes** and shoes?
3 Was there a clothing shop near his home?
4 Did he buy any shoes from that shop?
5 What did he think of the suit?
6 How much did the suit cost?
7 Why didn't John buy that suit?
8 What did he decide to buy at last?

2 Choose the right answer.

1 John decided to buy some new clothes and shoes because ______________.
A. he was going to leave school the following week
B. he had got a job and made a lot of money
C. he was going to start work the following week

2 The new shop near his home sells ______________.
A. men's shoes only B. men's shoes and clothes
C. shoes and clothes

3 John didn't buy any shoes from that shop because ____________.
A. the shop didn't have his size B. he didn't have enough money
C. they were all too expensive

4 John was very surprised when he heard ______________.
A. how much the shoes cost B. how much the suit cost
C. how much the jackets cost

5 At last John decided to buy ____________.
A. a jacket B. a pair of shoes C. a suit

3 Fill in the blanks with proper words. Then put the sentences into Chinese.

1 A young man named John decided to ______ some new clothes and a ______ ______ ______ shoes.
2 The shoes were ______ too big ______ too small for John.
3 "We've ______ ______ the shoes in your size," said the shopkeeper.
4 John ______ ______ the suit and went to look ______ ______ in a mirror.
5 John ______ ______ several jackets and at last ______ a very nice one.
6 Have you got anything ______? This suit is too expensive.
7 This is just the ______ size for me. I'll ______ it.

***4 Retell the story on page 82 of the Students' Book in your own words.**

Lesson 83

1 Answer these questions. Write down the answers in your exercise books.

1 Who did John meet before he left the shop?
2 How did they feel when they saw each other?
3 What were they busy doing in the shop?
4 What did they decide to do together?
5 What did John do then?
6 What did the shopkeeper ask John?
7 Did John know why the shopkeeper called him at first?
8 What did John say?
9 What had John forgotten to do?

2 Fill in the blanks with *in, towards, on, up, at, for, of, with, off* or *into* and then retell the story.

John was trying _____ the new jacket. He looked _____ himself in the mirror and thought it was very nice. He picked ____ the jacket and told the shopkeeper to put it _____ a bag. _____ that moment his old friend Ron came _____ the shop. They hadn't seen each other_____ months. They were so pleased to see each other. They talked _____ and _____.

It was late, so they decided to go and have dinner. John picked _____ the bag, and walked _____ the door _____ the shop. The shopkeeper stopped them and asked John to pay _____ the jacket. John looked _____ him _____ surprise _____ first, but soon he remembered that he hadn't paid _____ it. He said sorry and paid _____ the jacket. Then he left the shop _____ his friend.

3 Combine the two sentences by *so ... that ....*

Model: The shoes are too small. I can't wear them. →
The shoes are *so* small *that* I can't wear them.

1 This pair of trousers are too long. I can't wear them.
2 The colour TV is too expensive. We can't buy it.
3 He is running too fast. I can't catch up with him.
4 Some stars are too far away. We can't see them with our eyes.
5 She is speaking too fast. I can't follow her.

4 Read and learn.

care — care**ful**	happy — **un**happy	health — healthy
use — use**ful**	usual — **un**usual	thirst — thirsty
forget — forget**ful**	lucky — **un**lucky	rain — rainy
wonder — wonder**ful**	true — **un**true	snow — snowy

Lesson 84

1 Listen to the tape and choose the right answer.

The girl's name is	Alice.	Lisa.
She has bought	a skirt.	a coat.
She likes	green.	red.
It costs	250 dollars.	280 dollars.
It is	just the right size.	a bit large.
It is made of	cotton.	wool.

2 Fill in the blanks with the right words in the box.

well	slowly
loudly	badly
tired	weak
lazy	young
hard	cold

1 He is so ______ that he cannot go to school.
2 I am so ______ that I cannot go any further.
3 He is becoming so ______ that he doesn't do any housework at home.
4 John's father is so ______ that he often gets up after eight.
5 The weather is getting so ______ that many of us have caught a cold.
6 She worked so ______ that she got the first in the examination.
7 He slept so ______ that I couldn't wake him up.
8 She walked so ______ that she missed the last bus.
9 The little boy hurt himself so ______ that they took him to hospital right away.
10 That woman was talking so ______ that you could hear her from far away.

3 Practise the dialogues with the words in the boxes.

GIRL: Can I help you, sir?
MAN: Yes, please. I want a kilo of *duck*, please.
GIRL: Here you are. Is that all?
MAN: Yes. How much does it cost?
GIRL: *6 dollars*, please.

pork	5 dollars / kilo
mutton	3 dollars / kilo
beef	4 dollars / kilo
fish	4 dollars / kilo
chicken	3 dollars / kilo

What can I do for you, madam?
WOMAN: I would like one and a half kilos of *potatoes*, please.
GIRL: Certainly. Here you are.
WOMAN: How much is it?
GIRL: *2 dollars*.

carrots	1 dollars / kilo
tomatoes	2 dollars / kilo
cabbages	1 dollars / kilo
peas	3 dollars / kilo
nuts	4 dollars / kilo

Unit 22 Lesson 85

1 Fill in the blanks with the sentences in the box and act out the dialogue.

MOTHER: Why don't you get up, Kate? It's time for school.
KATE: Sorry, Mum! ________________
MOTHER: Oh dear! ________________
KATE: I've got a headache and a cough.
MOTHER: ________________
FATHER: What's wrong with Kate?
MOTHER: ________________ I told her to stay in bed till tomorrow.
FATHER: Nothing serious, I hope!
MOTHER: I hope not. ________________

1 What's the trouble?
2 I don't feel very well.
3 She's not feeling well.
4 Perhaps she's caught a cold.
5 You'd better stay in bed till tomorrow.

2 Match the sentences (句子配对).

1 I feel a little thirsty.	A. We'd better take her to hospital.
2 I've forgotten to bring my pen.	B. You'd better stop to have a drink.
3 I couldn't sleep well these days.	C. You 'd better turn on the lights.
4 I feel very warm in here.	D. You'd better go and borrow one.
5 His radio is very noisy.	E. You'd better ask him to turn it down.
6 It's rather dark in this room.	F. You'd better take off your coat.
7 Linda is very ill now.	G. You'd better go and see a doctor.

***3 Write your English teacher a note asking for a sick leave (病假). The words in the box will help you.**

Dear Mr / Miss.................,

I'm sorry to tell you that I'm not feeling well today. ....

....

....

....

....

....

catch a bad cold
doctor tell me
stay in bed for two days
can not go to school
today and tomorrow
hope get well
very soon thank you

Lesson 86

1 Read the dialogue on page 86 of your Students' Book and answer the questions. Write the answers in your exercise books.

1 Where were Tom and his mother?
2 What was wrong with Tom?
3 Did Tom have a temperature?
4 What did Tom have for breakfast that morning?
5 Would Tom stay at home or go to school?
6 Did the doctor think Tom was terribly ill?

2 Puzzle dialogue

A: ____________
B: Good morning. What's your trouble, young man?
A: ____________
B: How long have you been like this?
A: ____________
B: Have you taken your temperature?
A: ____________
B: Well, you have caught a cold.
A: ____________
B: No, nothing serious. Take these pills and stay in bed for two days.
A: ____________
B: Yes. You must stay at home for two days.
A: ____________
B: It'll be a pity if you can't go. But health is better than wealth (财富), young man.

1 Oh, no, I can't stay in bed. We'll have a football match next Monday. And if we win the match, each of us will get a T-shirt!
2 Good morning, doctor.
3 I've got a headache and a cough. I'm feeling terrible now.
4 Do you mean I can't go to school for two days, doctor?
5 Since last night.
6 Yes, the nurse has. She said it was a little high.
7 Is it serious, Doctor?

3 Fill in the blanks with *something, everything, anything* or *nothing*.

1 There is ____________ wrong with the computer. It doesn't work.
2 Is there ____________ to eat in the fridge, Mum? I'm so hungry.
3 ____________ is difficult if you put your heart into it.
4 ____________ is all right at my place. Please don't worry!
5 **A**: Do you have ____________ to say at this meeting?
B: No, I have ____________ to say.
6 ____________ has a hard beginning.
7 "____________ serious! You've just caught a bit of cold," said the doctor.

Lesson 87

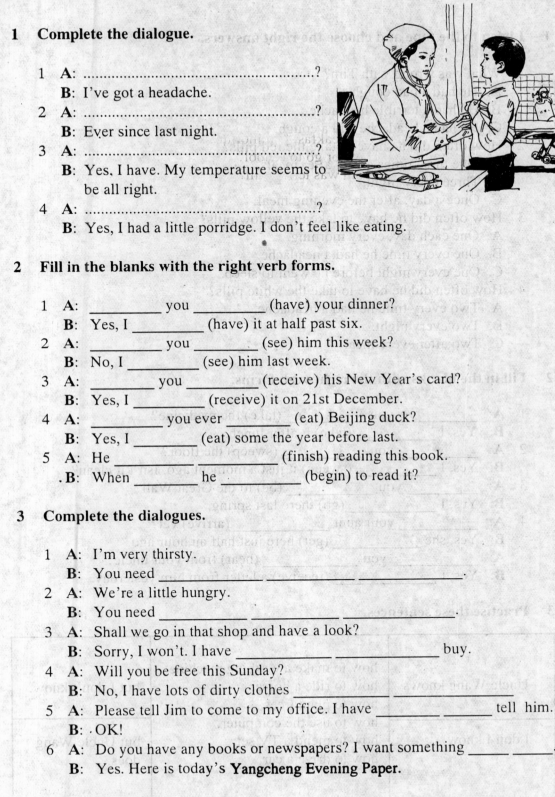

1 Complete the dialogue.

1 **A**: ....?

B: I've got a headache.

2 **A**: ....?

B: Ever since last night.

3 **A**: ....?

B: Yes, I have. My temperature seems to be all right.

4 **A**: ....?

B: Yes, I had a little porridge. I don't feel like eating.

2 Fill in the blanks with the right verb forms.

1 **A**: ________ you ________ (have) your dinner?

B: Yes, I ________ (have) it at half past six.

2 **A**: ________ you ________ (see) him this week?

B: No, I ________ (see) him last week.

3 **A**: ________ you ________ (receive) his New Year's card?

B: Yes, I ________ (receive) it on 21st December.

4 **A**: ________ you ever ________ (eat) Beijing duck?

B: Yes, I ________ (eat) some the year before last.

5 **A**: He ________ ________ (finish) reading this book.

B: When ________ he ________ (begin) to read it?

3 Complete the dialogues.

1 **A**: I'm very thirsty.

B: You need ________ ________ ________.

2 **A**: We're a little hungry.

B: You need ________ ________ ________.

3 **A**: Shall we go in that shop and have a look?

B: Sorry, I won't. I have ________ ________ buy.

4 **A**: Will you be free this Sunday?

B: No, I have lots of dirty clothes ________ ________.

5 **A**: Please tell Jim to come to my office. I have ________ ________ tell him.

B: OK!

6 **A**: Do you have any books or newspapers? I want something ______ ______.

B: Yes. Here is today's **Yangcheng Evening Paper**.

Lesson 88

1 Listen to the tape and choose the right answers.

1 What was wrong with Tim?
A. He had a bad cough.
B. He had a terrible headache.
C. He had a headache and a cough.

2 How often did he have to take the red pills?
A. One three times a day, after meals.
B. Three every night.
C. Once a day, after the evening meal.

3 How often did he have to take the yellow pills?
A. One each day, every morning.
B. One every time he had a headache.
C. One every night before he went to sleep.

4. How often did he have to take the white pills?
A. Two every time he had a headache.
B. Two every night.
C. Two after every meal.

2 Fill in the blanks with the right verb forms.

1 **A**: ________ you ________ (take) the medicine?
B: Yes, I ________ (take) it after lunch.

2 **A**: ________ you ________ (sweep) the floor?
B: Yes, I ________ (sweep) it just a moment ago. Isn't it clean?

3 **A**: ________ you ________ (be) to the Great Wall?
B: Yes, I ________ (go) there last spring.

4 **A**: ________ your aunt ________ (arrive) yet?
B: Yes, she ________ (get) here just half an hour ago.
A: ________ you ________ (hear) from your uncle?
B: Yes, I ________ (receive) a letter from him yesterday.

3 Practise these sentences.

Uncle Wang knows	how to make a washing machine, how to ride a horse, how to plant trees, how to use the computer, how to mend a TV set, how to drive a car,	but I don't know.
I don't know		but Uncle Wang does.

Unit 23 Lesson 89

1 Join the two sentences after the models.

Model 1: Lily may go with you, or Lucy may. →
Either Lily ***or*** Lucy may go with you.

1 My father will go to the evening party, or my mother will.
2 You may stay here tonight, or he may.
3 Wei Hua can have this English book, or Meimei can.
4 You can get the film tickets, or I can.
5 Mr Wang may move out, or Mr Wu may.

Model 2: He won't spend his holiday anywhere else,
and his wife won't, either. →
Neither he ***nor*** his wife will spend their holiday anywhere else.

1 Liu Mei doesn't want to go there on foot, and Xiao Hai doesn't, either.
2 He doesn't like mutton, and she doesn't, either.
3 My father won't come to see me tomorrow, and my mother won't, either.
4 Ma Lin hasn't seen him for long, and Gao Feng hasn't, either.
5 His father can't help him with **his** English, and his mother can't, either.

2 Practise the dialogues in pairs, and then make a similar dialogue.

A: Which would you like, madam, ***tea*** or ***orange***?
B: Neither, thanks. I'd like ***a glass of water***, please.
A: OK. Anything else?
B: No, thanks.
A: Which would you like, sir, ***beer*** (啤酒) or ***water***?
C: Either is OK.
A: Would you like anything else?
C: ***A hamburger***, please.

3 Choose the right answer.

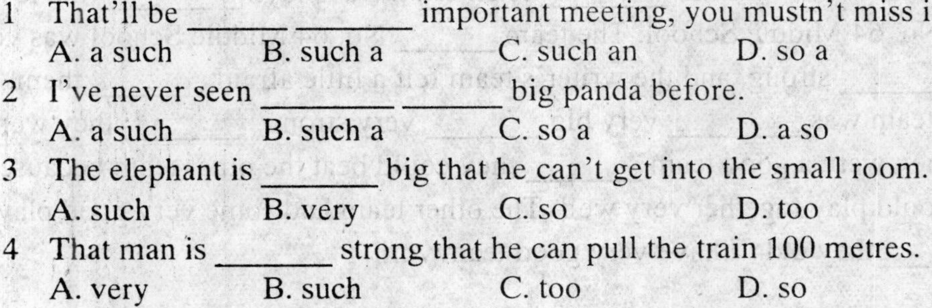

1 That'll be ______ ______ important meeting, you mustn't miss it.
A. a such B. such a C. such an D. so a
2 I've never seen ______ ______ big panda before.
A. a such B. such a C. so a D. a so
3 The elephant is ______ big that he can't get into the small room.
A. such B. very C. so D. too
4 That man is ______ strong that he can pull the train 100 metres.
A. very B. such C. too D. so

Lesson 90

1 Read the page of diary on page 90 of your Students' Book and then answer the questions.

1 When was the football match held?
2 What was the weather like that day?
3 Was the writer's team top of the league before that match?
4 Why did the writer find it difficult to work in class that day?
5 Which team did the writer's team play against?
6 What was No. 64 Middle School's football team like?
7 What was the writer's team like?
8 Who was the P.E. teacher of the writer's team?
9 What did their P.E. teacher ask them to remember?
10 What was the weak point of the other team?

2 Fill in the blanks with the phrases in the box.

A as often as possible
B as many as you like
C as much as you can
D as well as you can
E as far as you can
F as quickly as possible
G as soon as possible
H as fast as you can

1 I'm waiting for your letter, please write me ____.
2 If you like the fish, please have ________.
3 Don't be afraid! Please play ________.
4 He's fallen ill. Please send for a doctor ____.
5 Please run ________. You'll be the winner.
6 These books are for you, please choose ______.
7 Try to speak English with your friends ______.
8 Please jump _______.

3 Read the diary on page 90 of the Students' Book and fill in the blanks with the proper words.

The writer had a quick breakfast and then went _______ school. He found it difficult ______ work ______ class because he kept on thinking _______ the match _______ the afternoon.

School ended a little _______. Their team was playing _______ the team from No. 64 Middle School. The team ______ No. 64 Middle School was very big _______ strong, and the writer's team felt a little afraid _______ them. Their team was ________ very big ________ very strong. _______ they were sure they were a good team _______ they could beat the other team because they could play together very well. The other team had some very good players, ________ they didn't have very good teamwork.

***4 Retell the story in the student's diary.**

Lesson 91

1 Find the answer with the same meaning as the underlined part in each sentence.

1 If we won this match, <u>we would be top</u>!

A. we would be the last B. we would be the best

C. we would be the worst D. we could lose all games

2 <u>It was a draw</u> when we played against them last time.

A. We were beaten by them B. We won the match

C. They lost the game D. We kicked the same goals as they did.

3 But still we weren't sure <u>we could beat them</u>.

A. we could win the game B. we would lose the game

C. they could win the game D. they would lose the game

4 Mr Wu told his team to remember — <u>TEAMWORK</u>!

A. to learn from each other B. to play together very well

C. to help each other in work D. to work with friends

5 Early in the first half of the match <u>he kicked a goal</u>.

A. he kicked the ball out B. he fell down on the ground

C. he broke one of his legs D. he got a goal

6 <u>By the end of the match</u>, they had kicked two goals and we had kicked four.

A. Before the match nearly ended, B. Before the match began,

C. After the match started, D. When the match was going on,

2 Fill in the blanks with *such, both, or, neither, nor,* or *either*.

1 I have never eaten ______ delicious noodles before.

2 We ______ have got tickets. You'd better give it to somebody else.

3 There's only one bike here. ______ you ______ he can use it.

4 ______ she ______ I know his telephone number, because it has been changed.

5 We didn't go to see him yesterday, because ______ of us had his home address.

6 **A**: Are you ______ the same age?
B: No, I am two years older than her.

3 Give the past and past participle forms of the verbs.

break <u>broke</u> <u>broken</u>	read ______ ______	sleep ______ ______
beat ______ ______	make ______ ______	become ______ ______
write ______ ______	be ______ ______	see ______ ______
fight ______ ______	give ______ ______	choose ______ ______
keep ______ ______	begin ______ ______	know ______ ______

Lesson 92

1 Fill in the blanks with the phrases in the box.

A a pair of
B a cup of
C a glass of
D a piece of
E a bottle of
F a plate of
G a bag of

1 **A**: Would you like ____________ tea?
B: No. I'd like ____________ water.
A: How about you?
C: I want __________ orange.
2 Would you please pass me ________ paper and a pen?
3 I was very hungry, so I had ________ fish and some bread.
4 Uncle bought me __________ sports shoes for my birthday.
5 We three people cannot finish such __________ rice in one month.

2 Fill in the blanks with the words in the box.

because
since
kept on raining
afraid of
against
in time

1 **A**: It's a long time _____ we last met. How are you?
B: I'm very well. Thank you.
2 **A**: Has the film begun?
B: Not yet, you are just _______ _______.
3 **A**: Why did you end your school so early today?
B: ________ there's going to be a football match.
4 **A**: Who are you going to play ________?
B: No. 60 Middle School.
5 **A**: Are you ________ ________ tigers?
B: Ahh, terrible!
6 **A**: Did you have a good holiday?
B: No, it ______________________ all the time.

3 Fill in the blanks with the right verb form.

1 When I got to the station, the train ________ ________ (leave). So I had to come back and wait for the next.
2 **A**: Did you see him last night?
B: No. When I got to his home, he ______________ (go) to bed.
3 It ________ __________ (stop) raining when I woke up this morning.
4 **A**: You watched the TV play last night, didn't you?
B: Yes. But I missed the beginning. When I turned on the TV, it ________ ________ (begin).
5 Xiao Wang's mother was ill. Somebody called him back home at once. When Xiao Wang _________ (hurry) home, he found that his mother ________ already _________ (go) to **hospital**.
6 The little boy said that he _______ never _________ (hear) such an interesting story.

Unit 24 Lesson 93

1 Join the two sentences after the model.

Model 1: He doesn't have a computer. She doesn't have a computer, either. →
Neither of them has a computer.

1 He hasn't got a brother. She hasn't got a brother, either.
2 I don't have much money. You don't have much money, either.
3 She isn't a scientist. He isn't a scientist, either.
4 Lisa hasn't been to the Great Wall. Bob hasn't been to the Great Wall, either.
5 I don't know his telephone number.
You don't know his telephone number, either.

Model 2: John was ill yesterday. Ann was ill yesterday, too. →
Both John and Ann were ill yesterday.

1 Lily has got a new dress. Lucy has got a new dress, too.
2 Jim is good at drawing. Tom is good at drawing, too.
3 Mr Wang is going to the USA. Mr Wu is going to the USA, too.
4 Bill has got a penfriend. Jill has got a penfriend, too.
5 America is an English-speaking country. Australia is an English-speaking country, too.

2 Fill in the blanks with *though* or *but*. Put the sentences into Chinese.

1 Lily can speak some Chinese, __________ Linda can't.
2 __________ it's getting dark, the farmers are still working in the fields.
3 It was raining hard, __________ we went on with our work in the rain.
4 Jim has passed the maths exam, __________ Bill hasn't.
5 __________ the doctor has told Mr Smith not to smoke, he still smokes as much as before.
6 __________ he is over sixty, he goes to work by bike.
7 Mr Bush hates travelling, __________ Mrs Bush doesn't.
8 She is not the boy's mother, __________ she loves him as much as she loves her own child.

3 Ask and answer.

1 **A:** How often do you write to your penfriend? **B:** ....
2 **A:** How often do you have English classes? **B:** ....
3 **A:** How often do you have meetings? **B:** ....
4 **A:** How often do you see films? **B:** ....

Lesson 94

1 Read the letter on page 94 of your Students' Book and answer the questions. Write down the answers in your exercise books.

1 Who is this letter from and who is this letter to?
2 When and where did Bob White write this letter?
3 When did Bob receive Wei Hua's letter?
4 Where is Ayers Rock?
5 How did Bob and his family go to Ayers Rock?
6 Why didn't they reach the top?
7 How do the sand and the sky look when the sun goes down?
8 How many sheep does Australia have?

2 Choose the right answers.

1 Bob White went to Ayers Rock ________.
A. to buy something B. to spend a holiday C. to see mountains
2 They went to Ayers Rock ________ most of the way.
A. by land B. by sea C. by air
3 Ayers Rock is in the ________ of Australia.
A. southwest B. southeast C. middle
4 Ayers Rock is the name of ________.
A. a city B. country C. a mountain
5 They started climbing the mountain before the sun rose, because ________.
A. it gets too cloudy later B. it gets too hot later C. it gets too cold later.
6 The population of Australia is about ________.
A. 1,700,000 B. 17,000,000 C. 170,000,000

3 Fill in the blanks with proper words.

Ayers Rock is a ____ mountain, but not very ______. It is in the ______ of Australia. It's nearly two thousand ________ ________ Sydney. Bob White and his family went there for ______ ______. They ______ ______ a line of mountains. Then they found most of the land below ______ like ______. Dad told Bob that there were a lot of ______ down there, but ________ any people.

The next day, they started climbing up the mountain ______ the sun ______. If they started late, the weather would get too ______ for climbing. ______ the foot of Ayers Rock they found most of the ground was covered with ______ and ______. But when they climbed ________, they found nothing ________ at all. They didn't ______ the top, because it was too ______. When the sun ______ ______, both the ______ and the ______ turned red. It looked really ________.

Lesson 95

1 Match the sentences.

1 Though I like English very much,
2 I didn't have my breakfast this morning,
3 Though they've won the first game,
4 I have never seen him before,
5 Though he is old,

A. but I have heard a lot about him.
B. it will be rather difficult for them to win the second.
C. he never stops learning.
D. I can't remember the words well.
E. but I don't feel hungry now.

2 Fill in the blanks with *neither* ... *nor*..., or *either* ... *or*....

1 ______ he ______ I knew about this accident because it was kept as a secret.
2 ______ Lily ______ Lucy will go with you because one of them must be at home to help her mother.
3 ______ the black one ______ the blue one is mine. Mine was borrowed by Li Lei.
4 ______ Tuesday ______ Wednesday is OK. I'll be free on these days.
5 ______ he ______ I know his address because he moved just a week ago.

3 Choose the right country for each city.

1	Paris is the capital of ______.	A. the USA	B. Japan	C. France
2	Toronto is a city of ______.	A. Canada	B. the USA	C. Australia
3	London is the capital of ______.	A. Japan	B. England	C. Australia
4	Tokyo is the capital of ______.	A. Australia	B. France	C. Japan
5	New York is a city in ______.	A. the USA	B. France	C. Japan
6	Sydney is a city in ______.	A. England	B. France	C. Australia

4 Look at the colour page iv, and write something about the Ayers Rock.

*** 5 Read and talk.**

The building is on fire. There are six people on the top floor. They are a farmer, a doctor, a teacher, a scientist, an old worker and a little boy. The building seems to fall down very soon. The firemen (消防队员) have a ladder. There is only enough time for them to save one of the six people. Do you know whom the firemen will save first? Why do you think so?

Lesson 96

1 Look at the picture. It is a picture of a very common animal in Australia — a kangaroo (袋鼠). Talk about the picture with your teacher. Then listen to the tape, and choose the right answers.

1 How many different kinds of kangaroo are there?
A. Seven. B. Forty-seven. C. Only one.
2 How large is a big kangaroo?
A. Smaller than a man. B. Bigger than a man.
C. The same size as a man.
3 How often does a kangaroo have a baby?
A. Twice a year. B. Once a year. C. Once every two years.
4 How long does a baby kangaroo stay in its mother's pocket?
A. One month. B. Three months. C. Six months.
5 What do kangaroos eat?
A. Anything. B. Other animals. C. Fruit, leaves and grass.
6 **Fill in the blanks:**
The biggest kangaroos stand more than ________ metres tall, and can jump more than _________ metres. They are very fast, and can travel at more than _________ kilometres an hour.

2 Rewrite the sentences using *neither* or *both*.

1 She doesn't like French. He doesn't like French, either.
2 He hasn't seen an elephant. She hasn't seen an elephant, either.
3 He is not at work. She is not at work, either.
4 He has had his lunch. She has had her lunch, too.
5 I would like a cup of tea. He would like a cup of tea, too.

3 Write an envelope in English and draw a stamp in the right place.

* Your address:

...

* The receiver's name and address:

Miss Nancy Pattis
407 M Street NW
Washington D.C.
USA

***4 Write a letter about yourself to your penfriend.**

Revision exercises

I 语音、语法和词汇练习

1 Read each group of the words and find the word with a different vowel sound.

( )	1	A. n*a*me	B. pl*a*ce	C. th*a*nk	D. l*a*te
( )	2	A. tr*ee*	B. sh*e*	C. m*ee*ting	D. sp*e*nd
( )	3	A. sh*i*p	B. t*i*me	C. l*i*fe	D. n*i*ce
( )	4	A. h*o*me	B. sh*o*p	C. ag*o*	D. *o*ver
( )	5	A. st*u*dent	B. h*u*rry	C. s*u*mmer	D. s*u*n
( )	6	A. h*ea*d	B. str*ee*t	C. m*ea*l	D. p*ie*ce
( )	7	A. c*are*	B. cl*ear*	C. h*air*	D. wh*ere*
( )	8	A. wea*th*er	B. *th*an	C. ear*th*	D. mo*th*er
( )	9	A. bru*sh*	B. wa*sh*ing	C. *s*ure	D. *s*outh
( )	10	A. *c*ry	B. *c*loud	C. *c*entre	D. *c*atch
( )	11	A. *h*our	B. *h*orse	C. *h*eart	D. *h*oliday
( )	12	A. shop*s*	B. leg*s*	C. desk*s*	D. park*s*

2 Pronounce these words and spell them out. Then put the words into Chinese.

1 [tʃi:p] ________	11 [bə:d] ________	21 [dɔg] ________
2 [bred] ________	12 ['brʌðə] ________	22 [si:t] ________
3 [bʌs] ________	13 ['beibi] ________	23 [geit] ________
4 [lɑ:dʒ] ________	14 [krai] ________	24 [plei] ________
5 [ki:p] ________	15 [baik] ________	25 ['veri] ________
6 [bɔks] ________	16 [rɔŋ] ________	26 [ʃɔ:t] ________
7 ['meni] ________	17 [bɔi] ________	27 ['wə:kə] ________
8 [buk] ________	18 ['hɔspitl] ________	28 [tri:] ________
9 [tʃu:z] ________	19 [kɛə] ________	29 ['bizi] ________
10 [brait] ________	20 [kliə] ________	30 ['siŋə] ________

3 Pronounce these words and spell them out. Then put them into Chinese.

1	[wi:k] ________	[weik] ________	[wɔ:k] ________	[wə:k] ________
2	[mʌtʃ] ________	[mɑ:tʃ] ________	[mætʃ] ________	[mauθ] ________
3	[big] ________	[bæg] ________	[bed] ________	[bæd] ________
4	[θiŋ] ________	[θin] ________	[θiŋk] ________	[θæŋk] ________

4 Tick the correct vowel sound for each group of the words.

1 p*a*ss h*ar*d cl*a*ss f*a*st he*ar*t
A. [ɑ:] B. [ɔ:] C. [ei] D. [æ]

2 sp*or*t m*ore* fl*oor* s*aw* w*ar*m
A. [əu] B. [uə] C. [ɔ:] D. [ɑ:]

3 sh*ir*t t*ur*n p*er*son w*or*d l*ear*n
A. [ɔ:] B. [ə:] C. [ɛə] D. [iə]

4 br*ea*k aw*ay* t*a*ke w*ai*t afr*ai*d
A. [i:] B. [ei] C. [ai] D. [e]

5 wh*ere* th*ere* p*ear* c*are* *air*
A. [iə] B. [ə:] C. [uə] D. [ɛə]

6 h*u*ngry bec*o*me m*o*ney s*u*n s*u*mmer
A. [u] B. [ɔ] C. [ʌ] D. [ɑ:]

7 br*ow*n t*ow*n l*ou*d h*ou*se cl*ou*d
A. [ɔ] B. [əu] C. [ʌ] D. [au]

5 Put the right letters in the following words, then read them out.

1 e ea ee ie ei ey
f_____ld rec_____ve agr_____ b_____t _____ven k_____

2 a ai ay eigh ey ea
br_____k _____teen p_____ ag_____nst h_____te th_____

3 o oa ow oo oi oy
j_____n h_____ld r_____d ch_____se enj_____ sh_____

4 ar er ir or ur ear
w_____ld d_____k d_____ty _____ly b_____n p_____son

6 Form new words.

foot<u>ball</u>	book_____	class_____	pen_____
every_____	moon_____	birth_____	home_____
some_____	any_____	black_____	grand_____
south_____	shop_____	pencil-_____	loud_____

7 Change these words as the models, and then put them into Chinese.

1 Models: swim → swim**mer** teach → teach**er**

clean dance keep listen sing drive make

jump	learn	lose	work	own	play	build
run	sell	speak	tell	use	read	travel

2 **Models:** kind → kind**ly** lucky → luck**ily**

bad	easy	bright	busy	careful	safe	usual
quick	quiet	angry	happy	heavy	hungry	noisy

3 **Models:** use → use**ful** sun → sun**ny**

care help hope cloud rain wind snow

4 **Models:** house → houses factory → factor**ies** man → men

season	week	nurse	friend	match	brush	glass	library	
fish	family	story	woman	child	foot	knife	leaf	sheep

8 Complete the sentences.

1 The woman in a red coat is ________________ (王琳的妈妈).
2 (露西的裙子) ________________ is more beautiful than yours.
3 (格林先生的办公室) ________________ is on the second floor.
4 The shop near the post office sells ________________ (男鞋).
5 (王大伯的家) ________________ is near a river.
6 (日本的首都) ________________ is Tokyo.
7 Shall we meet at 9:00 tomorrow morning in front of ________________ ________________ (人民公园的门口)?
8 (这本书的纸张) ________________ is not good enough.
9 Before the sunrise the farmer and the scientist took the eagle to ________________ ________________ (山顶).
10 (这棵树的叶子) ________________ will turn yellow and fall down in autumn.

9 Choose the right answer for each blank.

1 My parents are teachers. ________ both teach English.
A. Them B. They C. He D. She
2 Aunt Liu is a doctor. ________ works in the People's Hospital.
A. He B. She C. Him D. Her
3 My skirt is more expensive than ________.
A. she B. her C. hers D. him
4 He told ____ in the letter that he would meet ________ at the station.
A. I ... we B. my ... our C. his ... her D. me ... us
5 The two girls are crying. ________ cannot find ________ mother.
A. Her ... she B. They ... them C. They ... her D. They ... their

6 Mrs Green hates travelling. ______ is going to stay at home with ______ children for the summer holiday.

A. She ... their B. She ... her C. He ... their D. He ... his

7 The red dress is ________ and the blue one is ________.

A. me ... you B. my ... your C. mine ... yours D. mine ... your

8 ________ school is much larger than ________.

A. They ... our B. Theirs ... ours C. Theirs ... our D. Their ... ours

9 **A**: Excuse me! Is this bike ________?

B: No, it's not ________. ________ bike is at home.

A. yours ... mine ... My B. your ... mine ... My

C. yours ... my ... Mine D. mine ... yours ... My

10 Fill in the blanks with *myself, yourself, himself, herself, ourselves, yourselves* and *themselves.*

1 The girl put on her new dress and then went to the mirror to look at ______.

2 Li Ming's grandfather is so old that he cannot look after ________.

3 "I'm poor, but I always enjoy ____________," said Mr Thin.

4 "Please take good care of __________ while you are away from home," Mother said to her son.

5 "Please help __________ to the fish," Mrs Read said to us.

6 **A**: Did you have a good time last night?

B: Yes, we all enjoyed ____________ very much. Thank you.

7 They said that they had done this work by ______________.

8 **A**: Your English is very good. How did you learn it?

B: I taught ____________.

9 Oh, she fell off her bike. I hope she didn't hurt __________.

10 After he left middle school, he stayed at home for a year and learned medicine all by ____________.

11 Fill in the blanks with the words in the brackets.

1 **A**: What would you like to drink, please?

B: I'd like ________ water. (any, some, many, much)

2 There isn't _______ paper in the box. Will you go and get _______ for me? (some, any, many, much)

3 I'm very busy because I've so ______ books to read and so ________ work to do every day. (many, much)

4 **A**: How ______ money do you spend on food each month?

B: About sixty *yuan*. (many, much)

5 Her parents are _______ doctors, so she wants to be a doctor, too. (both, all)

6 ______ of the students in our class want to go to plant trees. (both, all)

7 Class is over. That's _______ for today. (both, all)

8 Don't rush. There's still ____________ time left. (little, a little, few, a few)

9 **A**: Do you have any friends in Beijing?

B: Yes, I have __________ there. (little, a little, few, a few)

10 This question is so difficult that very _________ people in our class can answer it. (little, a little, few, a few)

11 We have __________ milk for the baby. You'd better go and buy some. (little, a little, few, a few)

12 These shoes are too small for me. Would you please show me ______ pair? (one, another, other, the other)

13 I have two sisters. __________ is a doctor, and __________ is a nurse. (one, another, other, the other)

14 I study Chinese, English, maths and some __________ subjects. (one, another, other, the other)

12 Write out the numbers in English and read them aloud.

12 20 28 80 92 101 1,000 1,350

58,600 694,320 1,008,000 85,002,000 3,000,000,000

13 Write these in numbers.

1 six thousand seven hundred and eighty-nine ( )

2 thirty-four thousand five hundred and sixty-four ( )

3 seven hundred and eighty thousand and thirty two ( )

4 five million three hundred thousand ( )

5 one billion one hundred million ( )

14 Read and write these dates, years and telephone numbers in English.

1662 1774 1840 1900 1911 1949

1980. 1. 1 1992. 7. 23 1995. 5. 12 2001. 11. 18

4016633 5505824 3388691 4433275

9843150 3017755 5016789 7556076

15 Write out the numbers in English. Pay attention to *9th, 12th, 20th, 21st, 32nd, 43rd,* and *101st*.

1st ________ 2nd ________ 3rd ________ 4th ________ 5th ________

6th ________ 7th ________ 8th ________ 9th ________ 10th ________

11th ________ 12th ________ 20th ________ 21st ________ 32nd ________

40th ________ 43rd ________ 100th ________ 101st ________

16 Fill in the blanks with the prepositions in the box.

from of with except by round about on at in
behind for without along across between to

1 I often go shopping with my mother ________ Sundays.
2 We'll have a meeting ________ 9:30 tomorrow morning.
3 This story happened ________ March, 1979.
4 He found himself fall ________ the others after he came back from Britain.
5 The satellites go ________ the earth, and help us to learn more ________ the earth, the weather and other things.
6 Many ________ the stars cannot be seen because they are too far away ________ us.
7 It was very interesting to eat, live and work ________ farmers for a week.
8 All of us, ________ Xiao Ming, went to Xiangshan Park last Sunday because he had caught a bad cold.
9 **A**: It was raining hard this morning. How did you come here?
B: I came here ________ train.
10 I had studied English ________ 3 years before I went ________ Australia.
11 ________ your help we cannot finish the work.
12 Go ________ this road, turn left at the second crossing and go ________ the bridge. You'll find a tall green building ________ a hospital and a school.

17 Choose the right answer.

1 This programme was sent to the USA ________ China ________ satellite.
A. in ... of B. of ... in C. from ... by D. by ... from
2 Many people say I look ________ my father.
A. after B. up C. at D. like
3 China has built a Great Green Wall ____ the northern part ____ the country.
A. to ... in B. across ... of C. across ... on D. at ... in
4 Before 1980 there was no airline ________ the two cities.
A. across B. along C. between D. among
5 It's not good to be late ________ school.
A. for B. on C. about D. to
6 She asked me to sit ________ her and help her ________ Chinese.
A. beside ... with B. between ... at
C. below ... on D. before ... in
7 Which team are you going to play ________?
A. by B. up C. about D. against
8 Please leave ________ 7:00, then you'll be able to get there ________ time.
A. till ... in B. after ... on C. before ... on D. behind ... in

18 Fill in the blanks with the words in the box.

before	when	since	because	until	while	and	so	if	or

1 I cannot go home ________ I finish my homework.
2 I had worked for three years ________ I joined the P.L.A.
3 She has never come back to see her daughter again ________ she left in 1975.
4 He is listening to the music ________ he is washing clothes.
5 My father cannot come to see you ________ he is too busy.
6 Where were you ________ it began to rain hard yesterday afternoon?
7 My mother is good at cooking, ________ my father is good at cooking, too.
8 ________ I have time next Sunday, I'll go and visit your new house.
9 **A**: Do you want to stay at home ________ go shopping with us, my children?
B: I want to go shopping. What about you?
C: ________ do I.

19 Give the opposites of the following words.

difficult ________	small ________	black ________
same ________	happy ________	wrong ________
poor ________	thin ________	far ________
high ________	weak ________	warm ________
wet ________	bad ________	clean ________
fast ________	safe ________	empty ________
new ________	long ________	bright ________
inside ________	after ________	down ________
late ________	no ________	noisy ________
last ________	best ________	cheap ________
go ________	lend ________	buy ________
start ________	hate ________	forget ________
pull ________	bring ________	give ________

20 Fill in each blank with a proper adjective or adverb.

1 Many students cannot answer this question. It is very ________.
2 He is such a strong man that he can lift the heavy stone ________.
3 This bottle is ________. Would you please give me a full one?
4 We can't hear you. Speak ________, please.
5 Is there anything to eat? I'm very ________.
6 She got up very ________ so that she could catch the first bus.
7 This skirt is too ________. Do you have any cheap ones?
8 In the old days many children couldn't go to school because their families were very ________.
9 Eating more vegetables will keep you ________.
10 That apple is too high. I am not ________ enough to reach it.

21 Fill in the blanks with the opposites of the adjectives.

1 I don't like *dark* blue. Could you let me have a __________ blue dress?
2 It is *dangerous* to play here. Let's find a __________ place.
3 This room is a little *dark*. Shall we go and find a __________ one?
4 My shirt is *dirty*. I'll change into a __________ one tomorrow.
5 The weather in Beijing is usually *dry* in spring and __________ in summer.
6 These blouses are *expensive*, but these T-shirts are __________.
7 He felt *sad* when he found himself lying in bed, but when the doctor told him there was nothing serious, he began to feel __________.
8 Canada is a *large* country. New Zealand is a __________ country.
9 This question is quite *easy* for us Chinese students, but __________ for Jim.
10 My sports shoes are *old* and worn out. I'll ask my mother to buy me a __________ pair.
11 I think having too much meat is *bad* for health, but having more vegetables is __________ for health.

22 Give the comparative and superlative degrees of the adjectives and adverbs.

weak ________ ________ deep ________ ________ clear ________ ________
busy ________ ________ dirty ________ ________ clever ________ ________
few ________ ________ wide ________ ________ fast ________ ________
low ________ ________ bad ________ ________ well ________ ________
little ________ ________ carefully ________ ________
difficult ________ ________ important ________ ________

23 Fill in the blanks with the right form of the adjectives and adverbs.

1 Their house is a little __________ (small) than ours.
2 Travelling by train is much __________ (safe) than by plane.
3 My brother is two years __________ (old) than I.
4 I hope you're well. You look much __________ (thin) than before.
5 Which do you like __________ (well), tea, orange or water?
6 Which is the __________ (large) city, Shanghai, Beijing or Tianjin?
7 Beijing is one of the seven __________ (old) capital cities in China.
8 I came here just a little __________ (early) than you.
9 The seats in the middle of the cinema are the __________ (good).
10 Which city is ________ ________ (beautiful), Beijing or Shanghai?
11 Chinese is one of the ________ ________ (important) subjects in middle schools.
12 Travelling by air is much ________ ________ (expensive) than by train.

24 Choose the right answer.

1 China and India are ____________ countries.
A. develop B. developed C. developing D. to develop

2 Germany and Great Britain are ____________ countries.
A. develop B. developed C. developing D. to develop

3 The population of Australia is ____________ than that of Canada.
A. fewer B. smaller C. larger D. more

4 Germany has ____________ people than France.
A. fewer B. smaller C. larger D. more

5 The population of France is almost as ____________ as Great Britain.
A. few B. many C. large D. more

6 India has the second ____________ population in the world.
A. larger B. largest C. most D. smallest

7 Which is the ____________ country, Japan or Australia?
A. more developed B. more developing
C. most developed D. most developing

25 Fill in the blanks.

1 **A**: Are things on the earth ____________ they are on the moon?
B: No, they are much ____________ on the earth than they are on the moon. (heavy, as heavy as)

2 **A**: Is this book ____________ that one?
B: No, this one is ____________ than that one because it has some ____________ beautiful pictures than that one. (interesting, more, as interesting as)

3 Lucy skates ____________ than Lily, but she doesn't skate ____________ Linda. (well, as well as)

4 Mr Read doesn't drive ____________ Mrs Read. But he drives ____________ ____________ than Mr King. (carefully, as carefully as)

26 Fill in the blanks with *what, when, where, how* or *why*.

1 **A**: Hello! May I ask you some questions, please?
B: Yes, please.
A: ____________ are you from?
B: Australia.
A: ____________ did you come to Beijing?
B: In 1980.
A: ____________ did you come to China, by sea or by air?
B: By air.
A: ____________ did you come to China?
B: I wanted to do something for China's education (教育).
A: ____________ are you going to leave Beijing?
B: On 10th of this September.
A: A happy journey home then!
B: Thank you.

2 **A**: Do you know _____ to do after the meeting?
B: Maybe we'll go out for lunch.
A: Did he tell you _______ to go?
B: To the same place as last time we went.
A: Do you know ______ to start our lunch?
B: I was told to get there at 11:30.

3 **A**: Could you tell me ______ to get to Zhongshan Road?
B: You can get there by bus No. 10.

4 **A**: Will you please show me _______ to drive a car?
B: Yes, of course. Now let me tell you _______ to do first.

27 Fill in the blanks with *a*, *an* or *the*.

1 Is Canada _______ English speaking country?
2 ________ Great Wall is _______ longest wall in the world.
3 Who's _______ man in a black coat sitting in _______ car?
4 January is _______ first month of the year.
5 What _______ hot day today! Let's go out and have _______ walk.
6 Is your child ______ boy or _______ girl?
7 Look at the picture! There's _______ house in _______ picture. In front of _______ house there's _______ old tree. Under _______ tree there is _______ woman reading _______ English story book.
8 Do you know _______ moon moves round _______ earth?

9 Once there were ____ lot of mice (老鼠) in ______ old house. They ate up _____ lot of food. So _____ owner of ______ house got ____ cat. The cat killed many of _____ mice. One day _____ oldest mouse said, "All _____ mice must come to my hole tonight, and we'll decide what to do about ______ cat."

All ____ mice came. They thought hard and tried to find _____ way to save their lives. Many of them spoke, but no one knew what to do. At last _____ young mouse stood up and said, "Why not tie _____ bell round _____ cat's neck? Then, when ____ cat comes near, we'll hear _____ bell and run away. Then ____ cat won't be able to catch any more of us."

"Good idea! Can anyone here tie _____ bell round _____ cat's neck?" the oldest mouse asked. None of _____ mice answered.

He waited but still no one said anything.
At last he said, "It's easy to say something, but not so easy to do it."

28 Fill in the blanks with articles where necessary.

Once____ man wanted to go from one side of ____ river to the other in ____ boat. He had to take with him _____ sheep, _____ wolf and _____basket of vegetables. But he could take only one of them at a time, because _____ boat was very small. "If I leave ____ wolf and ____ sheep together, ____ wolf may eat _____ sheep," he said to himself. "If I leave _____ sheep and _____ vegetables together, _____ sheep may eat _____ vegetables." He thought and thought. At last, he had _____ idea. And he was able to get to _____ other side of _____ river with ______ sheep, _____ wolf, and _____ vegetables . Do you know how he did it?

29 Give the past and past participle forms of the following verbs.

agree _______ _______	cry _______ _______	kill _______ _______
fly _______ _______	forget _______ _______	know _______ _______
pay _______ _______	burn _______ _______	blow _______ _______
drive _______ _______	buy _______ _______	dig _______ _______
can _______ _______	eat _______ _______	build _______ _______
give _______ _______	see _______ _______	mean _______ _______
sleep _______ _______	let _______ _______	break _______ _______
sweep _______ _______	read _______ _______	win _______ _______
rise _______ _______	wear _______ _______	speak _______ _______
think _______ _______	lend _______ _______	fall _______ _______

30 Fill in the blanks with *do, does, did, are, is, am, were, was, have, has,* or *will*.

1 A: _______ you often speak English? B: Yes, I _____.
2 A: What _____ you doing here? B: I ____ waiting for a friend.
3 A: _____your mother work in a school? B: Yes, she _____.
4 A: _____ you finished reading the book? B: No, I ____ still reading it.
5 A: When_____ he get up this morning? B: He ____ not get up until 9.
6 A: The baby ____ crying the whole night. B: Maybe he _____ ill.
7 A: ____ she going to come to see you? B: Yes, she _____.
8 A: _____ you be free tomorrow? B: I ____ afraid I won't.
9 A: What ____ you doing at nine last night? B: I ____ watching TV, I think.
10 A: Who ____ you living with now? B: I ___ living with Daddy.

31 Choose the best answer for each blank.

1 _________you mend my car? I _________ not start it.
A. Would ... would B. Must ... must C. Can ... can D. May ... may

2 You _______ go to see a doctor at once because you've got hurt so badly.
A. must B. may C. can D. would

3 _________ I open the window? It's so warm here.
A. Must B. Will C. Shall D. Would

4 You'd better go and ask Mr Wang. He______ know how to use the computer.
A. can B. may C. would D. could

5 She said that she ________ speak a little English when she was four.
A. might B. would C. could D can

6 ________ you please tell me how to get to the station?
A. Shall B. May C. Might D. Will

7 What ________ you like for breakfast?
A. may B. will C. would D. can

32 Fill in the blanks with the phrases in the box.

1 Jim, go and see who's ________ the door, please.
2 Have you ________ the jacket? It's forty *yuan*.
3 I haven't ________ my uncle for a long time.
4 It's not polite to ________ others.
5 The bus moved away as soon as he ________ it.
6 When I ________ this morning, it was 9 o'clock.
7 If you don't work hard, you'll ________ others.
8 I've ________ China's Great Wall a lot, but I've never been there.
9 Don't worry! I'm sure you'll ________ others in your class if you study harder than before.
10 Would you please ________ my name and my telephone number?
11 I'm sorry you have to ________ your shoes before you get into the computer room.
12 I often ________ late on Sunday mornings.
13 Smoking ________ your health.
14 His daughter ________ singing and dancing.
15 I'm sorry. All the tickets have been ________.
16 Could you ask him to ______ me ________ tonight?
17 She's very ill. Has her mother ________ a doctor?
18 Time ________ no man.

1 got on
2 knocking at
3 paid for
4 heard of
5 fall behind
6 waits for
7 woke up
8 laugh at
9 catch up with
10 heard from
11 write down
12 sent for
13 take off
14 is bad for
15 sold out
16 get up
17 is good at
18 ring ... up

33 Choose the right phrase for each blank.

1 He ________________ the radio at six o'clock every morning.
A. listens on B. listens to C. listens in D. listens at

2 As soon as he walked into the room, he ______ his heavy coat and sat down.
A. took off B. took out C. took away D. took down

3 He ________________ spaceship and knows a lot about it.
A. is interested on B. is interested in
C. is interesting about D. is interesting with

4 Most of the tables ____________ wood.
A. are made in B. are made of C. are made for D. are made by
5 "Mum, have you __________ the party? It's time to leave now," said Dick.
A. waited for B. looked for C. got ready for D. heard from
6 I think that teachers are the most hard-working people. Do you ______ me?
A. go on with B. catch up with C. agree with D. laugh at
7 That's too expensive. I'll ______________ it.
A. think about B. hear about C. talk about D. worry about
8 It's not right to ______________ other people.
A. get on with B. play games with C. **laugh at** D. ring up

34 Choose the right phrase for each blank.

1 **She has just bought _____ trousers from that shop.**
2 Excuse me. Could you please pass me ________ paper?
3 Yesterday afternoon they didn't have any lessons ________ the football match.
4 On May Day there were many ________ beautiful flowers at Tian An Men Square.
5 A: Where did you meet him yesterday?
B: I met him ________ the Great Wall Hotel (饭店).
6 The tiger was killed, so it could ________ come back to the village and eat pigs or babies.
7 Look! What happened over there? There are ________ people pushing around the policeman.
8 "How can it be true?" he said ________.

A. because of
B. **a pair of**
C. in front of
D. a piece of
E. kinds of
F. a lot of
G. no longer
H. in surprise

35 Fill in each blank with the right phrase. Then put the sentences into Chinese.

A | look at | look for | look like | look after | look over | look up |

1 If you don't know how to read a word, you'd better ______ it ______ in a dictionary.
2 The doctor ______ ______ the boy carefully and said, "Don't worry, my boy. There's nothing much wrong with you."
3 Aunt Li has gone to the post office. She asked me to ______ ______ her baby for a while.
4 This girl ______ ______ her mother. She has a round face and big eyes.
5 A: Have you found your bike?
B: No, not yet. I've ______ ______ it for several days.
A: Please go and ______ ______ that one in the corner. Maybe it's yours.
B: Yes, it is. It's my bike. You're great. Thank you very much.

B

turn on	turn off	turn down	turn up	turn white	turn left

1 Please remember to ______ ______ the light before you leave.

2 Go and ______ ______ the TV quickly. The women's football match has begun.

3 The baby is sleeping. Could you ______ ______ the TV a bit?

4 The radio is giving the weather report. I cannot hear it clearly. Could you please ______ it ______?

5 After the heavy snow, the whole fields ______ ______.

6 Go along this road until you get to the traffic lights, and then ______ ______.

C

go on	go back	go home	go shopping	go to bed
go away	go to school	go skating	go swimming	

1 Xiao Lin is a middle school student. He always gets up at six and ______ ______ ______ at seven in the morning from Monday to **Friday.** He has lunch at school. When the classes are over at four in the afternoon, he ______ ______ by bike. He finishes his homework before nine o'clock in the evening. He ______ ______ ______ at around ten o'clock.

Sometimes on Sunday, he ______ ______ with his mother. He often asks her to buy him some sports things. In summer holidays, he ______ ______ in the lake near his home with his good friends. And in winter he ______ ______ on the lake. Sometimes the lake is dangerous to skate on because the ice is not thick enough. Xiao Lin doesn't seem afraid. He still ______ ______ skating. That makes his parents worry about him.

2 Sorry! I've forgotten to bring my book. I have to ______ ______ home to get it.

3 "______ ______! The train is coming!" the policeman shouted at the children.

D

come back	come down	come from	come on
come round	come over	come in	come out

1 "______ ______!" the students were shouting. Wu Dong ran faster and faster. She won the girl's 100-metre race.

2 "______ ______," she said when she heard somebody knocking at the door.

3 I'll telephone you as soon as I ______ ______.

4 Mr Smith ______ ______ Australia. He often ______ ______ to my house and has a drink with me.

5 They went into the shop. The shopkeeper ______ ______ and asked if he could help them.

6 "Get a ladder, please. I can't ______ ______." Jim said in a tall tree.

7 The door was locked. The cat ______ ______ of the window and jumped into the garden.

E	give a call give the message give back give a talk

1 Please ________ my pen ________ when you finish writing the letter.
2 Doctor Clarke ________ ________ on medicine at the meeting yesterday.
3 "Lucy asked me to ________ ________ ________ to you when you come back," Kate said to Jim.
4 I'll ________ you ________ ________ when I arrive in London.

36 Find out the sentences with the same meaning as the underlined ones.

1 We'll have noodles for lunch instead of rice and vegetables.

A. We'll have noodles for lunch.
B. We'll have rice and noodles for lunch.
C. We'll have rice and vegetables for lunch.

2 They prefer Chinese food to Japanese food.

A. They like Chinese food better than Japanese food.
B. They like Japanese food better than Chinese food.
C. They like Chinese food as well as Japanese food.

3 All the students have passed the maths exam except Bill.

A. All the students have passed the maths exam.
B. Nobody has passed the maths exam.
C. Only Bill failed the maths exam.

4 You cannot cross the street until the light turns green.

A. You can cross the street before the light turns green.
B. You can cross the street after the light turns green.
C. You can cross the street while the light is turning green.

37 Write where each of the following people works and what each of them does.

1 A doctor works in a hospital. He saves people's lives.
2 A nurse ....
3 A teacher ....
4 A worker ....
5 A shopkeeper ....
6 A scientist ....
7 A street cleaner ....
8 A bus conductor ....
9 A car driver ....

10 A farmer ....

11 A postman..

12 A bookseller ....

38 Rewrite each of the sentences with the phrase in the bracket.

1 She was so weak that she couldn't take care of the child. (too ... to ...)

2 Sam was so tired that he couldn't walk farther. (too ... to ...)

3 Mr Hunt got up so late that he didn't catch the train. (too ... to ...)

4 The scientist had supper after he finished the work at midnight. (not ... until ...)

5 The town was able to build a school and a hospital after new China was founded. (not ... until ...)

6 Most of the shops are not open before nine o'clock. (not ... until ...)

39 Choose the right word for each blank.

1 "Did you ask me where the nearest post office is? Look! Can you see the two tall buildings over there? The nearest post office is _____ (between, among) them," said the policeman politely.

2 **A**: What's the ______ (day, date) today?
B: It's June 2nd.

3 You'd better not go ______ (through, across) the forest. It's dangerous.

4 "You must be careful when you go ______ (through, across) the street," Mabel said to her little son.

5 Walk straight and turn right ______ (in the end, at the end) of the street, you'll see a white tall building. That's the museum.

6 ______ (In the end, At the end), the lost child was found by a policeman in a small village.

7 The two foreigners are ______ (all, both) from America.

8 "Are you ______ (all, both) interested in climbing mountains, boys and girls?" the teacher asked.

9 **A**: What ______ (day, date) is it tomorrow?
B: It's Wednesday.

10 Jim prefers football to basketball. Bill prefers football, ______ (either, too).

11 Lucy doesn't like eating beef. Lily doesn't ______ (either, too).

12 "Are there any bridges ______ (over, above) the river?" asked a policeman. " I'm afraid not. You'll have to cross the river in a boat," Allan said.

13 When did his grandfather _______ (die, dead)?

14 That place is not interesting. ______ (Neither, Both) of us wants to go there.

15 John's a _____ (good, well) boy. He plays football very _____ (good, well).

40 Choose the right word for each blank. Change the verb forms if necessary.

1 "______ (See, Look) out of the window, you'll ______ (see, look) what you want," said Uncle Wang.

2 I don't want to go so far to ______ (see, watch) a film in the cold night. Let's ______ (see, watch) TV at home instead.

3 When the little girl ______ (hear, listen) someone coming upstairs, she stopped crying.

4 The people were sitting around the radio. They were ______ (hear, listen) to the important news.

5 "It's going to rain, Peter. You'd better ______ (take, bring) this raincoat with you," said Mary.
" Thank you. It's very kind of you. I'll ______ (take, bring) it back when I come next time," Peter said.

6 "Hi, Meimei!" said Li Lei. "Bill wants to ______ (lend, borrow) the book *A Terrible Monkey Island* from me. But mine isn't here. Could you ______ (borrow, lend) yours to him?"

7 Mr Smith is on his way to England. He ______ (arrive, reach, get) to Moscow on Tuesday morning. He ______ (arrive, reach, get) Paris in the afternoon and he will stay there for a few days . He will ______ (arrive, reach, get) in London on Saturday evening.

8 That's my watch. I lost it a week ago. Who ______ (look for, find) it?

9 Why, here's my pen! I ______ (look for, find) it just now, but I didn't ______ (look for, find) it.

10 He ______ (speak, say, tell) that he ______ (speak, tell, talk) with John the whole afternoon yesterday. John ______ (say, talk, tell) him that he should ______ (say, tell, talk) a few words about this at the meeting.

11 It's easy for some people to read English books, but difficult to ______ (speak, say, tell) English.

41 Fill in each blank with the right verb form.

1

There are six members in Jim's family. They ______ (be) Mr. Green, Mrs Green, Jim, Kate, Polly and the black cat Mimi. Mr Green usually ______ (get) up earliest. He ______ (cook) breakfast at 6:30. Then Mrs Green and the others ______ (get) up at ten to seven. They all ______ (have) milk and bread for breakfast except Polly. After breakfast, Mr Green ______ (go) to work. Mrs Green ______ (go) to work, too. But she always ______ (tidy) the house before she leaves home. Jim and Kate ______ (be) students. They ______ (go) to school together.

What ______ Polly and Mimi ________(do) every day? ______ they ______ (go) to school? No, they don't. Polly ______ (stay) at home. Mimi ______ (play) in the garden.

Today ______ (be) Sunday. Now it's eight o'clock in the morning. Mr Green ______ ______(read) the newspaper. Mrs Green ____ ______ (listen) to the radio. Jim and Kate ______ still ______ (sleep) in their bedrooms. Polly ____ ______ (sing) in the tree. Mimi ____ ______ (run) after a duck. The duck _____ ______ (shout) "Quack, quack, quack ...!"

2

In some foreign countries, some people ______ ______ (not like) the number 13. They ______ (not think) 13 is a lucky number. For example, they don't like to ______ (live) on the thirteenth floor.

My friend Jack ______ (have) got the same idea. He ______ ______ (not like) the number 13, either.

One day, he asked some friends to dinner. When all of his friends ______ (arrive), he ______ (ask) them to sit around the dinner table. He ______ (begin) to count the people in his mind while they ______ ______ (have) the delicious food. Suddenly, he ______ (cry) out,"Oh, there ______(be) thirteen people here!" Everybody's face ______ (turn) white except Mr Brown. He ______ (say) slowly with a smile on his face," ______ ______ (not worry), my dear friends! We ______ (have) fourteen people here. My wife Mrs Brown ______ ______ (have) a baby in a few weeks. She's in the family way (怀孕) now."

All of them______ (become) happy again.

"Congratulations!" they said to Mrs and Mr Brown. They ______ (enjoy) the nice food and ______ (have) a good time that evening.

3

I ______ just ______(receive) a letter from my brother, Tim. He is in Australia. He ______ ______ (be) there for six months. Tim ______ (be) a doctor. He ______ (work) for a big hospital and he ______ already ______ (visit) a great number of different places in Australia. He ______ just ______ (buy) an Australian car. He ______ ______ (be) to Alice Spring, a small town in the centre of Australia. He ______ already ______ (visit) Darwin. From there, he ______ ______ (fly) to Sydney. My brother ______ never ______ (be) to a foreign country before, so he ______ (find) this trip very interesting.

42 Fill in the blanks with the right verb forms.

1 He ________ ________ (see) the film twice already.
2 I ____________ (cough) a lot last night.
3 The children ________ (enjoy) themselves in the park last Sunday morning.
4 Most of the shops __________ (open) at nine o'clock in the morning.
5 The train ______ just ______ (arrive).
6 She _______ _______ (feel) terrible at this time yesterday.
7 Many foreign friends _________ (come) to visit China every year.
8 They ______ (join) the Young Pioneers six years ago.
9 The singer said, "Thank you very much. Now I _______ _______ (sing) another song for you."
10 She ____ ____ (pick) apples in her garden when I went to see her yesterday.
11 Mary _____ _____ (work) in the factory since she left school three years ago.
12 Mr Turner _________ _________ (give) a talk on spaceships next Thursday.
13 What _______ you ________ (do) at eight yesterday evening?
14 DOCTOR: Good morning, Dick. What ________ (be) wrong with you?
DICK: I _________ (get) a headache, I'm afraid.
DOCTOR: _________ you _________ (get) a temperature?
DICK: Yes, I _________ (have). My temperature _________ (reach) 39 yesterday evening.
DOCTOR: _________ you _________ (take) any medicine yet?
DICK: No, not yet. But I _________ (drink) a lot of water last night.

43 Here is a letter from Mike to his friend Peter. Please complete it with the right verb forms.

December 2nd, 199__

Dear Peter,

I ______ ______ (be) here in Beijing for half a year now. Beijing ______ (be) in the north of China, so it's quite cold in winter. It _____ just _____ (snow) twice here. I think I ______ _____ (have) the first "White Christmas" in my life! It's so warm in Australia and so cold here. It's hard to believe, isn't it?

Thank you for the wonderful stamps! I _______ _______ (get) over three hundred Chinese stamps since I came here. I _________ (send) some Monkey King stamps to you now. I think you __________ (like) them.

Now let me answer some of your questions. Yes, I ______ ________ (learn) Chinese. It is quite a difficult language for me. Mum is learning Chinese, too, and she ______ (like) using it here and there. One day Mum ______ (ask) for some cups in a shop. They ______ (show) her some quilts. Dad and I ______ (have) a good laugh over that. I ______ ______ (learn) about one thousand Chinese words. I can even ______ (write) them. ______ you ______ (look) at the words on the Christmas card? I ______ (write) them myself!

I _____ ______ (travel) to several places in South China with Mum and Dad since we _______ (come) to China. I______ _______ (see) a lot of interesting things. I ______ ________ (make) quite a few good friends, too.

I ______ (have) to ______ (finish) this letter now. ______ (Ask) Uncle John and Aunt Alice to ______ (bring) you to China when they ______ (come) in August. We ________ ______ (have) a good time together.

Yours,

Mike

44 Correct the mistakes in the following sentences.

1 His grandpa has died for two years.
2 Liu Huifang has joined the League for three years.
3 I have bought the dictionary half a year ago.
4 **A**: When have you visited the museum?
B: I've visited the museum last Sunday.
5 Where have you met him yesterday?
6 **A**: Where is Uncle Wang?
B: He has been to Guangzhou. He was asked to give a speech there.
7 If it will rain tomorrow, we won't hold the sports meeting.
8 I'll pass the message on to Lucy as soon as I'll meet her next week.
9 Peter won't go to see the film because he lost his ticket.
10 Mum cooked supper at six o'clock yesterday evening.

45 Guess the meaning of the underlined words and put the sentences into Chinese.

1 One tree can not make a wood.
2 The sun rises in the east and sets in the west.
3 Take down the picture and put up the world map.
4 Keep quiet! Don't make a noise!
5 How are you getting on? We often think of you.
6 We'll soon be on holiday. Are you going away?
7 We are terribly busy with our exams at the moment.
8 There are different kinds of vegetables in the shop, such as tomatoes, potatoes, carrots, peas, cabbages and so on.
9 I felt so tired that I went to sleep as soon as I lay down.

46 Change these sentences after the model and put them into Chinese.

Model: You have to dig a deep hole for the tree. →
You don't have to dig a deep hole for the tree.
Do you have to dig a deep hole for the tree?

1 These trees were planted in 1978.
2 The man cleans the toilet every morning.

3 They'll be ready in a few minutes.
4 She'll have to finish her homework before the class.
5 Mr Turner has received my letter.
6 Betty is going to the farm to help her uncle.
7 He was taking a walk in the park at 7:00 yesterday evening.

47 Ask questions about the underlined parts.

1 At nine o'clock the rich woman asked the singer to come upstairs. (what time)
2 The nurse passed a knife to the doctor when he began the operation. (what)
3 She decided to give art lessons to the poor girl. (whom)
4 They went out to look for the lost child. (why)
5 Li Lei went to visit the museum by bus yesterday. (how)
6 It's about 2 kilometres from my home to the nearest hospital. (how far)
7 The Yellow River is 5,464 kilometres long. (how long)
8 Her grandfather is over ninety years old. (how old)
9 The baby has four meals a day. (how many)
10 That's Mr Green's house. (whose)
11 She went to the station to meet her mother last night. (where)
12 This dictionary is six dollars. (how much)
13 It's Friday today. (what)
14 It's January 3rd tomorrow. (what)
15 He likes maths best. (which subject)
16 They studied in No. 11 Middle School. (which)

48 Complete the following sentences after the model.

Model: The computer is very useful to us, isn't it?

1 Our country has changed a lot since 1978, ____________?
2 It's going to rain this afternoon, ____________?
3 She teaches maths, ____________?
4 We're going to have an English exam next week, ____________?
5 You won't be away for long, ____________?
6 You won't have any classes tomorrow, ____________?
7 They can't walk there, ____________?
8 You haven't finished your work yet, ____________?
9 He knew how to mend the machine, ____________?

49 Change the sentences after the models.

Model A: We live a happy life today. → What a happy life we live today!

Model B: He is glad to see you again. → How glad he is to see you again!

1 She is a lucky girl.
2 Jeff is running fast.
3 Linda is watching carefully.
4 It is raining very hard.
5 He has a large garden.
6 It is a wonderful programme.
7 It is a clever dog.
8 You have done a good job.
9 She works very hard.
10 The building is very high.

50 Fill in the blanks with the infinitive or -ing form.

1 Do you know when ______ (go) to the farm?
2 Please remember ______ (lock) the door when you leave the room.
3 Please don't forget ______ (ask) Mr Johnson to come to my party.
4 It's good ______ (help) others when they are in trouble.
5 Jim decided ______ (leave) Polly to Ling Feng when he was back to England.
6 I want ______ (start) work at once.
7 The man downstairs told the man upstairs not ______ (drop) his shoes on to the floor at midnight any more.
8 You must be hungry. I'll get you something ______ (eat).
9 Uncle Wang told them how ______ (make) a plane with wood and metal.
10 The question is how ______ (get) to the top of the mountain quickly.
11 She didn't know what ______ (say) at the meeting the day before yesterday.

12 "Stop ______ (talk), please. The film has begun."
13 Can you tell me when you can finish ______ (read) these books?
14 I don't know whether she enjoys ______ (wear) sun glasses.
15 Did you hear her ______ (sing) in the next room last night?
16 No ______ (smoke), please!
17 Keep ______ (try). You are sure to get a good result.
18 A fridge is used for ______ (keep) vegetables and food cool.
19 He left angrily without ______ (say) a word.
20 He doesn't like ______ (dance) at all.

51 Find the end of these sentences and then put them into Chinese.

1 It's dangerous	A to give than to take.
2 It's not good	B to say than to do.
3 It's better	C to give food to animals in the zoo.
4 It's good	D to play football in the street.
5 It's easier	E to wash hands before meals.

52 Change the sentences after the model.

Model: We need more rice. → More rice is needed (by us).

1 The farm produces milk, meat, eggs and vegetables.
2 Chinese people built the Great Wall two thousand years ago.
3 We must plant more trees next year.
4 Uncle Wang invented a new machine last month.
5 You should clean and tidy your bedroom every day.
6 People in Australia speak English.
7 People may catch fish in the river.
8 Dalian produces big ships.
9 Farmers harvest rice in autumn.
10 We can see no stars in the day-time
11 Mr Henry heard a strange noise last night.
12 The nurse looked after those children very well.

53 Fill in the blanks with *when, but, if, because, before* or *and.*

Jenny was a good girl, ______ she was often late for school. One morning she was late again. Mr Black, her teacher, got angry ______ she came into the classroom.

"I'll write to your father ______ you aren't here on time tomorrow," he told her.

Jenny didn't want him to do that ______ her parents were very strict with her. The next day she got up very early ______ went to school without breakfast. She hurried to school. Just ______ she got to the school gate, she stopped. She found a small bag lying on the ground. She picked it up ______ she decided to give it to the headmaster. ______ she hurried into her classroom, Mr Black was already beginning his lesson.

"Jenny White," he said as soon as he saw her. "I've told you not to be late, ______ you're late again."

"I'm sorry, sir," Jenny said. "I was late ______ I found a small ...."

"I won't listen to any excuse, " Mr Black stopped her. "______ you can't get here on time, I'll write to your father."

Jenny could say no more. She sat down quietly, ______ she couldn't keep back her tears (眼泪).

As soon as the bell rang, the door opened. Mr Smith, the headmaster came in. He was holding a small bag in his hand.

"Excuse me, Mr Black," he said, "Is this yours?"

"Why, yes. It is mine, ______ I didn't know I lost it." Mr Black was surprised.

"Jenny White found it just ______ school started. She gave it to me ______ asked me to find out who had lost it," Mr Smith said.

Mr Black's face turned red. He looked at Jenny ________ said, "I'm sorry, Jenny. I take back what I said."

54 Fill in the blanks with *on, off, in, from, with, as, at* or *of*.

Mr White came home from work ____ six _____ the afternoon. He felt tired. As soon _____ he sat down _____ a chair, Mrs White brought him a cup _____ tea.

"Thank you, dear," said Mr White.

"Have you heard _____ Mr Green?" she asked.

"I've had another letter ____ him," Mr White said. "His leg is getting better." Mr White drank the tea and turned _____ the TV. "Um, what's wrong _____ the TV? There's no programme _____ any of the channels."

"I'm afraid it needs mending," Mrs White turned _____ the TV.

"Never mind. I'll see what I can do _____ the TV this weekend," said Mr White. "Now let's listen to the radio instead."

55 Join each pair of sentences after the model.

Model A: I'll go shopping. I finish washing the clothes. (as soon as) →
I'll go shopping *as soon as* I finish washing the clothes.

1 The soldiers will rush out. They receive the order.
2 I'll tell him about this. He comes back from work.
3 The children stopped playing. They saw the teacher coming in.

Model B: Tom has made a lot of friends.
He came to China last year. (since) →
Tom has made a lot of friends since he came to China last year.

1 A lot of things have happened here. You left in 1972.
2 I've never met a foreigner. I began to learn English.
3 He has changed a lot. He left school to work.

56 Join each pair of sentences, using *so...that*, and then put them into Chinese.

Model A: He was very friendly. We became friends soon. →
He was *so* friendly *that* we became friends soon.

1 The man was very angry. His face turned white.
2 He spoke very fast. I couldn't understand him.
3 It was very hot last night. I could hardly sleep.

Model B: He didn't come back. We were ready to leave. (until). →
He didn't come back until we were ready to leave.

1 The teacher didn't begin the lesson. All the students became quiet.
2 I couldn't ride a bike. I was sixteen.
3 I didn't know about this. He told me last night.

57 Fill in the blanks with the phrases in the box.

A

so ... that	both ... and	either ... or	as ... as
neither ... nor	as soon as	from ... to	so ... as

1 Jane's English is very good, but her French is not _____ good _____ her English.
2 The old man was ______ hungry ______ he couldn't walk any more.
3 There are ______ many League members in Class 1 ______ in Class 2.
4 We should learn ______ from books ______ from workers and farmers.
5 Bill's parents are going to travel ______ London ______ Paris next month.
6 The wall of the new building is ______ white ______ snow.
7 I like ________ English _______ Chinese.
8 You may ________ do it yourself ________ leave it to me.
9 I'll give the note to him _______ _______ _______ he comes.
10 This is ______ a Japanese book ______ an English one. It is a French book.
11 _______ Jim _______ Kate broke the glass. The cat did.
12 Lily was _____ thirsty _____ she had a bottle of orange and two cups of tea.
13 They jumped into the river and swam to the boy quickly _______ _______ _______ they saw him fall off the boat.
14 Grandma is often ill now. She's not ______ healthy ______ before.
15 They want just one of us. ________ you ________ he can join them.
16 It's 1460 kilometres ________ Shanghai ________ Beijing.

B

because	until	after	but	if	so
before	when	though	since	as	and

1 I'll go there by bike ____________ it is fine tomorrow.
2 He did not go home ____________ he finished the work.
3 I have learned a lot ____________ I came to this factory.
4 He went shopping yesterday, ____________ bought nothing.

5 He didn't tell me anything ____________ he left.
6 I didn't buy the dictionary yesterday ____________ my aunt said that she would give me one.
7 ____________ we said "Goodbye" to the farmers, we left the farm for school.
8 ____________ Mrs Turner passed the street corner, she saw the accident clearly.
9 ____________ the story is short and there are no new words in it, it is difficult to understand.
10 They ran to the teacher together ____________ gave the flowers to her.
11 You should do ____________ the teacher told you.
12 I was ill yesterday, ____________ I didn't come to school.

58 Change these sentences after the model.

Model A: What **did** they **fight** about? Do you know? →
Do you know what they **fought** about?

1 Where does she live? Do you know?
2 What can a computer do? The scientist told us.
3 How can I get to the station? Could you tell me?
4 Whose watch is this? Does anybody know?
5 When is our English teacher's birthday? I don't know.
6 Which one did you like best? She asked me.
7 When will the holiday begin? I asked the teacher.
8 When will the train arrive? He asked me.

Model B: **Does** Mr Brown **live** in Room 207? Could you tell me? →
Could you tell me *if / whether* Mr Brown lives in Room 207?

1 Did they have a picnic in the park last Saturday? Do you know?
2 Will a foreigner give a speech on computers next week? Can you tell me?
3 Is Lily coming to the museum? I don't know.
4 Were you at home before nine last night? The policeman wants to know.
5 Is there going to be a test this week? Do you know?
6 Will it rain **tomorrow**? Nobody knows.
7 Did they have a good **journey home?** He wants to know.
8 Has he come back from Guangzhou? I don't know.

59 Rewrite the following sentences after the model.

Model: Sit down. The teacher told me. → The teacher told me to sit down.
Don't play with fire. Mum told us. →
Mum told us not to play with fire.

1 Learn from Comrade Lei Feng. Our headmaster asked us.
2 Don't worry about the child. The doctor told her.

3 Wait at the gate of the museum. Mrs King asked the twins.
4 Don't be so noisy. The man downstairs told the children.
5 Please be quick! Mother told her daughter.
6 Don't jump the queue. The old woman asked Peter.

60 Complete the dialogues and then practise them.

1) TANG : Hello! John! How are you today?

JOHN : ________________. ________________?

TANG : I'm fine, too.

2) LIN : Mum, this is my friend, Jimmy.

MUM : __________________________, Jimmy.

JIMMY : Glad to meet you, too.

MUM : Sit down, please.

JIMMY : __________________________.

3) **A**: What's the time by your watch, please?

B: Half past four.

A: Oh, I think it's__________________ go now.

B: All right. See you tomorrow.

A: __________________________.

4) JIM : Hello! May __________________ Tim?

TIM : Speaking.

JIM : Hi, Tim. Could you come out for a moment? I want to show you something.

TIM: OK! Where shall ______________?

JIM: How about at No. 10 bus stop?

TIM: OK! __________________________.

JIM: See you later.

5) **A**: Hello! ______________ to Mr Hu?

B: ____________. He isn't in at this moment.

A: Could you ____________________ for him, please?

B: OK!

A: Please ask him to ring me up before nine tomorrow morning.

B: Could you tell me your ____________________, please?

A: Oh, yes. My name is Wan Da. W-A-N Wan, D-A Da, and my telephone number is 4357788

B: OK! I will write a note on his desk.

A: That's kind of you. ____________________. Goodbye!

B: ____________________.

6) **A**: Why are you in such a hurry?
B: My brother is in the hospital. I'm going to see him.
A: What's ________________ him?
B: He's broken his left leg.
A: Oh, dear. I'm ________________________ that.

7) **D**: What's ________________________ , madam?
M: I feel very weak. I can hardly do any work, doctor.
D: How long ________________ like this?
M: Ever since last month.
D: Have you ________________?
M: No, I haven't got a headache.
D: ________________________ at night?
M: Yes, I sleep very well.
D: Do you often ______________?
M: No, I don't often have breakfast. And I have a little food for lunch ________ I want to keep thin.
D: Oh. I see. There's nothing ________. You need to take ________ food and ________ meals a day. And do some ________ every day. Then you will get better soon.

8) GIRL: Can I ________________, sir?
MAN: Yes, please. I want to buy a pair of sports shoes.
GIRL: What size ____________________, please?
MAN: Size ten or eleven.
GIRL: OK! ______ ________ this pair?
MAN: Sorry! I don't like black. Have you got any other colours?
GIRL: Other colours? Oh, yes. We've also got blue, brown and white ones.
MAN: Can I ____________________ at the brown ones?
GIRL: Yes, please.
MAN: ________________ does each pair cost?
GIRL: Forty-six *yuan*.
MAN: It's too ________________. Can it be ____________?
GIRL: How about forty?
MAN: No, it's still ______________. What about thirty-five?
GIRL: Thirty-five? Er ... all right. Please take it!

9) **A**: ________________, may I have a look at the magazine?
B: ______________, it's not mine. Please ask that girl.
A: Excuse me, ______________________ your magazine?
C: Yes, please. But you should remember to return it before I get off the train.
A: ______________ get off?
C: The next stop.
A: OK! I'll have a quick look.
C: Please ____________ time. There are still about forty minutes to go.
A: ______________ very much.

10) **A**: Excuse me, Madam, could you please tell me how to get to the Children's Hospital?
B __________, I ____________. I'm new here. Please ask that man.
A: ____________, sir, could you tell me the way to the Children's Hospital?
C: ____________ this street until you reach the second traffic lights. Turn right. At the end of the street you'll see the _________.
A: Can I ________________________?
C: Sorry! There's no bus to go there.
A: ____________ will it take me to walk there?
C: Nearly an hour. You'd better call a taxi (出租汽车).
A: OK! ____________ very much. Taxi! Taxi!
D: What can I do for you, sir?
A: I want to ____________________________.
D: Please get in!
A: Thank you!

61 Make similar dialogues in pairs after the model.

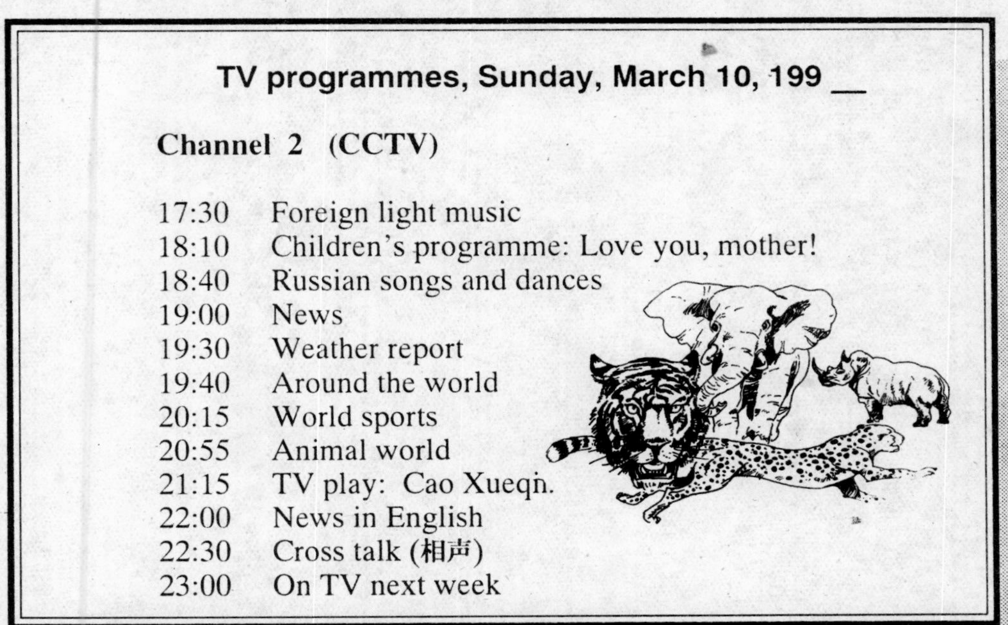

TV programmes, Sunday, March 10, 199 __

Channel 2 (CCTV)

17:30	Foreign light music
18:10	Children's programme: Love you, mother!
18:40	Russian songs and dances
19:00	News
19:30	Weather report
19:40	Around the world
20:15	World sports
20:55	Animal world
21:15	TV play: Cao Xueqn.
22:00	News in English
22:30	Cross talk (相声)
23:00	On TV next week

Model: **A**: Do you know when *Animal World* will begin?
B: Let's look at the TV newspaper. Here! It'll begin at *20:55*.
A: How long will the programme last?
B: It'll last *35 minutes*.
A: What's the next programme after *Animal World*?
B: A TV play about the famous writer Cao Xueqin.

62 Make similar dialogues after the model.

Model: FATHER: What do you want to do when you grow up, my son?
SON: I want to be *a teacher*.
FATHER: To be *a teacher*! That's very good. You must remember: whatever you do, do it well. Work hard, and then you'll live happily.

1 a farmer	4 a scientist	7 a film star
2 a singer	5 **a sportsman**	8 an inventor
3 a doctor	6 a soldier	9 a writer

II 听力练习

1 Listen to the tape. Read the questions and choose the right answers.

1 What's the time?
A. 3:30. B. 4:30. C. 5:30.

2 What day is it today?
A. Tuesday. B. Thursday. C. Wednesday.

3 How is Jim feeling?
A. A little better, but still tired. B. A little weak, but much better.
C. A little better, but still weak.

4 What did Lily have for lunch?
A. Rice and fish. B. Rice and eggs. C. Rice and chicken.

5 What did Bill want Tom to do?
A. He wanted Tom to see a film. B. He wanted Tom to play football.
C. He wanted Tom to go swimming.

6 Where did this dialogue happen?
A. It happened in a clothing shop. B. It happened in hospital.
C. It happened at home.

7 Where's the nearest post office?
A. At the first crossing. B. Between a fruit shop and a bookshop.
C. Between a bookshop and a clothing shop.

8 What's wrong with the young man?
A. He has got a headache. B. He is feeling quite weak.
C. He doesn't feel like eating and he cannot sleep well.

9 What will the weather be like tomorrow?
A. Very hot. B. Very cold. C. Very windy.

10 What's the speaker's name?
A. His name is JILES. B. His name is GIELS. C. His name is GILES.
What's the speaker's telephone number?
A. 3015577. B. 3017755. C. 3105577.

11 What was the man asked to do?
A. To stop smoking. B. To stop swimming. C. To stop eating.

12 Why was Bill late again for school?
A. Because he got up late. B. Because he was ill.
C. Because there was a traffic accident on his way to school.

2 Listen to the tape and choose the right answers.

1 Jeff was a ________________.
A. young man B. a little girl C. a little boy

2 Jeff's father took him to see ________________.
A. Jeff's uncle B. his father's uncle C. Jeff's grandpa

3 Jeff's father drove the car ________________.

A. slowly B. very fast C. carefully

4 The car was running ________________.

A. down a hill B. along a street C. through a forest

5 The car hit ________________.

A. a tall building B. a tall tree C. a bus

6 ________________ died in the accident.

A. Jeff B. The policmen C. Jeff's father

7 The doctor was ________________.

A. Jeff's uncle B. Jeff's mother C. Jeff's father

3 Listen to the world weather report for the next 24 hours and fill in the form.

	Fine	Cloudy	Windy	Rainy	Cool	Hot	Temperature
Beijing				√			20—30
Hong Kong (香 港)							
London							
Moscow							
New York							
Paris							
Sydney							
Tokyo							

4 Listen to the tape and then choose the right anwsers.

1 The children like Robert and Jane can't see their friends because ________.

A. they don't go to school B. they live too far away from each other

C. their families are too poor

2 The children can't study if they don't have ________________.

A. a car B. a bike C. a radio

3 The teacher teaches them ________________.

A. on TV B. over the radio C. over the telephone

4 When the children are having a lesson, ________________.

A. their teacher cannot see them B. their teacher cannot hear them

C. their teacher cannot talk to them

III 口语练习

1 Say a few words about one of the following topics.

1	Myself	5	My beautiful hometown
2	My family	6	What did I do last Sunday?
3	My school life	7	My English teacher
4	A friend of mine	8	My summer holiday

2 Look at this picture and say what they are doing.

Grandma Li lives alone. She is very ill. Han Meimei, Li Lei, Jim and the twins, Lin Tao have come .... (give food to, clean, sweep, wash, fill the thermos with ...)

3 Read the story on page 56 of Reading Practice Book 3. Now look at these pictures and retell the story in your own words.

4 Read the stories and have a talk with your classmates about each of the questions.

1 Turn back to page **107** of the Workbook, read the story in Exercise **28** again, and tell how the man got to the other side of the river with the sheep, the wolf and the basket of vegetables.

2 This story happened about one thousand and seven hundred years ago. One day somebody sent to Cao Cao, King of Wei, an elephant. Cao Cao wanted to know how heavy it was. "Who can think of a way to weigh (称重量) it?" he asked. But nobody knew what to do, because there was nothing big enough to weigh it. Read the story on page 12 of Reading Practice Book 3 and find out who got a way to weigh the elephant and tell how to weigh the big elephant.

5 Choose what you like and give your reason (理由).

1 If you get enough money, you can buy just one of the things (a black-and-white TV set, a washing machine, a bicycle, a radio set and a telephone). Which one would you like to buy? Why?

2 Here are some beautiful cities: Beijing, Qingdao, Guangzhou, Kunming, Nanjing, Hangzhou and Harbin. You can choose only one of them for tavelling this summer. Which one do you prefer? Please give your reasons.

3 Travelling by air is fast, but expensive and sometimes dangerous. Travelling by land is quite cheap and safe, but a bit slow. Sometimes it takes you several days from one city to another. Travelling by sea is not very expensive, you can have fresh air and enjoy beautiful scenes(风景), but sometimes it is not safe and a bit slow. And some people may feel seasick. How would you like to travel? Why?

4 As you know, there are four seasons in a year. They are spring, summer, autumn and winter. Which season do you like best? Why?

5 There are many kinds of jobs for you to choose, for example, a teacher, a scientist, a sportsman, a film star, a singer, a dancer, a doctor, a policeman, a postman, a soldier, a worker, a farmer and so on. What do you want to be when you grow up? Please give your reasons.

6 How many Chinese holidays or festivals can you name in English? Which one do you like best? Please give your reasons.

6 Why do you study English? Can you say something about the importance (重要性) of the English language?

7 Guess these riddles.

1 What has legs but cannot walk?

2 How can you turn a driver into a river?

3 If you cut off the head of a bear, what do you get?

4 It has cities but no people and houses; forests but no trees; rivers without water. What is it?

5 Which four letters can make everybody old?

IV 阅读练习

1 ROCKETS IN THE UNIVERSE

Scientists have always wanted to know more about the universe.

Years ago they knew many things about the moon. They knew how big it was and how far away it was from the earth. But they wanted to know more about it. They thought the best way was to send men to the moon.

The moon is about 384,000 kilometres away from the earth. A plane cannot fly to the moon because the air reaches only 240 kilometers away from the earth. But something can fly even when there is no air. That is a rocket (火箭).

How does a rocket fly? There is gas (气体) in the rocket. When the gas is made very hot inside the rocket, it will rush out of the end of the rocket, so it can make the rocket fly up into the sky.

Rockets can fly far out into space. Rockets with men in them have been to the moon. Several rockets without men in them have flown to another planet (行星) much farther away than the moon. One day rockets may be able to go to any place in space.

Choose the right answer.

1 Scientists have always wanted to know more about __________.
A. the stars B. the universe C. the sun and the moon

2 Scientists have known __________ the moon is.
A. how long B. how heavy C. how big

3 Scientists can be sent to the moon __________.
A. by rocket B. by plane C. by satellite

4 The earth is about 384,000 kilometres away from the __________.
A. sun B. moon C. universe

5 A plane cannot fly to the moon because __________.
A. there is no air above 240 kilometres away from the earth
B. there is no gas in the plane C. the plane must be driven by a man

6 The hot gas in the rocket is used for __________.
A. keeping the men in the rocket warm B. cooking food
C. making the rocket fly up

7 Several rockets without men in them have flown to __________.
A. the moon B. another satellite of the sun C. the sun

8 One day rockets may be able to go to any place in __________.
A. the sky B. the world C. the universe

2 EINSTEIN AND HIS DRIVER

Once Einstein ['ainstain] travelled to many places in America to give a lecture (演讲). He travelled in a car, and soon made friends with his driver.

Einstein gave the same lecture again and again. The driver always sat in the front of the lecture room and listened to the famous scientist carefully. One day, when they got to a small town in the south, the driver told Einstein that he knew the lecture so well that he was sure he could give it himself. Einstein smiled and said,"Why don't you give the lecture for me tonight?"

"All right. Let me try," answered the driver.

That evening, both Einstein and the driver went along to the lecture room. Nobody there had seen Einstein before. At first the driver was a bit afraid.

"Go on with your lecture. Don't be afraid," Einstein said with a smile. It made the driver feel better. Now he wasn't afraid any more.

When the driver took his place, everybody applauded (鼓掌). Then he began the lecture. He put his heart into it and gave a good lecture. When it was over, the people warmly applauded. The driver turned to look at Einstein. There was a smile on his face. He could see that the great scientist was quite pleased.

Then the driver started to leave and Einstein followed him quietly. Just when they got to the door, a man stopped them and asked the driver a very difficult question. The driver listened carefully. Of course, he did not understand it at all, but he smiled and said that the question was very interesting but really quite easy. "To show how easy it is, I'll ask my driver to answer it," the driver said.

Read the following sentences and answer right or wrong.

		Right	Wrong
1	Einstein got on well with his driver.	/ /	/ /
2	The driver didn't listen to Einstein carefully because he couldn't understand what Einstein said.	/ /	/ /
3	The driver was a clever man. He remembered the whole lecture.	/ /	/ /
4	One day the driver gave the lecture himself.	/ /	/ /
5	Everybody there knew Einstein so well that they gave him a warm welcome.	/ /	/ /
6	The driver gave a good lecture.	/ /	/ /
7	All of the people were pleased with the lecture except Einstein.	/ /	/ /
8	When Einstein heard the driver's lecture, he was very angry.	/ /	/ /
9	A man asked the driver a difficult question.	/ /	/ /
10	The driver thought that the question was very easy.	/ /	/ /
11	Einstein's driver is also a scientist.	/ /	/ /

3 Turn to page 34 of Reading Practice Book 3, read the play "The boy and his uncle", and then fill in the blanks.

A school inspector was coming to ______ a school. The school headmaster was ______. He sent a boy to the station to see ______ the inspector was ______ the train and he told the boy ______ run back to school if the inspector arrived.

When the boy got to the station, he was very ______ to meet his uncle there. He didn't see the inspector. His uncle didn't know ______ the boy wasn't at school at that time. The boy told his uncle the secret and he said the headmaster was waiting ______ the inspector.

The boy thought his uncle was coming to see his father. But his uncle came ______ him to his school. His uncle wanted to see the headmaster ______ he was the inspector.

4 Turn to page 68 of Reading Practice Book 3, read the story "A lesson from nature", and then fill in the blanks with the right verb form.

Many years ago, farmers ______ (get) very angry with hawks because they ______ ______ (eat) lots of their chickens. The farmers thought hawks must ______ ______ (kill). So many hawks ______ ______ (kill). After that, the farmers didn't have to ______ (worry) about their chickens. But field mice came out and ______ ______ (eat) up a lot of crops.

Hawks ate both chickens and field mice. They ______ (eat) more field mice than chickens. When the farmers ______ (kill) a lot of hawks, the balance of nature ______ ______ (change).

...

It is important for us to ______ (keep) the balance of nature. This lesson should ______ ______ (remember).

5 Turn to page 95 of Reading Practice Book 3, read the story "Peter's golden bridge", and then choose the right answer for each blank.

1 The colour of the Golden Gate Bridge is ______________.
A. yellow B. golden C. red D. white

2 The Golden Gate is an ______________ in the land.
A. gate B. opening C. river D. lake

3 The Golden Gate Bridge means ______________.
A. a gate made of gold B. a gate of golden colour
C. a gate to gold D. a gate to sea

4 The Golden Gate Bridge is in ______________.
A. Japan B. England C. France D. the USA

V 写作练习

1 Look at the four pictures and write several sentences about them.

2 There is a telephone call for Mr Smith, but he isn't in. You answer the telephone. After that, write a message to Mr Smith.

MAN: Hello! May I speak to Mr Smith?
YOU: Sorry! He isn't in at this moment. Could I take a message?
MAN: Yes, please. My name is Allan. A - double L- A - N. I'll go to the USA next Monday. I'm afraid I have no time to see him before I leave. Tell him I'll leave very early next Monday morning. Please ask him to give me a ring before then. And my telephone number is three zero one double five double seven.
YOU: OK! I'll tell him as soon as he comes back.
MAN: Thank you very much. Goodbye!
YOU: Bye!

TELEPHONE MESSAGE

FROM: TO:

DATE: TIME:

MESSAGE: ....

....

....

....

....

3 Write a note to your teacher to ask for a sick leave.

You have caught a bad cold. Last night you were not well. You had a .... You saw the doctor .... The doctor told you ....

4 Write a notice (通知) to your classmates.

Next Monday morning our class will go to the Red Star Farm. We'll help ....

We'll meet .... We'll go there by .... Please wear ... and take lunch .... Everyone should .... Thank you.

5 **Write eight or more sentences about the season you like best.**

Model: I like winter best. Though it is very cold, it's good for skating. I often go skating on Sundays with my father. When it snows everything turns white. Trees and houses are covered with thick snow. How beautiful the world looks! My friends and I like to make snowmen. Sometimes we make snow balls and throw them at each other That's a very interesting game. I like winter holiday very much because the Spring Festival is the happiest time of the year!

6 **Here is a letter from your penfriend, Catherine. Write a letter back to her.**

45 Gardener Street, APT. 24
Allston, MA 02134
USA
July 24th, 199__

Dear ...,

I haven't heard from you for a long time. How are you?

I have just finished the exams. Now I am glad I have time to write to you. Our teacher tells us that China is a large country. It has the largest population in the world. It is very far away from the USA. It is on the other side of the world. Now the sun is shining brightly while I am writing to you. But perhaps you are sleeping in the dark night. How interesting it is! I'm becoming more and more interested in China. I wish to know more about your life. Could you tell me what kind of food you often have for meals?

Please write me soon!

Best wishes to you!

Yours,

Catherine

7 **Write a letter to your penfriend about your English study. His address is: 27 York Street, Brooklyn, N.Y., USA.**

8 **Write about what you often do on Sundays.**

9 **Write about what you are going to do after you leave school.**

10 **Write a short passage on "My Happiest Day".**